OSINT Detective: Digital Tools & Techniques for Criminal Investigations

Algoryth Ryker

Criminals leave digital footprints everywhere—on social media, in financial transactions, across dark web forums, and even in the metadata of an image they thought was anonymous. Law enforcement agencies, private investigators, journalists, and intelligence analysts have increasingly turned to Open-Source Intelligence (OSINT) to track down suspects, solve cold cases, and uncover hidden criminal networks.

Unlike classified intelligence, OSINT leverages publicly available information to build investigative leads, identify persons of interest, and connect the dots in criminal cases. From tracking cyberstalkers and fraudsters to exposing human trafficking rings and extremist networks, OSINT has become an indispensable tool in the fight against crime.

But the digital age has also made criminals smarter. They use VPNs, burner accounts, encrypted messaging apps, and the dark web to hide their activities. The challenge for modern investigators is not just finding information—but finding it faster, verifying it efficiently, and using it legally.

This book is your field guide to criminal OSINT investigations. You'll learn how to:

✓ Unmask anonymous suspects using digital footprints

✓ Track financial fraud and money laundering trails

✓ Locate missing persons with geolocation intelligence

✓ Analyze social media patterns to expose threats

✓ Investigate organized crime syndicates and dark web activity

✓ Apply OSINT techniques in cold cases

✓ Navigate the ethical & legal boundaries of OSINT in law enforcement

Whether you're a law enforcement professional, cybersecurity expert, journalist, or digital investigator, this book will equip you with the advanced OSINT techniques needed to solve real-world crimes.

Now, let's dive into the world of digital detective work.

Chapter Breakdown

1. OSINT in Law Enforcement & Criminal Cases

- How OSINT is used in modern criminal investigations

- The difference between open-source and classified intelligence
- The role of OSINT in law enforcement agencies
- Overview of OSINT tools used in criminal casework
- **Case Study**: How OSINT cracked a high-profile criminal case
- The challenges & limitations of OSINT in law enforcement

2. Digital Identity Investigations

- Tracking suspects through their online footprints
- Investigating aliases, usernames, and digital personas
- Analyzing social media profiles for intelligence
- Cross-referencing multiple online accounts
- Mapping digital behavior patterns for suspect profiling
- **Case Study**: How OSINT unmasked an anonymous cybercriminal

3. Tracking Stalkers, Harassers & Cybercriminals

- Identifying cyberstalkers and online harassers
- Using OSINT to track perpetrators across platforms
- Gathering legal evidence from social media, emails & forums
- Behavioral analysis to predict escalation risks
- OSINT's role in cybercrime investigations
- **Case Study**: How OSINT helped law enforcement arrest a cyberstalker

4. OSINT in Financial Crimes & Fraud Investigations

- Identifying online financial fraudsters
- Tracking money laundering & shell companies
- Investigating Ponzi schemes and fake investment scams
- Exposing payment fraud & e-commerce scams
- OSINT tools for analyzing financial transactions & Bitcoin forensics
- **Case Study**: Unraveling a large-scale online fraud network

5. Geolocation OSINT for Missing Persons Cases

- How OSINT helps in missing persons investigations
- Tracking last-known digital locations
- Using social media check-ins & geotagged images
- Analyzing satellite & street view data for leads
- Collaborating with families, NGOs, and law enforcement

- **Case Study**: How OSINT helped locate a missing child

6. Criminal Networks & Organized Crime Intelligence

- Mapping out criminal organizations using OSINT
- Tracking drug trafficking networks and online markets
- Investigating gang activity & street crime networks
- Unraveling money laundering connections
- OSINT techniques for investigating human smuggling & trafficking
- **Case Study**: How OSINT exposed a global crime syndicate

7. Investigating Scams & Online Fraud Rings

- Identifying & tracking scammers operating online
- Investigating romance scams & social engineering fraud
- Unmasking phishing campaigns & email scam operations
- Tracking fake e-commerce websites & counterfeit stores
- Dark web markets for identity theft & fraud schemes
- **Case Study**: Breaking down a global fraud operation

8. Dark Web & Human Trafficking Investigations

- The dark web's role in human trafficking networks
- Using OSINT to track online trafficking operations
- Monitoring escort & classified ad websites for leads
- Tracking cryptocurrency transactions in trafficking cases
- OSINT's role in collaborating with NGOs & law enforcement
- **Case Study**: How OSINT disrupted a major trafficking ring

9. Terrorism & Extremist OSINT Monitoring

- Understanding how extremist groups recruit online
- Identifying radicalization patterns & warning signs
- Tracking propaganda networks & online hate groups
- Investigating domestic terrorism & extremism
- Monitoring deep & dark web forums for threat intelligence
- **Case Study**: How OSINT helped prevent a terrorist attack

10. Case Study: Using OSINT in a Cold Case

- Reopening a cold case with digital evidence
- Using OSINT to track new leads & suspects
- Collaboration between OSINT experts & forensic investigators
- How data correlation & public records solve old crimes
- Lessons learned from applying OSINT in unsolved cases

11. OSINT & Law Enforcement Collaboration

- How OSINT analysts work with law enforcement
- Turning OSINT findings into actionable intelligence
- Cross-agency collaboration & challenges
- Legal & ethical considerations in law enforcement OSINT
- Using OSINT for court evidence & prosecution
- **Case Study**: How OSINT helped convict a major criminal

12. Ethical & Legal Challenges in Criminal OSINT

- Understanding privacy laws & data protection
- Ethical concerns in criminal investigations
- The boundary between OSINT & private investigation
- Legal risks of conducting OSINT on criminals
- Best practices for ethical & responsible OSINT investigations
- **Case Study**: When OSINT crossed ethical & legal boundaries

Conclusion: OSINT as the Investigator's Superpower

The digital age has revolutionized crime—and also how we fight it. OSINT has become a game-changer in tracking criminals, solving cases, and gathering intelligence.

✅ OSINT helps uncover hidden connections in financial fraud, human trafficking, and organized crime

✅ Digital footprints make it easier to track suspects, even when they try to hide

✅ Publicly available intelligence can be the missing piece in criminal cases

✅ The ethical and legal landscape of OSINT is complex, but mastering it ensures responsible investigations

This book has given you a practical roadmap to using OSINT in criminal cases. Whether you're an investigator, cybersecurity analyst, journalist, or law enforcement officer, your ability to harness OSINT can mean the difference between an unsolved crime and bringing a criminal to justice.

The tools are at your fingertips. Now, it's time to investigate.

1. OSINT in Law Enforcement & Criminal Cases

In this chapter, we delve into the pivotal role Open Source Intelligence (OSINT) plays in law enforcement and criminal investigations. With the digital age transforming how crimes are committed and investigated, OSINT has become an indispensable tool for uncovering evidence, tracking suspects, and solving cases. We will explore how law enforcement agencies are increasingly leveraging digital tools and online resources to gather critical information, enhance investigative efforts, and navigate the complexities of modern criminal cases. Through real-world examples and practical insights, this chapter highlights how OSINT is reshaping the landscape of criminal justice.

1.1 The Role of OSINT in Modern Criminal Investigations

In the age of digital connectivity, criminal investigations have undergone a significant transformation. Gone are the days when investigators relied solely on physical evidence or witness testimony. Today, Open Source Intelligence (OSINT) has emerged as a cornerstone of modern criminal investigations, enabling law enforcement agencies, security professionals, and intelligence agencies to harness publicly available digital data for critical insights into criminal activity.

What is OSINT?

Open Source Intelligence refers to the process of collecting, analyzing, and utilizing publicly available data from various sources to support intelligence gathering and investigative efforts. OSINT differs from traditional intelligence sources like classified government reports or surveillance data because it focuses on information that is freely available to the public—such as social media posts, public records, news articles, websites, forums, and even metadata. With the rapid expansion of the internet and digital technologies, OSINT has become an indispensable resource in tracking and uncovering criminal behavior.

The Importance of OSINT in Modern Investigations

The rise of digital technologies has significantly altered the landscape of crime. Criminals now utilize online platforms for activities such as money laundering, identity theft, trafficking, fraud, and cybercrime. As traditional investigative methods, such as physical surveillance or interrogations, face limitations in the digital age, OSINT has become a vital tool for modern law enforcement.

OSINT is essential because it offers a way to track and gather real-time intelligence, identify patterns of behavior, and uncover hidden connections between suspects, criminal organizations, and illicit activities. Digital platforms like social media provide an unprecedented level of insight into an individual's behavior, location, relationships, and interests, all of which can be valuable in solving cases. This wealth of publicly accessible information, when combined with traditional investigative techniques, increases the chances of solving crimes and identifying perpetrators.

OSINT Applications in Criminal Investigations

Cybercrime and Fraud Investigations

One of the most notable uses of OSINT in criminal investigations is in the realm of cybercrime. The internet has given rise to an array of new criminal activities, from phishing scams and identity theft to hacking and online fraud. By monitoring online marketplaces, forums, and social media, investigators can track illegal transactions, uncover stolen data, and identify criminal networks responsible for operating in the digital shadows.

For example, in a case involving financial fraud or money laundering, OSINT tools can be used to analyze digital footprints such as payment histories, cryptocurrency transactions, and online discussions. Platforms like Bitcoin blockchains, social media pages, and hidden forums are often where criminals exchange information or conduct business, making them critical sources for investigators. By leveraging OSINT, investigators can trace the flow of illicit funds, discover shell companies, and track criminal movements within the dark web.

Tracking and Monitoring Criminal Networks

OSINT is also instrumental in tracking criminal networks and understanding their structure. Organized crime syndicates, gangs, and trafficking networks often use online platforms to communicate, recruit members, and organize criminal activities. OSINT enables investigators to monitor these platforms for digital clues that can help identify key players, dismantle networks, and disrupt criminal operations.

Through careful analysis of social media profiles, encrypted messaging apps, and publicly accessible databases, investigators can trace connections between individuals and uncover the relationships that fuel criminal enterprises. A prime example is the use of OSINT in drug trafficking investigations. By tracking patterns in online communications and mapping out digital interactions, investigators can identify drug suppliers, buyers, and even drug routes, bringing them closer to busting large-scale operations.

Locating Missing Persons

Another vital application of OSINT in modern investigations is in locating missing persons. OSINT allows investigators to track the online activities of individuals who may have disappeared, including posts, photos, and location-based data. This method is particularly useful when traditional investigation methods, such as interviewing witnesses or checking physical locations, have not yielded results.

For instance, by reviewing an individual's last known interactions on social media or analyzing location data from their smartphone, investigators can trace a person's movements before they went missing. This data might also reveal whether the individual voluntarily left or was abducted, aiding in the development of new investigative leads.

Digital Evidence in Violent Crimes and Terrorism Investigations

OSINT has also proven invaluable in solving violent crimes, including homicides and domestic violence cases, as well as monitoring terrorist activities. Social media platforms like Facebook, Twitter, and Instagram often serve as spaces for individuals to express their thoughts, share experiences, or document actions that could provide investigators with critical evidence. In violent crime cases, posts or videos related to the crime scene, witness accounts, or confessions can provide pivotal leads for investigators.

When it comes to terrorism investigations, OSINT plays a central role in monitoring extremist propaganda, recruitment efforts, and radicalization processes. Terrorist organizations and extremist groups have increasingly turned to social media and encrypted messaging platforms to disseminate their ideology, recruit members, and plan operations. By analyzing these online spaces, law enforcement can gain early warnings of potential threats, track terrorist financing, and even thwart attacks before they occur.

Enhancing Traditional Investigative Techniques

OSINT does not replace traditional investigative methods but instead complements them. By incorporating OSINT into the investigative process, law enforcement agencies can enhance the effectiveness of their operations. For example, OSINT can be used to verify alibis, trace suspects' movements, or corroborate witness statements. Additionally, OSINT enables investigators to access valuable background information on suspects or individuals of interest, such as their social connections, previous criminal activities, and even online behavior patterns that may not have been accessible through conventional methods.

The synergy between OSINT and traditional tools like surveillance, wiretaps, and forensic evidence helps investigators build a more complete picture of a crime and its perpetrators, increasing the likelihood of securing a conviction.

Challenges and Limitations of OSINT

While OSINT provides investigators with powerful resources, it is not without its challenges. The sheer volume of publicly available information can be overwhelming, and not all digital data is relevant or accurate. Investigators must sift through vast amounts of information, ensuring that the intelligence they gather is reliable and applicable to their case.

Additionally, the legal and ethical considerations surrounding OSINT are significant. Investigators must respect privacy laws and ensure that they are not infringing upon individuals' rights when collecting and using open-source data. Proper training and adherence to legal guidelines are necessary to ensure that OSINT is used ethically and within the confines of the law.

The Future of OSINT in Criminal Investigations

As technology continues to evolve, so too will the role of OSINT in criminal investigations. The advent of artificial intelligence, machine learning, and advanced data analytics will enhance OSINT capabilities, enabling investigators to process vast amounts of data quickly and accurately. Predictive analytics will allow law enforcement to identify potential criminal activity before it occurs, providing a proactive approach to preventing crimes.

In conclusion, OSINT has become an invaluable tool in modern criminal investigations, offering new ways to gather, analyze, and utilize publicly available information. Whether in cybercrime, missing persons cases, or the fight against terrorism, OSINT enables investigators to work smarter and faster, improving their chances of solving cases and bringing perpetrators to justice. As digital technologies continue to shape the future of crime and investigation, the role of OSINT will only grow, ensuring that law enforcement stays ahead of emerging threats in an increasingly digital world.

1.2 Understanding Open-Source vs. Classified Intelligence

Intelligence gathering is a crucial component of criminal investigations, law enforcement, and national security efforts. Within the intelligence community, information is categorized based on its accessibility, source, and sensitivity. Two primary types of intelligence are open-source intelligence (OSINT) and classified intelligence. Understanding the distinction between these two types is essential for investigators, analysts, and law enforcement professionals as they navigate the digital landscape in pursuit of critical information.

This chapter explores the differences between open-source and classified intelligence, their respective roles in investigations, and how OSINT complements classified intelligence in modern law enforcement and intelligence operations.

What is Open-Source Intelligence (OSINT)?

Open-Source Intelligence (OSINT) refers to intelligence gathered from publicly available sources. It includes any information that is legally and ethically accessible to the public, without requiring special permissions or security clearances. OSINT sources include:

- **Social Media** – Public posts, comments, geotags, and interactions on platforms like Facebook, Twitter, Instagram, and LinkedIn.
- **News & Media** – Online news articles, television broadcasts, blogs, and press releases.
- **Public Records & Government Databases** – Court records, business registries, patents, and publicly available legal filings.
- **Academic & Scientific Publications** – Research papers, white papers, and industry reports.
- **Websites & Online Forums** – Information shared in public discussion boards, blogs, and community forums.
- **Satellite Imagery & Geospatial Data** – Data obtained from public mapping services like Google Earth or NASA's open-data programs.

The strength of OSINT lies in its accessibility, allowing investigators to collect intelligence without engaging in covert or classified operations. With the right tools and methodologies, OSINT provides actionable intelligence that can support criminal investigations, cybersecurity efforts, and counterterrorism operations.

However, OSINT requires verification and analysis. Because it is publicly available, misinformation, outdated data, and intentional deception can complicate investigations. Analysts must employ cross-referencing techniques to ensure accuracy and reliability.

What is Classified Intelligence?

Classified intelligence, on the other hand, refers to sensitive information that is restricted from public access due to its importance to national security, law enforcement operations, or intelligence gathering. This information is typically collected through covert means and is safeguarded by various security measures. Classified intelligence can be divided into several categories:

- **Human Intelligence (HUMINT)** – Information gathered through human sources, such as undercover agents, informants, or defectors.
- **Signals Intelligence (SIGINT)** – Intelligence collected from intercepted communications, including emails, phone calls, and encrypted transmissions.
- **Geospatial Intelligence (GEOINT)** – Classified satellite imagery, aerial surveillance, and geographical data used for military and security purposes.
- **Measurement and Signature Intelligence (MASINT)** – Data collected through scientific analysis, such as radiation detection, seismic monitoring, or weapons testing.
- **Cyber Intelligence (CYBINT)** – Information related to cyber threats, digital espionage, and cyber warfare activities.

Classified intelligence is protected under strict governmental regulations and is only accessible to authorized personnel with the proper security clearances. Governments and intelligence agencies use classified intelligence to prevent terrorist attacks, counter espionage, and safeguard national security interests.

However, classified intelligence has limitations. Its restricted nature makes it less accessible to frontline law enforcement officers or private investigators. Additionally, obtaining classified intelligence often requires bureaucratic approval, which can delay urgent investigations.

Key Differences Between OSINT and Classified Intelligence

Feature	OSINT (Open-Source Intelligence)	Classified Intelligence
Accessibility	Available to the public, legally accessible	Restricted, requires security clearance
Sources	Social media, news, websites, public records	HUMINT, SIGINT, GEOINT, CYBINT
Collection Methods	Passive, based on existing public data	Active, includes covert operations
Legal Considerations	Must comply with data privacy laws but is generally open	Highly regulated, must follow strict legal and security protocols
Verification Challenges	Misinformation and disinformation risk	Generally vetted through secure intelligence channels
Speed & Flexibility	Quick access to information without approvals	Bureaucratic processes may delay access
Usage	Law enforcement, journalists, cybersecurity, private investigators	National security, counterterrorism, military operations

How OSINT and Classified Intelligence Work Together

Although OSINT and classified intelligence differ in their sources and accessibility, they are not mutually exclusive. In fact, modern investigations and intelligence operations benefit from an integrated approach where OSINT complements classified intelligence.

Enhancing Intelligence Gaps – OSINT can help fill gaps in classified intelligence by providing additional context, verifying details, or tracking evolving situations in real time. For example, while classified SIGINT might intercept terrorist communications, OSINT can provide supporting intelligence by analyzing public social media activity or monitoring extremist propaganda forums.

Corroborating Evidence – OSINT can validate or contradict classified intelligence findings. Analysts often cross-check classified data with open-source reports to confirm details, assess credibility, and identify false information.

Identifying Emerging Threats – While classified intelligence is crucial for counterterrorism and security operations, OSINT allows investigators to track emerging threats before they reach the attention of intelligence agencies. Trends in cybercrime, online radicalization, and fraud often surface in public domains before being flagged as national security risks.

Supporting Criminal Investigations – OSINT plays a key role in everyday law enforcement investigations. Detectives, prosecutors, and forensic analysts use publicly available records, social media evidence, and digital footprints to build cases against criminals. If necessary, this intelligence can be escalated for classified investigation.

Public Awareness and Security – Unlike classified intelligence, OSINT findings can be shared with the public to raise awareness about security threats, cyber risks, or criminal activities. Government agencies frequently use OSINT to issue warnings about scams, fraud schemes, or terrorist threats.

Challenges and Ethical Considerations

Both OSINT and classified intelligence come with their own ethical and legal challenges.

- **Privacy Concerns** – OSINT must be collected responsibly, ensuring that investigators do not infringe upon individuals' privacy rights. Data scraping, social media monitoring, and surveillance techniques should adhere to legal guidelines.
- **Misinformation Risks** – Since OSINT is publicly available, false or misleading information can be spread intentionally. Analysts must verify sources and cross-reference data to avoid basing investigations on unreliable intelligence.
- **Legal Limitations** – Investigators handling classified intelligence must navigate legal frameworks, ensuring they comply with governmental regulations on handling sensitive information. Unauthorized disclosure of classified data can lead to severe penalties.
- **Ethical Use of Intelligence** – Both OSINT and classified intelligence should be used responsibly, ensuring they serve public safety and do not infringe on civil liberties.

Conclusion

Understanding the distinction between open-source and classified intelligence is critical for investigators and intelligence professionals. OSINT provides a powerful and accessible tool for gathering intelligence in real time, while classified intelligence remains essential for national security and covert operations. By combining the strengths of both intelligence types, law enforcement agencies and analysts can develop a more comprehensive approach to criminal investigations and security threats.

As technology continues to evolve, OSINT will play an even greater role in bridging the gap between public data and classified intelligence, offering new opportunities for law enforcement, cybersecurity experts, and intelligence analysts to stay ahead of criminal activities in the digital age.

1.3 How Law Enforcement Uses OSINT for Investigations

Law enforcement agencies across the world increasingly rely on Open-Source Intelligence (OSINT) to support criminal investigations, enhance situational awareness, and proactively prevent crimes. OSINT allows officers, analysts, and investigators to leverage publicly available information to uncover criminal activities, track suspects, and gather critical intelligence—all without requiring warrants or classified resources.

This chapter explores how law enforcement integrates OSINT into investigations, the tools and techniques they use, and the impact of digital intelligence on modern policing.

The Growing Role of OSINT in Law Enforcement

The digital revolution has transformed crime, with criminals operating across multiple platforms, leaving digital footprints that investigators can analyze. As a result, OSINT has become a cost-effective, legal, and efficient method of gathering intelligence.

Law enforcement agencies use OSINT to:

- Identify suspects and locate persons of interest
- Monitor social media for threats or criminal behavior
- Investigate fraud, cybercrime, and financial crimes
- Track missing persons and human trafficking victims
- Map out criminal networks and gang affiliations
- Counter terrorism and extremism

Gather intelligence for undercover operations

By combining OSINT with traditional investigative methods, law enforcement agencies can build stronger cases, respond to threats more effectively, and ensure public safety.

Key OSINT Techniques Used in Investigations

Law enforcement officers and OSINT analysts rely on a variety of digital techniques to collect, analyze, and verify intelligence. Below are some of the most commonly used OSINT methods:

1. Social Media Intelligence (SOCMINT)

Social media platforms serve as gold mines for OSINT investigations. Suspects often leave behind valuable digital footprints, including location check-ins, photos, videos, and interactions. Investigators use SOCMINT to:

- Identify suspects and associates based on posts, tags, and geolocation data
- Monitor threats such as planned attacks, gang activity, or public disturbances
- Track criminal behavior by analyzing suspect communications and social patterns
- Verify alibis through social media activity timestamps

For instance, if a suspect claims they were in one location at a specific time but a social media post places them elsewhere, this can serve as digital evidence in a case.

2. Geolocation Tracking & Mapping

By analyzing publicly available geolocation data—such as photos with embedded metadata, check-ins, and GPS coordinates—law enforcement can:

- Reconstruct crime scenes and track a suspect's movements
- Locate fugitives or missing persons by identifying their last known locations
- Monitor illegal activities in specific areas, such as drug trafficking routes

Google Earth, OpenStreetMap, and geolocation metadata extracted from social media posts provide valuable insights for investigations.

3. Dark Web & Cybercrime Investigations

The dark web is a hub for illegal activities, including drug sales, human trafficking, and cybercrime. Law enforcement agencies use OSINT to:

- Monitor hidden forums and marketplaces for illegal transactions
- Track cryptocurrency movements in financial crimes
- Uncover digital identities of cybercriminals operating anonymously

By analyzing dark web discussions and marketplaces, investigators can infiltrate criminal networks and disrupt illicit operations.

4. Public Records & Database Searches

OSINT enables investigators to access publicly available records, including:

- Court filings and arrest records
- Business registrations and financial disclosures
- Property ownership records
- Leaked data from past breaches

These records help law enforcement connect suspects to businesses, assets, or prior criminal activities, strengthening their cases.

5. Image and Video Analysis

Law enforcement agencies use OSINT tools to analyze images and videos shared online. This includes:

- Reverse image searches to identify locations, faces, or objects
- Video metadata extraction to verify timestamps and sources
- AI-based facial recognition to match suspects to known databases

By examining images from social media, news reports, and security footage, investigators can uncover key evidence that may have been overlooked.

Real-World Applications of OSINT in Law Enforcement

1. Criminal Investigations

OSINT plays a crucial role in identifying suspects, verifying alibis, and gathering digital evidence. For example, in homicide investigations, social media interactions, location data, and public records can help detectives piece together motives and suspect movements.

2. Human Trafficking & Missing Persons Cases

Law enforcement agencies use OSINT to track victims and perpetrators of human trafficking. Analysts monitor escort websites, social media ads, and online forums to identify potential trafficking rings. By geolocating images and cross-referencing missing persons databases, investigators can rescue victims more effectively.

3. Fraud & Financial Crimes

OSINT is instrumental in exposing fraudulent activities such as:

- Online scams that defraud individuals through fake investment schemes
- Identity theft where criminals steal personal data to commit financial fraud
- Money laundering by tracing digital transactions and offshore companies

Investigators often analyze financial records, online transactions, and dark web discussions to uncover fraud schemes.

4. Counterterrorism & Extremism Monitoring

Terrorist groups and extremists often use social media and encrypted platforms to recruit, communicate, and spread propaganda. OSINT enables law enforcement to:

- Monitor extremist activity on social media
- Identify radicalized individuals before they act
- Track terrorist financing through crowdfunding and cryptocurrency transactions

Governments worldwide use OSINT to prevent terror attacks and monitor high-risk individuals.

5. Gang & Organized Crime Surveillance

Street gangs and organized crime groups often communicate through online platforms. Investigators use OSINT to:

- Identify gang affiliations through tattoos, hand signs, and coded language
- Map out rivalries and territorial disputes based on online threats
- Monitor social media for recruitment efforts and planned attacks

By understanding gang structures, law enforcement can anticipate violence and prevent crime before it happens.

Challenges & Ethical Considerations in Law Enforcement OSINT

While OSINT provides valuable intelligence, law enforcement must navigate challenges such as:

- **Privacy concerns** – Investigators must ensure they are legally collecting and using publicly available data without violating privacy laws.
- **Misinformation and fake news** – Criminals sometimes spread false information online to mislead authorities. Verification and cross-referencing are crucial.
- **Legal boundaries** – Law enforcement must operate within the law when collecting OSINT, avoiding unauthorized surveillance or data breaches.
- **Encryption and anonymity** – Some criminals use encrypted messaging apps and VPNs, making it difficult to track their activities.

To address these challenges, law enforcement agencies must implement clear policies, ethical guidelines, and proper training for OSINT investigations.

Conclusion

OSINT has revolutionized modern law enforcement, providing an efficient, legal, and cost-effective way to gather intelligence. By leveraging social media analysis, geolocation tracking, dark web monitoring, and public records, law enforcement agencies can solve crimes faster, locate suspects, and prevent threats before they escalate.

As technology continues to evolve, OSINT will play an even greater role in criminal investigations, counterterrorism, and cybersecurity. However, responsible use, adherence to legal standards, and ethical considerations will be crucial to ensuring that OSINT remains a powerful yet lawful tool for law enforcement agencies worldwide.

1.4 Common OSINT Tools for Criminal Casework

Open-Source Intelligence (OSINT) plays a crucial role in modern criminal investigations, allowing law enforcement, analysts, and private investigators to gather intelligence from publicly available sources. A key aspect of OSINT is the use of specialized tools that automate data collection, analysis, and visualization, making investigations more efficient and accurate.

This chapter explores some of the most commonly used OSINT tools in criminal casework, categorized by their functions, such as social media analysis, geolocation tracking, dark web monitoring, and digital forensics.

1. OSINT Tools for Social Media Investigations (SOCMINT)

Social media platforms are a goldmine of intelligence for criminal investigations, providing insights into suspect activities, affiliations, and locations. Here are some of the top tools used to analyze social media data:

a) Maltego

- **Function**: Link analysis and relationship mapping
- **Use Case**: Helps investigators visualize connections between individuals, social media profiles, organizations, and websites
- **Strengths**: Provides deep-link analysis and can integrate multiple data sources

b) Social Links & Echosec

- **Function**: Social media and deep web monitoring
- **Use Case**: Tracks conversations, posts, and images shared on social media and deep web forums
- **Strengths**: Can analyze hidden data, including deleted posts and metadata

c) Twint (for Twitter Investigations)

- **Function**: Twitter data scraping without an API key
- **Use Case**: Monitors tweets, geolocation data, and user interactions for investigative purposes
- **Strengths**: Useful for tracking criminal discussions, extremist activity, and sentiment analysis

d) OSINT Combine Social Network Analysis

- **Function**: Social media footprint analysis
- **Use Case**: Helps map relationships and online behaviors of persons of interest
- **Strengths**: Used extensively in law enforcement for monitoring criminal networks

2. Geolocation OSINT Tools

Tracking a suspect's location or mapping out criminal activity often requires geospatial intelligence. The following tools are widely used for geolocation tracking and analysis:

a) Google Earth & Google Maps

- **Function**: Satellite imagery and street-level mapping

- **Use Case**: Crime scene analysis, tracking suspect movements, and mapping out locations linked to criminal activity
- **Strengths**: Provides high-resolution imagery for visualizing places of interest

b) EXIF Tools (Metadata Extraction)

- **Function**: Extracts metadata from images
- **Use Case**: Determines location and device information from suspect-shared photos
- **Strengths**: Useful in verifying alibis and tracking digital footprints

c) Mapchecking & SunCalc

- **Function**: Time and location verification
- **Use Case**: Analyzes sun position and shadows to confirm the authenticity of images and videos
- **Strengths**: Helps debunk falsified media evidence

d) GeoSpy & OpenStreetMap

- **Function**: Open-source geolocation tracking
- **Use Case**: Identifies crime hotspots and monitors suspect movements based on geotagged social media posts
- **Strengths**: Works well in tracking missing persons and criminal hideouts

3. Dark Web & Cybercrime OSINT Tools

The dark web is often used for illicit activities, including drug sales, human trafficking, and cybercrime. OSINT tools help law enforcement monitor hidden marketplaces, track cybercriminals, and investigate digital footprints.

a) Tor & OnionScan

- **Function**: Dark web scanning
- **Use Case**: Helps law enforcement monitor illicit activities, forums, and marketplaces
- **Strengths**: Provides insights into cybercriminal networks operating anonymously

b) SpiderFoot

- **Function**: Automated OSINT reconnaissance
- **Use Case**: Collects data on suspects, including domains, IP addresses, and online activities
- **Strengths**: Ideal for cybersecurity investigations

c) DarkOwl Vision

- **Function**: Dark web intelligence gathering
- **Use Case**: Tracks leaked credentials, fraud schemes, and criminal activities in hidden networks
- **Strengths**: Provides real-time monitoring of dark web activity

d) Have I Been Pwned

- **Function**: Data breach monitoring
- **Use Case**: Checks if a suspect's credentials have been leaked in data breaches
- **Strengths**: Helps identify compromised accounts and potential fraud risks

4. OSINT Tools for Financial Crimes & Fraud Investigations

Tracking financial fraud, money laundering, and illicit transactions requires specialized OSINT tools.

a) CipherTrace & Chainalysis

- **Function**: Cryptocurrency transaction tracking
- **Use Case**: Investigates illegal cryptocurrency transactions linked to fraud and money laundering
- **Strengths**: Helps law enforcement follow the money trail in crypto-related crimes

b) OpenCorporates

- **Function**: Business registry and corporate tracking
- **Use Case**: Identifies shell companies, fraudulent business activities, and criminal financial operations
- **Strengths**: Accesses global corporate records

c) LittleSis

- **Function**: Political and financial network analysis

- **Use Case**: Investigates corruption, financial fraud, and hidden corporate relationships
- **Strengths**: Maps financial connections between criminals and businesses

d) Offshore Leaks Database

- **Function**: Tracks offshore accounts and financial records
- **Use Case**: Identifies tax evasion, fraud, and money laundering schemes
- **Strengths**: Helps law enforcement trace hidden assets

5. Digital Forensics & Cyber Investigations

Digital forensic tools help investigators analyze devices, recover deleted data, and extract digital evidence in criminal cases.

a) Autopsy & FTK Imager

- **Function**: Digital forensic investigation
- **Use Case**: Recovers deleted files, emails, and logs from suspect devices
- **Strengths**: Used extensively in cybercrime investigations

b) Cellebrite UFED

- **Function**: Mobile device forensics
- **Use Case**: Extracts and analyzes data from seized smartphones in criminal cases
- **Strengths**: Helps recover messages, call logs, and hidden files

c) Magnet AXIOM

- **Function**: Digital evidence collection
- **Use Case**: Gathers evidence from computers, cloud storage, and mobile devices
- **Strengths**: Supports complex cyber investigations

d) Wireshark

- **Function**: Network traffic analysis
- **Use Case**: Monitors suspect network activity for cybercrime investigations
- **Strengths**: Used for tracking hackers and cybercriminals

Conclusion

OSINT tools have transformed criminal investigations, providing law enforcement with powerful capabilities to track criminals, analyze digital footprints, and prevent crimes. Whether investigating fraud, cybercrime, human trafficking, or terrorism, these tools enhance intelligence gathering and improve case resolution rates.

As technology evolves, OSINT will continue to play a critical role in criminal casework, requiring law enforcement professionals to stay updated on the latest tools and techniques to stay ahead of criminals in the digital age.

1.5 Case Study: OSINT in a High-Profile Criminal Investigation

The power of Open-Source Intelligence (OSINT) in criminal investigations has been demonstrated in numerous high-profile cases, where digital footprints, social media activity, and public records played a crucial role in identifying suspects, tracking movements, and gathering evidence. This case study explores how law enforcement used OSINT to crack a major criminal case, highlighting the tools, techniques, and impact of digital intelligence.

Case Study: The Capture of Luka Magnotta

Background:

In 2012, an international manhunt was launched for Luka Magnotta, a Canadian fugitive accused of the brutal murder and dismemberment of a university student, Jun Lin. The case gained international attention due to the suspect's disturbing online activity, use of multiple identities, and an attempt to evade capture by fleeing across multiple countries.

Phase 1: Identifying the Suspect Through OSINT

Before the murder, Magnotta had already drawn attention from online communities and law enforcement. He was known for posting graphic animal abuse videos, which led to a crowdsourced OSINT investigation by internet sleuths on platforms like Reddit and Facebook.

Key OSINT Techniques Used:

- **Reverse Image Search**: Investigators and online users traced Magnotta's images and videos across multiple platforms to uncover locations and aliases.
- **Social Media Analysis**: His past activity on Facebook, YouTube, and personal blogs revealed his obsession with fame and his tendency to taunt authorities.
- **Public Records & Leaks**: Investigators accessed old forum posts, past employment records, and online comments linking Magnotta to multiple fake identities.

Phase 2: Tracking Magnotta's Movements

After committing the murder in Montreal, Magnotta mailed body parts to Canadian political offices and fled the country. OSINT played a crucial role in tracking his movements across continents.

Key OSINT Techniques Used:

CCTV & Geolocation Analysis:

- Surveillance footage from airports and bus stations helped law enforcement confirm Magnotta's escape route.
- OSINT investigators used Google Street View to match locations seen in his previous online videos with real-world places, leading to better predictive tracking.

IP Address & Online Activity Monitoring:

- Despite being on the run, Magnotta continued using the internet, searching for news about himself.
- Investigators monitored his digital footprint and found that he frequently checked news articles about the manhunt, revealing his location patterns.

Hotel & Travel Records Scraping:

- Magnotta booked one-way tickets and cheap hostels, leaving behind digital breadcrumbs through booking websites and online reviews.
- OSINT tools were used to cross-reference his email IDs and aliases against public reservation data.

Phase 3: Arrest in Berlin – OSINT in Action

The final breakthrough in the case came when Magnotta was located in Berlin, Germany. Law enforcement used OSINT to pinpoint his exact location before moving in to make the arrest.

Key OSINT Techniques Used:

Wi-Fi & Network Tracing:

- Magnotta was found using a public computer at an internet café, where he was reading articles about himself.
- Investigators cross-referenced login timestamps with his suspected locations to confirm his presence in Berlin.

Facial Recognition & Public Reporting:

- German authorities used facial recognition software on surveillance footage.
- A café employee, who had seen news reports and images of Magnotta, recognized him and alerted the police.

The OSINT-led investigation ended with Magnotta's arrest without incident.

Impact of OSINT on the Investigation

1. Speed & Efficiency

Without OSINT, tracking an international fugitive could have taken months or even years. OSINT allowed investigators to:

- Quickly identify Magnotta's online presence and behavior
- Monitor his movements in real time
- Predict his next locations based on his digital patterns

2. The Power of Crowdsourced OSINT

One of the most significant aspects of this case was the role played by internet sleuths and online communities.

- Before law enforcement got involved, online investigators had already identified Magnotta as a suspect in previous animal abuse videos.

- These online communities provided law enforcement with valuable intelligence, proving how OSINT can democratize investigations.

3. The Role of Digital Footprints in Criminal Cases

This case demonstrated how even the most cautious criminals leave behind digital evidence:

- Social media posts, even if deleted, can be retrieved through OSINT archives.
- Online searches and browsing habits can be traced back to physical locations.
- Public databases and leaked records make it difficult for criminals to stay hidden forever.

Key Takeaways for OSINT Investigators

1. OSINT is Essential in International Investigations

Magnotta traveled across multiple countries, but OSINT tools allowed law enforcement to track him in real time. Future criminal investigations must leverage:

- **Geolocation OSINT tools** (Google Maps, satellite imagery)
- **Airline and hotel booking analysis** (leaked databases, travel monitoring)
- **Dark web & forum tracking** (for criminals using aliases online)

2. Criminals Always Leave a Digital Trail

Despite using multiple fake identities, Magnotta made mistakes:

- He continued using the internet, leading to his eventual capture.
- He left behind digital traces in booking records and CCTV footage.
- He repeatedly searched for himself online, providing investigators with useful behavioral insights.

3. Crowdsourced OSINT is a Game-Changer

- The public played a major role in uncovering Magnotta's identity before law enforcement got involved.
- Future cases can benefit from online volunteers analyzing evidence, using tools like reverse image search, social media monitoring, and dark web tracking.

Conclusion

The Luka Magnotta case is a textbook example of OSINT-driven law enforcement. It highlights how publicly available information, digital footprints, and social media intelligence can be leveraged to track and apprehend criminals—even across international borders.

In the modern era of digital crime, OSINT has become an indispensable tool for law enforcement agencies worldwide. By effectively using social media monitoring, geolocation tracking, and digital forensics, investigators can solve complex cases faster, bringing fugitives to justice even in the most challenging scenarios.

1.6 Challenges & Limitations of OSINT in Law Enforcement

Open-Source Intelligence (OSINT) has revolutionized criminal investigations by providing law enforcement agencies with access to vast amounts of publicly available data. However, despite its effectiveness, OSINT comes with significant challenges and limitations that can impact the reliability, legality, and ethical use of intelligence in investigations. This chapter explores the key obstacles law enforcement faces when using OSINT and discusses potential solutions for overcoming them.

1. Legal & Ethical Challenges

a) Privacy Concerns & Ethical Boundaries

- OSINT operates in the grey area between public and private information.
- Law enforcement must balance investigative needs with privacy rights, ensuring compliance with laws like the General Data Protection Regulation (GDPR) and the Fourth Amendment (U.S.).
- Ethical concerns arise when covert monitoring of individuals occurs without explicit consent, even if data is publicly accessible.

Example:

Scraping social media profiles may be legal in some jurisdictions but could violate terms of service agreements, leading to legal disputes or evidence being inadmissible in court.

b) Jurisdictional & International Legal Barriers

- OSINT investigations often cross international borders, creating legal conflicts.
- Different countries have varying privacy laws, which can restrict how law enforcement agencies collect and use OSINT data.
- Collaboration with foreign governments may be required, slowing down investigations.

Example:

A criminal may use a foreign-based social media platform that does not cooperate with law enforcement, making it difficult to access critical evidence.

2. Data Overload & Verification Issues

a) Information Overload & False Positives

- OSINT generates massive amounts of data, making it difficult to filter relevant intelligence.
- Investigators risk drowning in irrelevant data, leading to inefficient investigations.
- False positives can misidentify suspects, wasting valuable law enforcement resources.

Example:

Searching for a suspect's name on social media or public databases may yield hundreds of unrelated individuals, leading to misidentifications.

b) Misinformation & Disinformation

- Criminals use fake identities, manipulated images, and deepfakes to mislead investigators.
- Disinformation campaigns can create false narratives, diverting law enforcement from real threats.

Example:

Terrorist groups use social media to spread misleading propaganda, making it difficult for investigators to distinguish between genuine threats and hoaxes.
Solution:

- Use cross-referencing techniques to verify information.

- Employ AI-driven analytics to detect fake accounts, bots, and deepfakes.

3. Technical Limitations & Data Access Issues

a) Rapidly Changing Technology & OSINT Evasion Tactics

- Criminals adapt quickly, using encrypted communication platforms, VPNs, and burner phones to evade detection.
- Social media restrictions on data access make it harder for law enforcement to collect intelligence.
- AI-generated content (e.g., deepfake profiles) complicates digital investigations.

Example:

Human traffickers use encrypted messaging apps like Signal and Telegram, making OSINT tools ineffective for intercepting communications.

Solution:

- Law enforcement must continuously update OSINT tools and methodologies to stay ahead of evolving criminal tactics.
- Use dark web monitoring tools to track illicit activities in hidden online communities.

b) Data Fragmentation Across Multiple Platforms

- Criminals operate on multiple platforms, including mainstream social media, dark web forums, and encrypted apps.
- OSINT tools may not always provide comprehensive coverage, forcing investigators to manually search multiple sources.

Example:

A cybercriminal may discuss illicit activities on Reddit, Telegram, and a dark web forum, requiring investigators to track conversations across all platforms.

Solution:

Use automated OSINT aggregation tools like Maltego, Social Links, and ShadowDragon to consolidate intelligence from multiple sources.

4. Admissibility of OSINT Evidence in Court

a) Chain of Custody & Digital Evidence Integrity

- OSINT evidence must be collected, stored, and presented in a legally acceptable manner.
- Courts may reject OSINT findings if they are improperly sourced or manipulated.
- Screenshots and scraped data may not be considered primary evidence unless properly verified.

Example:

A screenshot of a suspect's social media post may be dismissed in court unless metadata and forensic validation are provided.

Solution:

Follow forensic evidence handling protocols and use certified data collection tools like Hunchly to preserve OSINT findings.

b) Challenges in Attribution & Identity Confirmation

- Criminals use aliases, burner phones, and fake social media accounts, making it difficult to prove digital activity belongs to a specific individual.
- Courts require solid proof linking a suspect to online evidence.

Example:

A suspect may claim that a fraudulent financial transaction was carried out by an imposter using their stolen identity.

Solution:

Use digital forensic analysis to cross-check IP addresses, device fingerprints, and geolocation data.

5. Resource Constraints & Training Gaps

a) Lack of OSINT Training in Law Enforcement

- Many law enforcement agencies lack specialized OSINT training, leading to inefficient investigations.
- Without proper skills, investigators may misinterpret data or miss key intelligence.

Example:

An investigator unfamiliar with dark web OSINT may struggle to track illicit activities on Tor networks.

Solution:

- Implement regular OSINT training programs for law enforcement personnel.
- Utilize public-private partnerships to leverage expertise from cybersecurity firms and OSINT professionals.

b) Limited Budgets for OSINT Tools

- Many agencies lack the budget to access premium OSINT tools.
- Free OSINT tools may provide limited features, making it harder to conduct comprehensive investigations.

Example:

A police department may be unable to afford enterprise-level tools like Palantir or Maltego, limiting their investigative capabilities.

Solution:

- Leverage open-source OSINT tools like OSINT Framework, SpiderFoot, and The Harvester for cost-effective intelligence gathering.
- Collaborate with government agencies and private-sector partners to access advanced tools.

Conclusion

While OSINT is an invaluable tool in modern criminal investigations, it comes with legal, ethical, technical, and operational challenges. Investigators must navigate privacy laws, data overload, misinformation, and evolving criminal tactics while ensuring OSINT findings are admissible in court.

To maximize OSINT's effectiveness, law enforcement agencies must:

✓ Stay updated with emerging OSINT tools & methodologies

✓ Ensure ethical and legal compliance

✓ Improve training and resource allocation

✓ Use AI-driven automation to filter and verify data

By addressing these challenges, OSINT can continue to be a powerful force in solving crimes, tracking criminals, and enhancing public safety in the digital age.

2. Digital Identity Investigations

This chapter focuses on the intricate process of digital identity investigations, a critical aspect of modern criminal investigations. In an era where almost every aspect of a person's life is online, tracing digital footprints has become essential for uncovering true identities, verifying alibis, and uncovering criminal activity. We will explore the methods used to investigate digital identities across various platforms, from social media and email accounts to online purchases and IP addresses. By examining real-world applications and case studies, this chapter reveals how OSINT tools can be utilized to piece together the puzzle of a suspect's digital persona, enabling investigators to make informed decisions in their pursuit of justice.

2.1 Identifying Suspects Through Online Footprints

In the digital age, almost every individual leaves behind an online footprint—a trail of digital activity across social media, forums, websites, and public records. For law enforcement and OSINT investigators, these footprints serve as crucial pieces of evidence in identifying suspects, confirming identities, and uncovering hidden connections. This chapter explores how digital footprints are created, key OSINT techniques for identifying suspects, and real-world case examples where online traces have led to successful criminal apprehensions.

Understanding Digital Footprints

A digital footprint is the collection of data an individual leaves behind through their online activities. This can be classified into two main types:

1. Active Footprints

Data that a user deliberately shares online.

Examples:

- **Social media posts, comments, and interactions** (Facebook, Twitter, Instagram).
- **Public profiles and usernames** (LinkedIn, Reddit, gaming platforms).
- **Uploaded photos and videos** (YouTube, TikTok, image-hosting sites).

2. Passive Footprints

Data that is collected without direct user input.

Examples:

- IP addresses and geolocation data collected by websites.
- Metadata in images and videos revealing location or device details.
- Browsing history and online tracking cookies stored by websites.

These footprints, when analyzed correctly, can lead investigators to a suspect's identity, location, and network of associates.

Key OSINT Techniques for Identifying Suspects

1. Username & Alias Tracking

Many criminals use unique or recurring usernames across multiple platforms. By tracking these usernames, OSINT investigators can link social media profiles, forums, and email addresses to a suspect.

Tools & Techniques:

- **Namechk / KnowEm** – Checks username availability across multiple platforms.
- **Sherlock & Maigret** – OSINT tools for identifying usernames across social networks.
- **Google Dorking** – Search queries to find linked accounts (e.g., inurl:profile "suspect_username").

Example:

A cybercriminal running online scams used the same alias on Reddit and PayPal forums. Investigators linked his username to a Twitter handle, revealing his real identity.

2. Social Media Analysis

Social media platforms are rich sources of personal information, behavior patterns, and location data. Investigators can use:

- Facebook Graph Search alternatives (e.g., IntelTechniques tools) to map social connections.
- Reverse image search to trace profile pictures across different accounts.
- Geotagged posts to track movements and location history.

Example:

A suspect bragging about a robbery on Instagram posted a selfie near the crime scene. Investigators extracted EXIF metadata from the image, confirming his location.

3. Geolocation & Image Analysis

Many criminals unknowingly reveal their location through images, videos, or public posts.

Tools & Techniques:

- **Google Reverse Image Search / Yandex** – Finds where an image has been used online.
- **EXIF Data Extraction (ExifTool)** – Retrieves metadata like GPS coordinates from photos.
- **Geoguessr-style OSINT** – Identifies locations using background details in photos.

Example:

Investigators found a missing person by analyzing their last known selfie, identifying distinctive buildings and street signs in the background.

4. Email & Phone Number Tracing

Criminals often leave behind email addresses and phone numbers in leaked databases, forum posts, and website registrations.

Tools & Techniques:

- **Have I Been Pwned / Dehashed** – Checks if an email appears in data breaches.
- **Phoneinfoga** – Traces phone numbers for linked accounts.
- **Hunter.io / OSINT.email** – Finds associated email domains and contact details.

Example:

A fraudster used an anonymous Gmail account to scam victims. Investigators checked data leaks and found the same email linked to an old Facebook profile with his real name.

5. Deep Web & Dark Web Investigations

Some criminals operate on the dark web, believing they are anonymous. However, they often make mistakes—reusing usernames, email addresses, or wallets that can be traced.

Tools & Techniques:

- **Dark Web Search Engines (Ahmia, OnionLand)** – Index .onion sites for suspect activity.
- **Bitcoin Address Analysis** – Tracing cryptocurrency transactions linked to crimes.
- **Pipl / Skopenow** – Aggregates deep web data to find hidden identities.

Example:

A hacker selling stolen credit card data was tracked when he reused a Bitcoin wallet for personal transactions, revealing his real-world identity.

Case Study: Tracking a Human Trafficker Through OSINT

Background:

A suspected human trafficker was recruiting victims through fake job ads on social media. He used burner accounts and encrypted messaging apps, making traditional investigative methods ineffective.

How OSINT Led to His Arrest:

Username Linkage:

Investigators used Sherlock to find that his alias was used on escort forums.

Reverse Image Search:

He had posted a fake profile picture on his job ad. A Google Reverse Image Search revealed the real source, proving the ad was fraudulent.

Phone Number Tracing:

The suspect used multiple phone numbers but reused one in a rental agreement found in a public database.

Social Media & Geolocation Analysis:

- Investigators checked his old Instagram posts and identified a unique hotel lobby in the background.
- Using Google Maps, they confirmed the exact location, leading to his arrest.

Result:

OSINT techniques exposed the trafficker's identity, allowing law enforcement to rescue multiple victims.

Challenges & Limitations in Identifying Suspects with OSINT

Despite its power, OSINT investigations face obstacles:

1. Privacy Restrictions & Data Protection Laws

- GDPR & CCPA limit access to personal data.
- Social media platforms restrict data scraping, requiring law enforcement subpoenas.

2. False Identities & Misinformation

- Criminals use fake profiles, burner phones, and VPNs to mislead investigators.
- Deepfake technology makes visual identification harder.

3. Data Overload & Verification Issues

- Investigators must sift through huge amounts of data, increasing the risk of false positives.
- Cross-verification with multiple OSINT sources is crucial to avoid mistakes.

Conclusion

Identifying suspects through online footprints is a critical aspect of modern OSINT investigations. By leveraging social media tracking, geolocation analysis, email tracing, and dark web investigations, law enforcement can uncover identities, track movements, and build strong cases against criminals.

To stay ahead, OSINT investigators must:

✔ Continuously adapt to emerging technologies and criminal evasion tactics.

✔ Use automation & AI tools to filter and analyze vast amounts of data.

✔ Ensure compliance with privacy laws to maintain ethical and legal integrity.

As digital footprints continue to grow, OSINT will remain a powerful tool for law enforcement—turning online traces into real-world arrests.

2.2 Investigating Aliases, Usernames & Digital Personas

In the digital world, criminals rarely use their real names. Instead, they create aliases, usernames, and digital personas to mask their identities and operate anonymously across multiple platforms. However, OSINT techniques can uncover hidden connections between these pseudonyms, exposing the real individuals behind them. This chapter explores how investigators track usernames, analyze digital personas, and link aliases to real-world identities using OSINT tools and methodologies.

Understanding Digital Personas & Aliases

A digital persona is the online identity an individual creates, often comprising:

- Usernames and nicknames used across different sites.
- Profile pictures and avatars (which may be reused elsewhere).
- Email addresses and contact details linked to multiple accounts.
- Posting patterns and language styles, which reveal behavioral traits.

Many criminals maintain multiple online identities for different purposes:

- Scammers use fake business profiles to trick victims.
- Hackers create anonymous personas to sell stolen data.
- Terrorist recruiters use multiple social media aliases to spread propaganda.

- By analyzing patterns in usernames, profile data, and activity logs, OSINT investigators can connect separate aliases to a single individual.

Key OSINT Techniques for Tracking Aliases & Usernames

1. Username Enumeration Across Platforms

Criminals often reuse usernames across multiple websites. OSINT investigators can search for a suspect's alias across:

- **Social media** (Twitter, Instagram, Facebook, Reddit, TikTok, LinkedIn).
- **Gaming platforms** (Steam, Xbox Live, PlayStation Network).
- Dark web forums and hacker communities.

Tools for Username Tracking:

- **Sherlock & Maigret** – Search for usernames across hundreds of platforms.
- **WhatsMyName** – A web-based tool for finding usernames on different sites.
- **Google Dorking** – Advanced search queries to find username links (e.g., site:instagram.com "suspect_username").

Example:

A cybercriminal using the alias "DarkXHunter" on a hacking forum was also found using the same username on Twitter, where he posted personal photos.

2. Reverse Image Search for Profile Pictures

Many criminals reuse the same profile picture across multiple accounts. Investigators can use reverse image searches to find linked profiles.

Tools for Reverse Image Search:

- **Google Reverse Image Search / Yandex** – Finds where an image appears online.
- **TinEye** – Compares profile pictures across websites.

Example:

A fraudster's WhatsApp profile picture was reverse-searched, revealing the same image on a LinkedIn profile with his real name.

3. Email & Phone Number Correlation

Aliases are often linked to email addresses and phone numbers, which can expose real identities.

OSINT Tools for Email & Phone Lookup:

- **Have I Been Pwned / Dehashed** – Checks if an email has been exposed in data breaches.
- **PhoneInfoga** – Finds details about a phone number's origin and linked accounts.
- **Hunter.io** – Searches for email addresses associated with a domain.

Example:

A hacker's email "anon_h4ckr@mail.com" was found in a data breach, linking it to an old Facebook account with his real name.

4. Behavioral Analysis & Writing Style

Even when criminals use different usernames, their writing style, slang, and posting habits often remain consistent.

Methods for Analyzing Writing Style:

- **Linguistic fingerprinting** – Analyzing word choice and grammar.
- **Activity patterns** – Checking posting times to determine timezone or routine.
- **Hashtag and emoji usage** – Comparing stylistic patterns across multiple accounts.

Example:

A terrorist recruiter used multiple aliases but had a distinctive way of writing, which allowed OSINT analysts to link his accounts.

5. Cross-Referencing Social Media Data

Suspects often mention other platforms in their social media bios, leading investigators to new accounts.

OSINT Techniques for Social Media Linkage:

- Check bios and about sections for linked accounts.
- Look for username variations (e.g., DarkXHunter_97 on one site, DarkXHunter97 on another).
- Analyze friends and followers for mutual connections.

Example:

A scammer's Telegram bio mentioned his Instagram handle, allowing investigators to find his personal profile.

Case Study: Unmasking a Cybercriminal's Alias

Background:

A hacker known as "ShadowByte" was selling stolen credit card data on a dark web forum. Law enforcement needed to identify his real-world identity.

OSINT Investigation Steps:

Username Search:

Sherlock found that "ShadowByte" was also active on GitHub and Twitter.

Reverse Image Search:

His Twitter profile picture matched a gaming forum account with the username "ShadowB97".

Email Lookup:

A leaked database from an old hacking site revealed that "ShadowB97" was linked to shadowbyte97@gmail.com.

Social Media Analysis:

Investigators searched the email on Facebook and found a profile under his real name.

Result:

By connecting multiple usernames, profile pictures, and emails, investigators uncovered ShadowByte's real identity, leading to his arrest.

Challenges in Investigating Aliases & Usernames

Despite the effectiveness of OSINT, investigators face several challenges:

1. Use of VPNs & Anonymity Tools

- Criminals use VPNs, Tor, and burner emails to hide their identity.
- **Solution**: Look for behavioral patterns and reused data points.

2. Fake or Stolen Identities

- Some criminals use hacked accounts or identity theft to mislead investigators.
- **Solution**: Verify profiles using cross-referencing techniques.

3. Social Media Privacy Restrictions

- Platforms like Facebook and Instagram limit profile searches.
- **Solution**: Use OSINT tools that work within legal and ethical boundaries.

Conclusion

Tracking aliases, usernames, and digital personas is a fundamental part of modern OSINT investigations. By leveraging username search tools, reverse image searches, email tracing, and behavioral analysis, investigators can link online personas to real-world identities.

To enhance success, OSINT professionals should:

✓ Cross-reference multiple data points (usernames, emails, IP addresses).

✓ Utilize AI-driven analytics to detect writing patterns and account similarities.

✓ Stay updated on privacy laws to ensure ethical investigations.

As criminals continue to evolve their anonymity tactics, OSINT investigators must adapt and refine their techniques, ensuring that no alias remains truly hidden.

2.3 Social Media Profile Analysis for Criminal OSINT

Social media platforms are a goldmine for OSINT (Open-Source Intelligence) investigations, providing vast amounts of publicly available data that can reveal identities, locations, and connections. Criminals often leave digital traces—whether through direct posts, interactions, or metadata—that can be analyzed to build intelligence profiles. This chapter explores how OSINT investigators analyze social media profiles, extract useful data, and link digital personas to real-world identities in criminal investigations.

The Role of Social Media in Criminal Investigations

Criminals and suspects frequently use social media for:

✓ **Communication** – Planning crimes, coordinating with accomplices.

✓ **Recruitment & Radicalization** – Especially in terrorism and human trafficking.

✓ **Fraud & Scams** – Creating fake accounts for financial crimes.

✓ **Bragging & Evidence Leaks** – Posting images or videos that incriminate them.

By systematically analyzing social media accounts, interactions, and digital footprints, OSINT investigators can uncover hidden connections and behavioral patterns that lead to arrests.

Key OSINT Techniques for Social Media Profile Analysis

1. Profiling a Suspect's Social Media Presence

Investigators start by collecting and mapping a suspect's social media activity.

What to Look For:

- **Username & Alias Consistency** – Is the suspect using the same or similar usernames across platforms?
- **Profile Photos & Background Images** – Are they reused on other sites? Reverse image search can link profiles.

- **Bio & Contact Information** – Email addresses, phone numbers, links to other accounts.
- **Connections & Followers** – Who do they interact with? Are there known associates?
- **Location & Check-Ins** – Posts, tagged locations, and geotagged images can provide crucial leads.

OSINT Tools for Profile Mapping:

- **Social Mapper** – Automates searches for social media profiles linked to a name or photo.
- **Namechk / WhatsMyName** – Checks if a username exists on multiple platforms.
- **Google Dorking** – Advanced search queries for profile discovery (e.g., site:instagram.com "suspect_username").

Example:

A gang member using the alias "StreetKing47" on Twitter was found using the same username on Snapchat, where he shared images of stolen goods.

2. Analyzing Posts & Content for Investigative Clues

Criminals often reveal critical details through posts, images, and status updates.

Key Indicators in Social Media Posts:

✓ **Crime-Related Content** – Posts bragging about illegal activities.

✓ **Images & Videos with Identifiable Backgrounds** – Street signs, landmarks, license plates.

✓ **Slang & Hashtags** – Common in gang-related or extremist communication.

✓ **Mentions & Replies** – Conversations that may link the suspect to accomplices.

Metadata & Image Analysis:

- **ExifTool** – Extracts metadata from images (e.g., GPS coordinates, camera details).
- **Yandex Reverse Image Search** – Finds where an image appears online.
- **FotoForensics** – Analyzes image tampering and hidden metadata.

Example:

A drug dealer posted a photo of cash and narcotics on Instagram. Investigators extracted GPS metadata from the image, leading them to his apartment.

3. Tracking a Suspect's Digital Behavior & Patterns

Behavioral analysis can reveal a suspect's routine, time zone, and activity peaks.

Key Behavior Analysis Techniques:

✓ **Post Timing & Frequency** – When does the suspect post? This can indicate their location/time zone.

✓ **Preferred Platforms** – Criminals often favor encrypted or niche platforms (e.g., Telegram, Discord).

✓ **Friend & Follower Patterns** – Frequent interactions with known criminals or organizations.

✓ **Code Words & Emojis** – Criminal networks use coded language to communicate.

AI & Automation Tools for Pattern Recognition:

- **TweetBeaver** – Analyzes Twitter user data for connections.
- **Silo for Research** – Secure OSINT browsing and data collection.
- **Creepy** – Maps geolocation data from social media posts.

Example:

A terrorist recruiter on Facebook frequently posted at specific hours, aligning with a foreign time zone, leading investigators to his operational base.

4. Identifying Fake Accounts & Sock Puppets

Many criminals create multiple fake profiles to spread misinformation, commit fraud, or hide their identity.

Signs of a Fake or Sock Puppet Account:

✓ **New or Recently Created Accounts** – Often made for scams or trolling.

✓ **Low Friend/Follower Count** – Few real interactions, mostly bot-like activity.

✓ **Stock or Recycled Photos** – Profile pictures found in multiple places via reverse search.

✓ **Inconsistent Posting Behavior** – Unusual gaps in posting history.

OSINT Tools to Detect Fake Accounts:

- **Botometer** – Detects automated/bot activity on Twitter.
- **FaceCheck.ID** – Compares profile images to known sources.
- **PimEyes** – AI-based facial recognition across the web.

Example:

A fraudster used multiple fake Instagram accounts to run investment scams. Investigators used Botometer and reverse image searches to prove all accounts were linked to the same person.

5. Cross-Referencing Social Media with Other OSINT Data

Linking social media profiles to real-world identities often requires cross-referencing with other OSINT sources.

Methods for Cross-Referencing:

✓ **Check Domain Registrations** – If the suspect has a personal website (Whois Lookup).

✓ **Search Leaked Databases** – Have I Been Pwned, Dehashed for linked email addresses.

✓ **Analyze Bitcoin & Crypto Transactions** – Blockchain analysis tools.

✓ **Public Records & Court Documents** – OpenCorporates, PACER for legal cases.

Example:

A scammer advertising fake jobs on Facebook was linked to a real-world business entity through his email address in leaked records.

Case Study: Catching a Human Trafficker Through Social Media Analysis

Background:

A human trafficker was luring victims via fake modeling job offers on Instagram. OSINT investigators needed to unmask his identity.

OSINT Investigation Steps:

Profile Analysis:

Username search revealed the same alias on Facebook & Telegram.

Reverse Image Search:

The suspect's profile picture matched an old social media account under his real name.

Geolocation Clues:

- Investigators analyzed his Instagram posts and found a specific hotel lobby in the background.
- Google Maps confirmed the location.

Cross-Referencing Email & Phone Number:

The suspect's contact info was found in a leaked scammer database.

Result:

By combining social media analysis, image metadata, and leaked data, law enforcement identified and arrested the trafficker, rescuing multiple victims.

Challenges in Social Media OSINT for Criminal Investigations

1. Privacy Restrictions & Data Protection Laws

- Many platforms restrict access to public data.
- Investigators must comply with laws (e.g., GDPR, CCPA) when collecting data.

2. Disappearing Content & Encryption

- Criminals use disappearing messages (Snapchat, Signal) to avoid detection.
- **Solution**: Real-time monitoring & archiving tools like Hunchly.

3. Fake Information & Misdirection

- Criminals create fake trails to mislead investigators.
- **Solution**: Cross-verify data with multiple OSINT sources.

Conclusion

Social media profile analysis is a critical OSINT technique for identifying criminals, tracking digital footprints, and gathering actionable intelligence. By leveraging username tracking, image forensics, behavioral analysis, and cross-referencing techniques, OSINT investigators can link online profiles to real-world identities.

To stay ahead, investigators must:

✓ Continuously adapt to evolving privacy settings & new platforms.

✓ Use automation & AI tools for large-scale data analysis.

✓ Ensure ethical & legal compliance when gathering OSINT data.

As criminals increasingly rely on social media, OSINT will remain one of the most powerful tools for modern law enforcement investigations.

2.4 Connecting Multiple Accounts Across Platforms

In modern OSINT investigations, criminals often use multiple social media accounts, email addresses, and online aliases to avoid detection. However, they frequently make mistakes—reusing usernames, profile pictures, email addresses, or posting habits—which can help investigators connect separate accounts and unmask real identities. This chapter explores OSINT techniques, tools, and methodologies for linking multiple accounts across different platforms.

Why Criminals Use Multiple Accounts

Criminals maintain multiple online identities for several reasons:

✓ **Avoiding detection** – Using separate accounts for different illegal activities.

✓ **Misdirection** – Creating fake identities to confuse investigators.

✓ **Scamming multiple victims** – Running fraud under different names.

✓ **Communication secrecy** – Using encrypted apps while maintaining public profiles.

However, despite their efforts, patterns emerge, allowing OSINT professionals to link seemingly unrelated accounts.

OSINT Techniques for Connecting Multiple Accounts

1. Username Reuse Across Platforms

Many criminals reuse the same or slightly modified usernames across different sites.

How to Identify Username Reuse:

- **Exact Matches** – The same username appears on multiple platforms.
- **Variations** – Small modifications (e.g., "DarkHunter47" vs. "DarkHunter_47").
- **Common Patterns** – Adding numbers, symbols, or location identifiers.

OSINT Tools for Username Tracking:

- **Sherlock** – Searches for a username across hundreds of platforms.
- **WhatsMyName** – Checks username availability across sites.
- **Google Dorking** – site:instagram.com "username" to find profile links.

Example:

A hacker known as "ShadowX" on a darknet forum was also found using "ShadowX_99" on Twitter, which led investigators to his real identity.

2. Email & Phone Number Linkage

Many social media accounts require email addresses or phone numbers for registration. If a suspect's email is found, it can be used to uncover linked accounts.

How to Find Email & Phone Linkage:

- **Check profile bios** – Many users list emails for business or contact purposes.
- **Look at password recovery pages** – Some sites reveal partial email addresses.
- **Search data breach databases** – Leaked credentials can show linked accounts.

OSINT Tools for Email & Phone Analysis:

- **Have I Been Pwned / Dehashed** – Finds if an email appears in data breaches.
- **PhoneInfoga** – Investigates phone numbers for associated accounts.
- **Hunter.io** – Checks email addresses linked to websites.

Example:

A fraudster's Instagram bio contained an email address. Searching it on Dehashed revealed a LinkedIn profile with his real name.

3. Reverse Image Search for Profile Pictures & Avatars

Many criminals reuse the same profile picture or avatar across multiple platforms, making image analysis a key OSINT technique.

How to Use Reverse Image Search:

- Download the suspect's profile picture.
- Use reverse image search tools to find where else it appears.
- Compare images to detect cropping, filters, or slight modifications.

OSINT Tools for Image Search:

- **Google Reverse Image Search** – Finds where an image appears online.
- **Yandex / TinEye** – More advanced reverse image searches.
- **FaceCheck.ID** – AI-powered facial recognition search.

Example:

A cybercriminal using an alias on Telegram was linked to a Facebook account with his real name by matching his profile picture.

4. Writing Style & Behavioral Analysis

Even when criminals change usernames, their writing style, emoji usage, slang, and posting times can expose them.

Key Behavioral Indicators:

✓ **Posting frequency & time zones** – Can indicate a suspect's location.

✓ **Language patterns** – Unique phrases, abbreviations, and spelling habits.

✓ **Hashtags & emojis** – Consistent usage across multiple accounts.

OSINT Tools for Behavioral Analysis:

- **TwiAnalyst** – Tracks Twitter behavior patterns.
- **Jupyter Notebook NLP Analysis** – Advanced linguistic fingerprinting.
- **TimeZone Convertor** – Matches post times to real-world time zones.

Example:

A terrorist recruiter changed usernames frequently, but his distinctive slang and emoji usage linked his Twitter and Telegram accounts.

5. Friend & Follower Network Analysis

Investigators can analyze a suspect's friend list, followers, and interactions to find linked accounts.

How to Analyze Social Networks:

- Compare friend lists across different platforms.
- Look for mutual connections who interact with multiple accounts.
- Track engagement patterns (likes, comments, shares).

OSINT Tools for Social Network Analysis:

- **TweetBeaver** – Analyzes Twitter connections.
- **Maltego** – Visualizes social media relationships.
- **Silo for Research** – Securely monitors suspect activity.

Example:

A human trafficker had separate accounts for recruiting victims and communicating with accomplices, but mutual followers exposed the connection.

6. Cross-Referencing IP Addresses & Location Clues

Even when criminals try to remain anonymous, their IP addresses, device metadata, and geolocation data can expose them.

How to Cross-Reference IP & Location Data:

✔ Check if different accounts log in from the same location.

✔ Analyze geotagged images and posts.

✔ Use leaked data breaches to find associated IPs.

OSINT Tools for IP & Location Tracking:

- **IPinfo.io** – Finds details on an IP address.
- **ExifTool** – Extracts GPS metadata from images.
- **Hunchly** – Archives web pages for geolocation evidence.

Example:

A scammer's Instagram post had hidden GPS metadata, linking it to a previously known email address used in financial fraud.

Case Study: Unmasking a Cybercriminal Using Multiple Accounts

Background:

A cybercriminal known as "GhostX99" was running multiple fraudulent e-commerce scams under different names. Investigators needed to prove the accounts were linked.

OSINT Investigation Steps:

Username Search:

Sherlock found that GhostX99 was also using Ghost_X99 on Reddit and GhostX_99 on Telegram.

Reverse Image Search:

His profile picture on Telegram matched a Facebook profile with his real name.

Email & Phone Analysis:

A leaked database showed his email address linked to multiple scams.

Friend Network Analysis:

His Twitter and Facebook accounts had mutual connections, linking them to the same person.

Result:

By combining username tracking, image analysis, and email cross-referencing, investigators proved that all accounts belonged to the same individual, leading to his arrest.

Challenges in Linking Multiple Accounts

1. Privacy Restrictions & Encryption

- Platforms like WhatsApp, Signal, and Telegram have strict privacy policies.
- **Solution**: Monitor public-facing accounts for slip-ups.

2. Fake Accounts & Identity Theft

- Criminals use stolen identities to create multiple accounts.
- **Solution**: Verify profiles through behavioral and metadata analysis.

3. VPN & Proxy Usage

- Some criminals use VPNs to hide their real IP address.
- **Solution**: Focus on non-IP-based identifiers (e.g., username reuse, image links).

Conclusion

Connecting multiple accounts across platforms is a crucial OSINT skill in criminal investigations. By analyzing usernames, emails, images, behavioral patterns, and network connections, investigators can trace digital identities back to real-world criminals.

To enhance success, OSINT professionals should:

✓ Use automation tools for large-scale username searches.

✓ Cross-reference data from multiple sources.

✓ Leverage AI-driven social network analysis.

As criminals become more sophisticated, OSINT investigators must continuously evolve their techniques to stay ahead.

2.5 Tracking Digital History & Behavioral Patterns

Every online action leaves behind a digital footprint, whether it's a social media post, search query, transaction, or website visit. Criminals often believe they can stay anonymous, but their behavioral patterns, online habits, and historical digital activity can reveal key insights. By analyzing timestamps, interactions, content, and browsing history, OSINT investigators can piece together a suspect's routine, network, and real-world identity.

Why Tracking Digital Behavior Matters in OSINT

Criminals try to erase their tracks, but they often:

✓ Reuse usernames, passwords, or email addresses across platforms

✓ Follow predictable daily posting or browsing habits

✓ Engage with the same groups, forums, or people

✓ Leave metadata in photos, videos, and documents

By tracking their patterns over time, investigators can:

✓ Predict their next move

✓ Identify alternate accounts or aliases

✓ Cross-reference online activity with real-world events

✓ Uncover hidden connections to criminal networks

Key OSINT Techniques for Tracking Digital History & Behavior

1. Analyzing Posting & Activity Patterns

A suspect's posting frequency, time zone, and content themes can reveal important details.

What to Look For:

- **Time of activity** – When does the suspect post? What time zone does this suggest?
- **Preferred platforms** – Do they use certain sites more frequently?
- **Content focus** – Do they post about the same topics across multiple accounts?
- **Hashtags & keywords** – Are specific words or emojis repeated?

OSINT Tools for Activity Tracking:

- **TwiAnalyst** – Analyzes Twitter user activity patterns.
- **Creepy** – Maps geolocation data from online posts.
- **Metapho** – Extracts metadata from images.

Example:

An online fraudster regularly posted on darknet forums between 2 AM and 5 AM UTC. Investigators cross-referenced this with known cybercriminal activity from Eastern Europe, leading to his identification.

2. Monitoring Browser & Search History

Even when criminals delete their posts, their search history, cookies, and cached data can be recovered from digital forensics or leaked databases.

How to Uncover Digital History:

✓ **Leaked database searches** – Look for past login activity.

✓ **Browser cache analysis** – Criminals may leave traces of visited sites.

✓ **Keyword search patterns** – What terms are frequently searched?

✓ **Dark web tracking** – Are they using hidden forums or marketplaces?

OSINT Tools for Digital History Analysis:

- **Have I Been Pwned / Dehashed** – Finds exposed emails and passwords.
- **Babel Street** – Tracks search engine activity.
- **OnionScan** – Maps dark web activity linked to a suspect.

Example:

A hacker was found using a leaked email address from a data breach. Searching the breach logs revealed his old search queries, which included instructions for malware development, proving intent.

3. Reverse Engineering Online Interactions

Even if criminals delete posts, their interactions (likes, comments, shares) can still be traced.

How to Track Interaction Histories:

✓ **Look for tagged posts** – Friends or victims may have tagged them.

✓ **Analyze conversation threads** – Have they interacted with known criminals?

✓ **Check old cached versions of websites** – Deleted profiles may still exist in archives.

OSINT Tools for Interaction Tracking:

- **Wayback Machine** – Recovers deleted social media pages.
- **Maltego** – Maps interactions between accounts.
- **Hunchly** – Archives suspect web pages for evidence collection.

Example:

A cyberstalker deleted his Twitter profile, but using Wayback Machine, investigators recovered old tweets where he harassed multiple victims, proving a history of abuse.

4. Identifying Device & Location Fingerprints

Even when criminals use fake profiles or aliases, their device and location data can expose them.

What to Track:

✓ **IP addresses & VPN usage** – Are they logging in from the same location?

✓ **Device metadata** – Are they using the same phone, laptop, or operating system?

✓ **Browser & cookie fingerprints** – Do they use a consistent browser setup?

OSINT Tools for Device & Location Analysis:

- **IPinfo.io** – Identifies locations from IP addresses.
- **ExifTool** – Extracts GPS metadata from uploaded images.
- **AmIUnique** – Analyzes browser fingerprinting for suspect identification.

Example:

A scammer used multiple fake accounts, but his device fingerprint (browser & OS details) remained identical across all logins, proving they were linked.

5. Cross-Referencing Dark Web & Surface Web Activity

Many criminals use the dark web for illegal transactions, but they often slip up by linking accounts to surface web activity.

How to Connect Dark Web & Regular Web Behavior:

✓ Check if usernames or emails appear on both networks

✓ Monitor forum & marketplace transactions

✓ Look for shared PGP keys or Bitcoin wallets

OSINT Tools for Dark Web Tracking:

- **DarkOwl Vision** – Searches dark web databases.
- **CipherTrace** – Tracks cryptocurrency transactions.
- **PGP Key Lookup** – Identifies connections via encryption keys.

Example:

An arms dealer used a PGP key on a darknet forum. Investigators found the same key on his LinkedIn profile, confirming his real identity.

Case Study: Uncovering a Cybercriminal's Digital Footprint

Background:

A cybercriminal was running multiple phishing scams under different aliases. Investigators needed to track his digital behavior and uncover his real identity.

OSINT Investigation Steps:

Analyzed usernames & posting habits

The suspect used the same phrase ("DM for details") across different platforms.

Checked browser fingerprinting & devices

AmIUnique showed all accounts used the same rare browser configuration.

Tracked leaked email credentials

A data breach revealed an old email address, which led to a real-world Facebook profile.

Cross-referenced IP & location metadata

The scammer uploaded an image with GPS metadata, revealing his location.

Result:

By analyzing digital behavior, metadata, and leaks, investigators linked multiple aliases to one person, leading to an arrest.

Challenges in Tracking Digital History & Behavior

1. Privacy & Anonymization Efforts

- Criminals use VPNs, encrypted messengers, and burner phones to evade tracking.
- **Solution**: Cross-reference non-anonymous data points (e.g., language use, posting habits).

2. Deleted & Disappearing Content

- Social media posts, messages, and transactions can disappear.
- **Solution**: Use archiving tools like Hunchly or the Wayback Machine.

3. False Trails & Identity Spoofing

- Criminals plant fake clues or hacked accounts to mislead investigators.
- **Solution**: Verify patterns across multiple independent sources.

Conclusion

Tracking digital history & behavioral patterns is one of the most powerful OSINT techniques for linking criminals to their online activity. By analyzing posting habits, search history, digital interactions, and device fingerprints, investigators can connect fake accounts, uncover hidden identities, and predict future actions.

To stay ahead, OSINT professionals should:

✓ Leverage AI & automation to analyze large datasets

✓ Continuously adapt to new privacy techniques used by criminals

✓ Use a combination of metadata, linguistic, and social network analysis

As online investigations become more sophisticated, tracking digital footprints will remain a crucial tool for law enforcement and intelligence agencies.

2.6 Case Study: Unmasking an Anonymous Online Offender

Background: The Rise of an Elusive Cybercriminal

In late 2022, law enforcement agencies across multiple countries noticed a spike in online harassment, cyberstalking, and extortion cases linked to an anonymous offender known as "ShadowReaper". This individual operated across dark web forums, encrypted messaging apps, and mainstream social media to target victims with doxxing, financial scams, and threats.

Despite ShadowReaper's use of VPNs, burner accounts, and encrypted services, OSINT analysts were tasked with uncovering their real-world identity and location.

Step 1: Identifying Patterns in Online Activity

The investigation began by compiling all available digital traces left by ShadowReaper, including:

✓ Forum posts on the dark web where they advertised hacking services

✓ Telegram messages where they demanded ransom from victims

✓ Fake social media profiles used to harass individuals

Using OSINT tools for behavioral analysis, investigators noted recurring language patterns, slang, and posting habits, revealing that:

ShadowReaper frequently used British slang and spellings

- Their activity occurred between 10 PM – 3 AM GMT, suggesting they were based in the UK
- They repeatedly used certain hashtags and emojis across different accounts

☐ OSINT Tools Used:

- **TwiAnalyst** – Tracked posting frequency and time zone indicators
- **Voyant Tools** – Conducted linguistic analysis of ShadowReaper's writing style

🔎 Key Finding:

The suspect's writing style matched posts on multiple platforms, linking separate aliases to the same individual.

Step 2: Tracking Username Reuse Across Platforms

Although ShadowReaper created new usernames for each platform, OSINT analysts discovered subtle naming patterns and variations, such as:

- "ShadowReaper007" (Twitter)
- "ReaperX_007" (Reddit)
- "ReaperH4X" (Dark Web Forum)

Using Sherlock and WhatsMyName, analysts searched for these usernames across hundreds of platforms, uncovering:

- A gaming forum profile under "ReaperX_007" that linked to an old Twitch account
- The Twitch account contained a partially visible email address

☐ **OSINT Tools Used:**

- **Sherlock & WhatsMyName** – Checked username availability
- **Google Dorking** – "site:forum.com "ReaperX_007" to find indexed accounts

🔎 **Key Finding:**

An old Twitch account linked to an email, which led to a real identity match in a leaked database.

Step 3: Extracting Email & Metadata from Leaked Databases

Using the email found from the Twitch account, analysts checked dehashed.com and Have I Been Pwned, revealing:

- The email appeared in a 2018 data breach from an old gaming forum
- The forum profile included a real name: "James Holloway"
- A linked profile contained a UK-based IP address from Manchester

☐ **OSINT Tools Used:**

- **DeHashed / Have I Been Pwned** – Checked email in breach databases
- **Hunter.io** – Verified associated websites for the email

🔎 **Key Finding:**

The email was tied to a real name and IP address, providing a location clue.

Step 4: Reverse Image Search & Social Media Cross-Checking

Although ShadowReaper used anonymous profile pictures, OSINT analysts extracted:

✔ A cropped profile picture from their Twitter burner account

✔ A WhatsApp profile image from an anonymous group chat

Using reverse image search tools (Google Reverse Image, Yandex, and TinEye), the same image appeared on a personal LinkedIn page for "James Holloway", listing:

A Manchester-based cybersecurity job

Publicly available conference appearances in 2021

☐ OSINT Tools Used:

- **Yandex & TinEye** – Found where profile images were reused
- **FaceCheck.ID** – Matched images to known social media profiles

🔎 Key Finding:

A LinkedIn profile confirmed ShadowReaper's real name, job, and city of residence.

Step 5: Connecting Financial Transactions & Cryptocurrency Activity

ShadowReaper demanded ransom payments in Bitcoin. Analysts tracked:

- Bitcoin wallets posted in Telegram chats
- Transaction history using blockchain explorers (BTCscan, CipherTrace)

By cross-referencing wallet activity with known exchange platforms, analysts identified:

- A withdrawal to a PayPal account under James Holloway's real name
- A credit card linked to an IP address in Manchester

☐ OSINT Tools Used:

- **CipherTrace & BTCscan** – Tracked Bitcoin wallet movements
- **PayPal Transaction Lookup** – Verified associated accounts

🔎 Key Finding:

ShadowReaper converted Bitcoin into real-world payments, linking financial records to his real identity.

Step 6: Final Geolocation & Confirmation

Even after uncovering James Holloway's identity, analysts needed final location confirmation.

Using public records and geolocation techniques, they:

✓ Checked public utility records & electoral registers for an address match

✓ Found a parking ticket issued to Holloway's car near his Manchester home

✓ Used Google Street View to confirm the address linked to his online delivery purchases

☐ OSINT Tools Used:

- **UK Public Records & Electoral Rolls** – Verified residential address
- **Google Maps & Street View** – Matched addresses with known delivery routes
- **License Plate Lookup** – Checked vehicle registration tied to his name

🔎 Key Finding:

Final geolocation placed ShadowReaper at a residential address in Manchester, confirming the investigation findings.

Outcome: Arrest & Conviction

With concrete OSINT evidence linking James Holloway to his online crimes, law enforcement obtained:

- A search warrant for his residence
- His personal devices, which contained chat logs, victim information, and hacking tools
- A full confession, leading to multiple cybercrime charges

☐ **Legal Action Taken:**

✓ Arrested & charged with cyberstalking, fraud, and extortion

✓ Digital evidence from OSINT used in court prosecution

✓ Victims received justice, and Holloway was sentenced to prison

Lessons Learned & OSINT Best Practices

This case highlights how OSINT can unmask anonymous offenders, even when they use VPNs, burner accounts, and encrypted services.

Key Takeaways:

✓ Behavioral analysis & time zone tracking help narrow down a suspect's location

✓ Username & email reuse across platforms can expose real identities

✓ Reverse image searches connect fake profiles to real ones

✓ Cryptocurrency tracing & financial records can lead to arrests

✓ Public records & geolocation tools confirm real-world identities

As criminals become more tech-savvy, OSINT techniques must evolve to stay ahead. This case proves that even the most anonymous online offenders can be unmasked through digital forensics and open-source intelligence.

Conclusion

The unmasking of ShadowReaper demonstrates the power of OSINT-driven criminal investigations. By leveraging multiple data points, cross-referencing digital traces, and applying advanced investigative techniques, analysts successfully identified and arrested a dangerous cybercriminal.

As OSINT tools and AI-driven analytics continue to advance, law enforcement agencies worldwide will increasingly rely on these methods to track, identify, and prosecute online offenders.

3. Tracking Stalkers, Harassers & Cybercriminals

In this chapter, we explore the critical role OSINT plays in tracking stalkers, harassers, and cybercriminals, who often operate under the radar of traditional investigative methods. With the rise of online harassment and cybercrime, law enforcement and investigators rely on digital intelligence to uncover the identities and locations of perpetrators who exploit the anonymity of the internet. Through advanced OSINT techniques, we examine how investigators track online behavior, analyze patterns, and connect digital footprints to real-world actions. This chapter provides practical tools and strategies for identifying and neutralizing threats from individuals who use the digital world to harm others, ensuring safer online environments.

3.1 Understanding Online Stalking & Cyber Harassment

The Digital Age of Harassment & Stalking

The rise of social media, instant messaging, and online forums has created new opportunities for cyberstalkers and online harassers to target victims. Unlike traditional stalking, online harassment can be persistent, anonymous, and global, making it harder to escape and easier for perpetrators to exploit. Cyberstalking involves the repeated use of digital tools to intimidate, monitor, or threaten someone, while cyber harassment includes a broader range of behaviors such as doxxing, threats, defamation, and unwanted contact.

Victims of online stalking can experience severe emotional distress, reputational damage, financial loss, and even real-world violence. For law enforcement and OSINT investigators, understanding the methods, motivations, and tools used by cyberstalkers is crucial for identifying and stopping them.

Types of Online Stalking & Cyber Harassment

1. Direct Online Stalking

This involves the perpetrator actively monitoring, messaging, or threatening a victim. Common tactics include:

✓ Excessive messaging (emails, texts, DMs) despite being ignored or blocked

✓ Harassing comments on social media posts or online forums

✓ Threats of violence, blackmail, or self-harm to manipulate the victim

✓ Persistent friend requests or fake accounts to maintain contact

☐ **Example Case:**

A woman reported a cyberstalker who sent over 500 messages in one month, tracked her social media activity in real time, and even created multiple fake accounts to bypass blocks.

2. Indirect Stalking & Digital Surveillance

Cyberstalkers often monitor victims without direct interaction by using:

✓ Social media tracking (watching posts, likes, and online presence)

✓ IP address tracking to approximate location

✓ Hacking into email, social media, or cloud accounts

✓ Using spyware or stalkerware on phones and computers

☐ **Example Case:**

An ex-partner installed spyware on a victim's phone, allowing him to track her messages, location, and even listen to her private conversations remotely.

3. Doxxing & Privacy Violations

Doxxing (or doxing) involves publishing private or personal information online to harass, threaten, or endanger a person. This can include:

✓ Home addresses, phone numbers, and personal emails

✓ Social Security numbers, financial records, or workplace details

✓ Family member information to threaten loved ones

☐ **Example Case:**

An activist was doxxed after speaking at a public event, leading to death threats, fake online reviews targeting her business, and repeated SWAT calls to her home.

4. Impersonation & Fake Accounts

Cyberstalkers sometimes create fake profiles or impersonate their targets online. This can be used for:

✓ Spreading false information or damaging reputations

✓ Catfishing victims for personal or financial gain

✓ Scamming friends and family under a victim's name

☐ Example Case:

A university student had their identity stolen on social media, with the stalker using fake accounts to harass classmates, post offensive content, and apply for jobs in their name.

5. Swatting & Real-World Escalation

Some cyberstalkers escalate online harassment into real-world threats, such as:

✓ Swatting (calling emergency services to a victim's home with a false report)

✓ Following or physically stalking a victim based on online information

✓ Ordering unwanted deliveries or services to a victim's address

☐ Example Case:

A Twitch streamer was swatted multiple times, with armed police responding to fake hostage situations at his home, causing severe trauma and public embarrassment.

The Motivations Behind Cyberstalking & Online Harassment

Understanding why cyberstalkers engage in harassment can help investigators predict their behavior and counteract threats.

1. Obsessive or Romantic Fixation

- Ex-partners who refuse to accept a breakup
- Strangers who develop parasitic attachments to influencers or celebrities
- Delusional beliefs in imaginary relationships (e.g., "They love me but don't know it yet")

☐ **Example:**

A famous TikToker had a cyberstalker who tracked her flight schedules, sent gifts to her home, and hacked her private messages, believing they were destined to be together.

2. Revenge & Retaliation

- Ex-friends, coworkers, or ex-lovers seeking emotional revenge
- Enemies posting false accusations to ruin reputations
- Harassers attempting to intimidate whistleblowers or activists

☐ **Example:**

A whistleblower was targeted by an organized cyber harassment campaign after exposing corporate fraud, receiving death threats and thousands of fake negative reviews on their business.

3. Financial & Criminal Intent

- Scammers use harassment to extort money (e.g., "pay or we leak your photos")
- Hackers use intimidation to steal accounts or personal information
- Ransomware groups send threats to coerce victims into paying in cryptocurrency

☐ **Example:**

A deepfake blackmail campaign used AI-generated fake nudes of victims to demand Bitcoin payments in exchange for not publishing them.

4. Political or Ideological Attacks

- Targeting activists, journalists, or public figures
- Coordinated mass harassment campaigns (e.g., hate groups, extremist groups)
- Spreading misinformation or conspiracy theories to discredit someone

☐ **Example:**

A journalist covering extremism was bombarded with death threats, fake accusations, and mass-reported social media bans as part of an organized harassment effort.

Key OSINT Techniques to Investigate Cyberstalking

Investigating online harassment requires identifying patterns, tracking digital footprints, and uncovering hidden connections between anonymous attackers and real-world identities.

1. Analyzing Message & Posting Patterns

✓ Identify recurring phrases, spelling mistakes, or emojis used in threats

✓ Cross-check timestamps & time zones to estimate location

✓ Monitor multiple platforms for linked accounts

☐ **Tools:**

- **TwiAnalyst** (tracks Twitter harassment campaigns)
- **Hunchly** (archives harassing messages as evidence)

2. Reverse Searching Usernames & Profile Images

✓ Run usernames across multiple platforms (Sherlock, WhatsMyName)

✓ Reverse-search profile pictures to uncover alternate accounts

☐ **Tools**:

- **Yandex & TinEye** (reverse image search)
- **Maltego** (visual mapping of connections between profiles)

3. Tracking Email, IP & Device Fingerprints

✓ Check leaked databases for registered emails

✓ Use tracert commands & IP lookup tools (if legal)

✓ Investigate metadata from messages, emails, or images

⬚ **Tools:**

- **DeHashed & Have I Been Pwned** (email leaks)
- **IPinfo.io** (IP address lookups)

Conclusion

Online stalking and cyber harassment are serious crimes that can have devastating consequences for victims. Understanding the types, tactics, and motivations of online harassers is essential for OSINT investigators, law enforcement, and cybersecurity professionals working to track and stop these criminals.

By leveraging OSINT techniques, analysts can uncover hidden connections, trace anonymous threats, and provide critical intelligence to protect victims and hold offenders accountable.

3.2 Identifying & Tracking Perpetrators Using OSINT

Introduction: Unmasking Cybercriminals & Stalkers

Cyberstalkers, harassers, and online criminals often believe they can act with impunity under the cover of anonymity, but OSINT (Open-Source Intelligence) techniques can expose their real identities, track their activities, and connect their digital footprints across multiple platforms.

By utilizing behavioral analysis, username tracking, metadata extraction, and geolocation tools, OSINT investigators can piece together fragmented data to identify perpetrators and assist law enforcement in holding them accountable. This chapter explores step-by-step methodologies to track and unmask cybercriminals using OSINT.

Step 1: Collecting & Organizing Initial Clues

Gathering Evidence from the Victim

Before launching an OSINT investigation, analysts should document all relevant information provided by the victim, including:

✓ Harassing messages, emails, or social media comments

✓ Screenshots of threats, abusive interactions, or impersonation attempts

✓ URLs of suspicious profiles, forums, or websites

✓ Timestamps & platform details of each attack

☐ **Best Practices:**

- Store evidence in Hunchly (for web scraping & archiving).
- Use Metadata2Go to extract metadata from images or documents.
- Preserve social media posts using archive.ph or Wayback Machine.

🔎 **Case Example:**

A journalist targeted by an anonymous Twitter harasser saved all messages and URLs. Using OSINT, investigators linked the attacker's Twitter profile to a real identity via username reuse.

Step 2: Analyzing Usernames & Email Patterns

Tracking Username Variations Across Platforms

Most cybercriminals create multiple accounts with slight variations of the same username across different platforms.

☐ **Tools to Identify Username Reuse:**

- **Sherlock** – Scans for username availability across 300+ websites.
- **WhatsMyName** – Finds matching usernames across forums, gaming sites, and social media.
- **Google Dorking** – "site:forum.com "username123" to find indexed results.

🔎 **Key Finding:**

A harasser using "ShadowHunter92" on Twitter also had accounts as "Shadow_Hunter92" on Reddit and "HunterX92" on Discord. OSINT analysts connected all three accounts and found a LinkedIn profile with the same username.

Step 3: Extracting Data from Email Addresses

If the suspect's email is available, OSINT tools can uncover:

✓ Past data breaches containing their real name or passwords

✓ Connected accounts on different platforms

✓ Hidden social media profiles

☐ **Email Intelligence Tools:**

- **DeHashed / Have I Been Pwned** – Check if an email has been exposed in breaches.
- **Hunter.io** – Finds associated company/work emails.
- **OSINT.email** – Extracts details from email headers.

🔎 **Key Finding:**

A cybercriminal's email appeared in a LinkedIn breach, revealing their full name and employer.

Step 4: Tracing IP Addresses & Digital Footprints

While VPNs and proxies help criminals hide, OSINT techniques can still reveal useful location data.

Finding IP Clues in Emails & Online Activity

- Some emails leak sender IPs in headers (check with MXToolbox).
- Torrenting & P2P file-sharing can expose IP addresses.
- IP lookup services (IPinfo.io, IPQualityScore) provide approximate locations.

Identifying VPN & Proxy Usage

- **iphey.com** – Checks if an IP belongs to a VPN or hosting service.
- **Shodan.io** – Finds devices & servers linked to an IP address.
- **Check-host.net** – Traces ping locations for websites & IPs.

🔎 **Key Finding:**

A stalker used a temporary email service, but OSINT investigators tracked an IP address from an email header, linking it to a city in Canada.

Step 5: Reverse Image Searching & Photo Metadata Analysis

Reverse Image Searches for Profile Pictures

Many cybercriminals reuse stock photos, stolen images, or edited versions of personal photos across accounts.

☐ **Best Reverse Image Search Tools:**

- **Yandex & TinEye** – Finds similar images across websites.
- **FaceCheck.ID** – Matches images with known profiles.
- **Google Lens** – Searches for visually similar images.

🔎 **Key Finding:**

A suspect's Twitter profile used a slightly modified LinkedIn photo of a real person, revealing their actual identity.

Extracting EXIF Metadata from Images

EXIF data (Exchangeable Image File Format) can expose:

✓ Geolocation (GPS coordinates if not stripped)

✓ Device type & camera settings

✓ Editing history & timestamps

☐ **Tools for EXIF Analysis:**

- **ExifTool** – Extracts metadata from images.
- **FotoForensics** – Checks for image tampering.

🔎 **Key Finding:**

A harasser uploaded a photo with GPS coordinates embedded, leading to a physical address in Germany.

Step 6: Geolocating the Perpetrator

Analyzing Location Clues from Social Media & Posts

Many criminals accidentally leak location data in photos, timestamps, or backgrounds.

☐ **Techniques for Geolocation:**

- **Google Earth & Street View** – Match background landmarks.
- **GeoSocial Footprint** – Extracts geolocation data from social media posts.
- **SunCalc.net** – Determines time of day & location based on shadows in photos.

🔍 **Key Finding:**

A stalker posted a selfie with a distinct bridge in the background. Using Google Earth, investigators matched the location to Madrid, Spain.

Step 7: Monitoring & Mapping Digital Behavior

Tracking Online Habits & Posting Patterns

- What time does the suspect post?
- Which platforms do they frequent?
- Do they engage in similar conversations across multiple sites?

☐ **Behavioral Analysis Tools:**

- TwiAnalyst – Tracks social media activity & peak posting hours.
- Maltego – Maps connections between social media profiles.

🔍 **Key Finding:**

A scammer posted threats between 6-9 PM EST daily, indicating they lived in the U.S.

Step 8: Correlating Data for Final Identification

Once all OSINT techniques have been applied, the final step is to connect all gathered data points into a clear suspect profile.

✓ **Real name** (from breaches, email searches, or username reuse)

✓ **IP address** / location clues (from metadata, ISP tracking, or time zones)

✓ **Social media accounts** (cross-referenced usernames, images, and posts)

✓ **Behavioral patterns** (posting times, linguistic analysis, or online habits)

🔎 **Final Outcome:**

Using OSINT, a cybercriminal who used multiple fake accounts, VPNs, and encrypted messaging was unmasked. Investigators provided law enforcement with full identity details, leading to an arrest.

Conclusion: OSINT as a Weapon Against Online Crime

Tracking cybercriminals, stalkers, and harassers requires meticulous data collection, pattern recognition, and digital forensics.

By leveraging OSINT tools & investigative techniques, analysts can uncover anonymous attackers, reveal their real identities, and support criminal cases with strong digital evidence.

✅ Username tracking & email searches expose linked accounts.

✅ Reverse image & metadata analysis uncover hidden clues.

✅ Geolocation & behavioral tracking narrow down a suspect's physical location.

✅ IP tracing & breach data analysis provide real-world identity matches.

In an era where criminals exploit digital anonymity, OSINT remains a powerful tool for justice and cybersecurity investigations.

3.3 Gathering Evidence from Emails, Social Media & Forums

Introduction: The Importance of Digital Evidence

Cybercriminals, stalkers, and online harassers often leave digital footprints in emails, social media interactions, and online forums. Gathering and preserving this evidence is crucial for identifying perpetrators, supporting law enforcement investigations, and building strong legal cases.

This chapter explores OSINT techniques for collecting, analyzing, and documenting emails, social media activity, and forum posts while ensuring evidence integrity for potential legal action.

Step 1: Collecting Evidence from Emails

Emails can provide critical information about a suspect's identity, location, and digital behavior.

Extracting Email Metadata

Many emails contain hidden metadata that reveals:

✓ Sender's IP address (sometimes masked by VPNs or relays)

✓ Email client and server information

✓ Timestamps and routing details

☐ **Tools for Email Header Analysis:**

- **MXToolbox** – Extracts sender details from email headers.
- **EmailHeaders.net** – Decodes email metadata.
- **OSINT.email** – Provides in-depth email analysis.

🔎 **Case Example:**

A stalker used a temporary email service to send threats, but header analysis exposed their real IP address, linking them to a city in France.

Checking If an Email is in a Data Breach

✓ **DeHashed / Have I Been Pwned** – Checks for email leaks in past data breaches.

✓ **Holehe** – Finds accounts registered with a specific email across multiple platforms.

🔎 **Key Finding:**

A scammer's email appeared in a LinkedIn data breach, revealing their real name and employer.

Step 2: Gathering Evidence from Social Media

Social media accounts can provide a wealth of information about cybercriminals, including usernames, interactions, locations, and digital patterns.

Archiving Social Media Posts & Profiles

✓ **archive.ph & Wayback Machine** – Saves webpages & social media profiles as legal evidence.

✓ **Hunchly** – OSINT browser tool for archiving online activity.

✓ **TweetBeaver & TwiAnalyst** – Analyzes Twitter interactions, mentions & relationships.

🔎 **Case Example:**

A harasser deleted abusive tweets, but OSINT analysts retrieved archived copies from archive.ph, proving their involvement in online threats.

Tracking Usernames Across Platforms

Cybercriminals often reuse similar usernames across different sites.

☐ **Tools for Username Research:**

- **Sherlock** – Finds matching usernames on 300+ sites.
- **WhatsMyName** – Cross-references usernames with online accounts.

🔎 **Key Finding:**

A harasser using "DarkWolf99" on Instagram also had Reddit and gaming forum accounts with the same username, leading to additional evidence.

Analyzing Social Media Connections & Patterns

✓ Who do they follow & interact with?

✓ Do they post from specific time zones?

✓ Do they mention locations or personal details in comments?

☐ **Tools for Social Media Analysis:**

- **Maltego** – Maps relationships between accounts.
- **Geosocial Footprint** – Extracts geolocation data from public social media posts.

🔎 **Key Finding:**

A scammer regularly posted between 7-10 PM PST, suggesting they lived in the U.S.

West Coast.

Step 3: Gathering Evidence from Online Forums & Dark Web

Tracking Forum Activity

Many criminals frequent forums related to hacking, cybercrime, and harassment.

✓ **Google Dorking** – "site:forum.com "username123" to find indexed posts.

✓ **BoardReader & Forum Search Engines** – Finds discussions related to a keyword or username.

🔎 **Case Example:**

A cyberstalker using the alias "Phantom97" was active on multiple forums, discussing methods for hiding identities.

Extracting Metadata from Forum Posts & Dark Web Activity

✓ Check post timestamps for time zones.

✓ Look for language patterns & writing style.

✓ Reverse search profile images to find alternate accounts.

☐ **Tools for Deep Web OSINT:**

- **Onion Search Engine** – Finds .onion sites on the dark web.
- **Dark.fail & Ahmia.fi** – Search for criminal forum discussions.

🔍 Key Finding:

A fraudster used the same writing style on a scam forum and a Twitter account, linking their identities.

Step 4: Preserving & Presenting Digital Evidence

✓ Save full-page screenshots with timestamps.

✓ Use metadata extractors for email, images, and posts.

✓ Document evidence in a report with links & descriptions.

☐ Tools for Evidence Preservation:

- **Hunchly** – Forensically saves online investigations.
- **ExifTool** – Extracts metadata from images & documents.
- **CaseFile / Maltego** – Organizes OSINT findings in visual charts.

🔍 Legal Consideration:

Always preserve the chain of custody when collecting evidence to ensure it holds up in court.

Conclusion: The Power of OSINT in Digital Investigations

By leveraging email tracking, social media monitoring, and forum intelligence, OSINT investigators can identify, track, and document cybercriminals' activities.

✓ Email analysis reveals IP addresses & hidden identities.

✓ Social media forensics uncovers usernames, locations & interactions.

✓ Forum intelligence links criminals to hidden communities.

✓ Evidence preservation ensures data is court-admissible.

With the right OSINT tools and methodologies, digital criminals can no longer hide in anonymity.

3.4 Analyzing Digital Footprints to Predict Behavior

Introduction: The Power of Digital Footprints

Every individual leaves behind a digital footprint—a trail of online activities, interactions, and behaviors across social media, forums, emails, and websites. For OSINT investigators, analyzing these footprints provides critical insights into a target's behavior, intentions, and possible next moves.

Understanding how cybercriminals, stalkers, or fraudsters operate can help law enforcement and analysts predict threats, prevent attacks, and identify hidden connections between accounts. This chapter explores the process of collecting, analyzing, and interpreting digital footprints to build behavioral profiles and anticipate future actions.

Step 1: Mapping an Individual's Digital Presence

Before predicting behavior, an OSINT analyst must map out a target's digital footprint across various platforms.

Key Data Sources for Digital Footprints

✔ **Social Media** (Facebook, Twitter, Instagram, LinkedIn, TikTok, Reddit, Discord, etc.)

✔ **Emails & Data Breaches** (Have I Been Pwned, DeHashed, Holehe)

✔ **Online Forums** (hacking forums, dark web sites, discussion boards)

✔ **Public Databases** (court records, business directories, WHOIS data, domain registrations)

✔ **Messaging Apps** (Telegram, WhatsApp, Signal, IRC chats, Discord servers)

☐ **Best Tools for Digital Footprint Mapping:**

- **Maltego** – Visualizes connections between online entities.
- **SpiderFoot** – Automates footprint collection across 100+ sources.
- **Social Links Pro** – AI-driven social media footprint analysis.

🔎 **Case Example:**

A cyberstalker operating under the username "ShadowHunter" was active on Twitter, Reddit, and a niche gaming forum. Investigators used OSINT tools to link all accounts, revealing common interests, peak activity times, and language patterns.

Step 2: Behavioral Pattern Analysis

Once a digital footprint is mapped, the next step is analyzing behavioral patterns to predict potential threats or actions.

Key Behavioral Indicators

✓ **Time of Activity:**

- What time does the suspect usually post or interact online?
- Does their activity align with a particular timezone or work schedule?

✓ **Content Analysis:**

- What topics do they frequently discuss?
- Do they express hostility, threats, or extremist views?
- Have they shown escalating aggression over time?

✓ **Engagement & Connections:**

- Who are their online associates and followers?
- Are they part of organized networks or groups?
- Do they frequently change usernames to avoid detection?

☐ **Tools for Behavioral Analysis:**

- **TwiAnalyst & TweetBeaver** – Analyze Twitter behavior, tweet patterns, and network connections.
- **GeoSocial Footprint** – Extracts geolocation insights from social media posts.
- **Obsidian OSINT** – Tracks user interactions across forums & deep web platforms.

🔎 **Key Finding:**

A fraudster posting fake investment schemes on Facebook and Telegram was most active between 8 PM and 11 PM UTC, suggesting their location in Europe. The scam peaked at the end of each month, aligning with salary days when people were more likely to invest.

Step 3: Predicting Behavioral Trends & Future Actions

By analyzing digital footprints over time, investigators can predict trends and potential threats.

Behavioral Indicators for Predictive Analysis

✓ **Escalation Patterns** – Is the suspect increasing aggression over time?

✓ **Repeated Targets** – Are they harassing the same individuals or groups?

✓ **Change in Digital Behavior** – Are they switching to new platforms, encryption tools, or aliases?

Using OSINT for Threat Prediction

- **Linguistic Analysis** – Detecting aggressive speech, coded threats, or radicalization signs.
- **Location Clues** – Monitoring if a suspect moves physically or shifts digital activities.
- **Financial Behavior** – Tracking sudden crypto transactions linked to criminal activities.

☐ **Tools for Predicting Threats:**

- **ThreatFox & IntelX** – Monitors dark web criminal discussions.
- **SunCalc** – Determines approximate time & location from social media photos.
- **Tracelabs OSINT Framework** – Provides AI-assisted behavioral tracking.

🔎 **Case Example:**

A known cybercriminal deleted all social media accounts after a law enforcement crackdown on his online fraud ring. OSINT analysts predicted he would reappear under a new alias on darknet forums—which he did three months later under a different username but with the same writing style and interests.

Step 4: Identifying Anomalies & High-Risk Indicators

Cybercriminals sometimes attempt to erase their tracks or alter behavior to avoid detection. Detecting anomalies helps investigators identify deception, burner accounts, and hidden activities.

Common Digital Anomalies to Investigate

✓ **Sudden Deactivation or Deletion of Accounts** – Attempt to evade detection?

✓ **Frequent Changes in Username & Profile Pictures** – Hiding past identity?

✓ **Switching Between Multiple IP Addresses & VPNs** – Trying to stay anonymous?

✓ **Shifting to Encrypted Communication (Telegram, Signal, ProtonMail)** – Hiding future plans?

🔎 **Key Finding:**

A dark web vendor selling stolen credit cards disappeared from a marketplace after increased law enforcement raids. OSINT analysts discovered he reappeared with a new profile on a different marketplace—using the same Bitcoin wallet address, confirming his identity.

Step 5: Visualizing Digital Footprints for Investigative Insights

Creating a visual representation of digital footprints helps investigators spot patterns, connections, and hidden links.

☐ **Best Tools for OSINT Visualization:**

✓ **Maltego** – Builds link analysis graphs for cybercriminal networks.

✓ **CaseFile** – Maps out investigative data points visually.

✓ **i2 Analyst's Notebook** – Helps law enforcement track criminal organizations.

🔎 **Case Example:**

An OSINT analyst tracking an online harasser mapped all known usernames, email accounts, social media profiles, and forum discussions into a Maltego graph. This visualization revealed multiple sock puppet accounts (fake identities used for harassment), leading to a single real identity.

Conclusion: The Power of OSINT in Predicting Criminal Behavior

By analyzing digital footprints, OSINT investigators can:

✓ Uncover hidden patterns & online behaviors.

✓ Predict future actions based on escalation trends.

✓ Identify high-risk individuals before they commit a crime.

✓ Support law enforcement with actionable intelligence.

In an era of increasing cybercrime, stalking, fraud, and digital harassment, OSINT-based behavioral prediction is a critical tool for proactive investigations and cyber defense.

3.5 Collaborating with Law Enforcement on Cybercrime Cases

Introduction: The Importance of OSINT in Law Enforcement Collaboration

As cybercrime continues to rise, collaboration between OSINT investigators and law enforcement agencies is more critical than ever. Many cybercriminals operate across multiple jurisdictions, utilizing anonymous online personas, encrypted communication, and darknet marketplaces to evade capture. OSINT analysts can play a crucial role by collecting, analyzing, and organizing publicly available intelligence that aids in identifying suspects, tracking criminal networks, and strengthening legal cases.

This chapter explores best practices for OSINT professionals working alongside law enforcement, including evidence-sharing, legal considerations, and maintaining ethical integrity in cybercrime investigations.

Step 1: Understanding Law Enforcement's Needs

Before collaborating with law enforcement, OSINT professionals must understand how law enforcement approaches cybercrime investigations and what type of intelligence is useful.

Types of Cybercrime Cases Where OSINT is Valuable

✓ **Online Harassment & Stalking** – Tracking perpetrators across multiple platforms.

✓ **Financial Fraud & Scams** – Identifying fraudulent websites, phishing campaigns, and scam networks.

✓ **Dark Web Investigations** – Unmasking criminals operating on darknet markets and forums.

✓ **Terrorism & Extremism** – Monitoring online radicalization and identifying extremist propaganda sources.

✓ **Human Trafficking** – Mapping out trafficker networks through classified ads, social media, and forums.

What Law Enforcement Needs from OSINT Investigators

✓ Identifying key suspects, their aliases, and online presence.

✓ Uncovering connections between cybercriminals and organized crime groups.

✓ Tracking cryptocurrency transactions linked to illicit activities.

✓ Collecting and preserving digital evidence for court-admissibility.

🔎 Example:

An OSINT analyst identified a scammer running fake tech support websites, which law enforcement later took down. The analyst provided screenshots, domain registration records, and transaction details to assist in the investigation.

Step 2: Gathering & Structuring OSINT for Law Enforcement Use

Law enforcement agencies often deal with large amounts of data and require information in a structured, actionable format.

How to Organize OSINT Findings for Investigators

✓ **Timeline-Based Reports** – Documenting the suspect's online activities over time.

✓ **Link Analysis Charts** – Mapping out connections between suspects, email accounts, social media profiles, and financial transactions.

✓ **Metadata Extraction** – Analyzing IP addresses, email headers, and domain registrations for key intelligence.

✓ **Threat Intelligence Summaries** – Providing concise profiles of suspects and their cyber activities.

☐ **Best Tools for Structuring OSINT Reports:**

- **Maltego** – Visual link analysis for cyber investigations.
- **i2 Analyst's Notebook** – Used by law enforcement for intelligence mapping.
- **Hunchly** – Automatically captures online investigations with timestamps.

🔎 **Example:**

An OSINT investigator built a timeline report detailing a hacker's movement across different online platforms over six months, helping law enforcement understand their behavioral patterns and preferred attack methods.

Step 3: Legal & Ethical Considerations When Assisting Law Enforcement

While OSINT focuses on publicly available data, investigators must adhere to legal and ethical guidelines to ensure their findings are admissible in court.

Legal Aspects of OSINT Collaboration

✓ **Privacy Laws & Data Protection** – Avoiding illegal data access (e.g., hacking, unauthorized logins).

✓ **Admissibility of Evidence** – Ensuring proper documentation and chain of custody for court cases.

✓ **Jurisdictional Challenges** – Cybercriminals may operate in multiple countries with different laws.

Ethical Guidelines for OSINT Analysts

✓ Avoid entrapment or illegal interactions with suspects.

✓ Ensure collected intelligence is verified and accurate.

✓ Be transparent with law enforcement about data collection methods.

🔎 Case Example:

An OSINT researcher investigating a phishing scam network ensured that all collected evidence came from publicly available sources and followed proper documentation procedures. This allowed the intelligence to be legally admissible in a multi-national law enforcement operation.

Step 4: Communication & Secure Information Sharing

OSINT professionals must establish secure communication channels when collaborating with law enforcement to protect sensitive intelligence from leaks or exposure.

Best Practices for Secure Collaboration

✓ **Use Encrypted Communication Channels** – PGP-encrypted emails, ProtonMail, Signal, or law enforcement-approved platforms.

✓ **Follow Chain of Custody Protocols** – Maintain proper logs for collected evidence.

✓ **Regularly Verify Intelligence** – Avoid spreading misinformation by cross-checking sources.

☐ **Secure OSINT Tools for Law Enforcement Collaboration:**

- **Keybase** – Encrypted team collaboration.
- **Tails OS** – Anonymized and secure investigative environment.
- **CryptPad** – Secure document sharing.

🔎 Example:

An OSINT analyst shared a leaked database of compromised accounts with law enforcement via a secure channel, preventing the data from being misused or falling into the wrong hands.

Step 5: Contributing to Multi-Agency Cybercrime Task Forces

In many cases, OSINT professionals work alongside law enforcement agencies, cybersecurity firms, and intelligence organizations to combat cybercrime.

How OSINT Experts Can Support Cybercrime Task Forces

✓ Providing specialized intelligence on cyber threats & tactics.

✓ Uncovering darknet and underground criminal networks.

✓ Assisting in digital forensics and attribution of cybercriminals.

✓ Training law enforcement on advanced OSINT techniques.

🔎 **Case Example:**

An OSINT analyst helped law enforcement unmask an anonymous dark web drug vendor by analyzing language patterns, cryptocurrency transactions, and social media leaks, leading to an international sting operation.

Conclusion: Strengthening Cybercrime Investigations with OSINT

OSINT professionals play a crucial role in assisting law enforcement with cybercrime investigations by gathering actionable intelligence, structuring evidence for legal use, and maintaining ethical standards.

✅ **Key Takeaways:**

✓ Understand law enforcement needs and structure OSINT findings accordingly.

✓ Ensure evidence collection follows legal and ethical guidelines.

✓ Use secure communication for intelligence sharing.

✓ Support multi-agency cybercrime task forces with specialized OSINT skills.

By strengthening OSINT and law enforcement collaboration, cybercriminals can be effectively tracked, identified, and brought to justice.

3.6 Case Study: Catching a Cyberstalker with OSINT

Introduction: The Rise of Cyberstalking

Cyberstalking is a growing crime where perpetrators use the internet to harass, intimidate, and monitor their victims. Unlike traditional stalking, cyberstalking leaves behind digital footprints—trails of usernames, emails, IP addresses, and online activities that investigators can track. In this case study, we examine how OSINT techniques were used to identify and apprehend a cyberstalker who had been tormenting multiple victims online.

Case Background: A Mysterious Online Harassment Campaign

In early 2023, a well-known journalist, Emma Carter, began receiving threatening emails, social media messages, and doxxing attempts. The harasser, using multiple anonymous accounts, had:

✓ Sent threats of violence via Twitter and Reddit.

✓ Created fake accounts impersonating Emma to spread false information.

✓ Leaked personal information, including her home address and phone number.

✓ Used burner email accounts to send threatening messages.

Despite blocking and reporting the accounts, the cyberstalker persisted and escalated their harassment. With limited options, Emma approached law enforcement and an OSINT investigator for help.

Step 1: Identifying the Cyberstalker's Digital Footprint

The OSINT analyst began by mapping out the cyberstalker's online activity. Since the suspect used multiple fake accounts, the investigator collected, cross-referenced, and analyzed publicly available data to find commonalities between accounts.

OSINT Techniques Used:

✓ **Username Pivoting**: Searching for the same or similar usernames across multiple platforms.

✓ **Reverse Image Search**: Checking profile pictures for reused images.

✓ **Metadata Extraction**: Analyzing email headers and social media post metadata for location clues.

✓ **IP Tracking**: Examining email headers for originating IP addresses.

✓ **Timeline Analysis**: Studying the time zones and posting patterns of the suspect.

☐ **Tools Used:**

- **WhatsMyName** – Checks username usage across multiple sites.
- **ExifTool** – Extracts metadata from images and files.
- **TweetBeaver** – Analyzes Twitter behavior and interactions.
- **Holehe** – Checks if an email address is linked to online services.

🔎 Key Finding:

One of the cyberstalker's Twitter accounts used the username "ShadowHunter91", which also appeared on Reddit, Discord, and an old gaming forum. The investigator found that the Reddit account had previously used an identifiable email address.

Step 2: Unmasking the Cyberstalker's Identity

By pivoting off the discovered email address, the OSINT investigator conducted a deeper analysis to reveal the suspect's real identity.

Analysis Steps:

✓ **Email & Data Breach Lookups** – Checking if the email appeared in previous data breaches.

✓ **Social Media Cross-Referencing** – Searching the email in Facebook and LinkedIn.

✓ **Domain & WHOIS Checks** – Looking up any registered websites linked to the suspect.

✓ **Phone Number & IP Analysis** – Verifying associated phone numbers and possible location.

🔎 Key Finding:

The email ShadowHunter91@gmail.com appeared in an old data breach, revealing a full name: Ryan Dawson and a secondary email address. The secondary email led to a LinkedIn profile showing that Ryan was a former classmate of Emma Carter in college.

This was a breakthrough—the cyberstalker had a personal connection to the victim.

Step 3: Tracking the Cyberstalker's Behavioral Patterns

The investigator conducted a behavioral analysis to predict the cyberstalker's next moves.

Behavioral Insights:

✔ The suspect posted threats at night (between 9 PM and 2 AM), suggesting his location.

✔ He primarily targeted Emma but also harassed her colleagues and friends.

✔ He used similar language patterns across different platforms, making it easier to confirm multiple accounts belonged to the same person.

✔ The cyberstalker frequently bragged about VPN use, but occasionally slipped up— posting from a real IP address on a less-secure forum.

🗆 **Tools Used for Behavioral Analysis:**

- **GeoSocial Footprint** – Mapped location clues from public social media posts.
- **Google Dorks** – Used advanced Google search queries to uncover hidden posts.
- **Maltego** – Created a link analysis map connecting all discovered accounts.

🔎 **Key Finding:**

The OSINT analyst discovered an IP address linked to a public Wi-Fi network near Ryan Dawson's workplace. This helped law enforcement pinpoint a physical location to verify his involvement.

Step 4: Providing Actionable Intelligence to Law Enforcement

With a strong digital footprint, timeline of harassment, and confirmed identity, the OSINT investigator compiled an evidence report for law enforcement.

Key Report Elements:

✔ **Timeline of Events** – Documenting the cyberstalker's online activities.

✔ **Link Analysis Chart** – Connecting accounts, emails, IPs, and behaviors.

✔ **Threat Assessment** – Analyzing risk level and likelihood of escalation.

✔ **Admissible Evidence** – Ensuring all OSINT findings were legally obtained.

Law enforcement used the OSINT report to obtain a warrant for Ryan Dawson's internet records, confirming he had been behind the cyberstalking. Shortly after, he was arrested and charged under cyber harassment laws.

Outcome & Lessons Learned

Final Case Resolution

✔ Ryan Dawson was convicted of cyberstalking and sentenced to community service, probation, and a restraining order preventing further contact with Emma Carter.

✔ The victim was able to regain control of her online presence, and the harassment completely stopped.

✔ The case demonstrated how OSINT techniques can be used to track, unmask, and prosecute cybercriminals.

Key OSINT Takeaways from This Case

✔ Digital footprints always leave clues – even anonymous attackers make mistakes.

✔ Username and email pivoting can uncover hidden connections.

✔ Time zone and posting behavior can reveal a suspect's location.

✔ Cross-referencing data breaches and old accounts can expose identities.

✔ OSINT reports help law enforcement take action with admissible evidence.

By combining OSINT techniques, behavioral analysis, and law enforcement collaboration, investigators can successfully track and stop cyberstalkers.

Conclusion: The Power of OSINT in Cybercrime Investigations

This case study illustrates how OSINT is a game-changing tool in combating cyberstalking and online harassment. By leveraging digital footprints, investigative tools, and analytical methods, law enforcement can identify, track, and prosecute cybercriminals, ensuring justice for victims.

OSINT remains a powerful ally in the fight against cybercrime—because on the internet, nobody is truly anonymous.

4. OSINT in Financial Crimes & Fraud Investigations

This chapter dives into the powerful application of OSINT in investigating financial crimes and fraud. As criminals increasingly exploit digital platforms to carry out illicit financial activities, from money laundering to identity theft, the need for sophisticated digital tools to trace and disrupt these crimes has never been greater. We will examine how OSINT techniques can be used to track suspicious financial transactions, uncover hidden assets, and expose fraudulent schemes by analyzing online records, social media interactions, and financial networks. Through case studies and practical insights, this chapter highlights how OSINT can provide a crucial edge in the fight against financial crime and fraud.

4.1 Identifying Online Financial Fraudsters

Introduction: The Growing Threat of Online Financial Fraud

Financial fraud has evolved dramatically in the digital age, with criminals leveraging anonymous transactions, social engineering, and sophisticated deception techniques to scam individuals, businesses, and financial institutions. OSINT (Open-Source Intelligence) plays a critical role in identifying, tracking, and exposing online financial fraudsters, helping investigators uncover illicit activities, follow digital money trails, and build actionable intelligence.

This chapter explores the key techniques and tools OSINT professionals use to identify online financial fraudsters, including fraud detection methodologies, link analysis, and case studies.

Step 1: Recognizing Common Financial Fraud Schemes

Fraudsters operate using a variety of deceptive tactics. Understanding these schemes is the first step in identifying suspicious actors and behaviors.

Types of Online Financial Fraud:

✓ **Phishing Scams** – Fake websites and emails designed to steal login credentials and financial information.

✓ **Ponzi & Investment Scams** – Fraudulent investment opportunities that promise high returns but rely on recruiting new victims.

✓ **Business Email Compromise (BEC)** – Cybercriminals impersonate executives or vendors to trick companies into transferring funds.

✓ **Cryptocurrency Fraud** – Fake crypto exchanges, rug-pull scams, and laundering through digital assets.

✓ **Money Mule Networks** – Criminals use unwitting individuals to transfer illicit funds through bank accounts or payment apps.

✓ **Carding & Payment Fraud** – Stolen credit card details sold and used for unauthorized purchases.

🔎 Example:

A fraudulent crypto investment platform promised guaranteed 200% returns, luring victims to deposit funds. OSINT investigators later found reused domain registrations and stolen testimonials, exposing the scam.

Step 2: Unmasking Fraudsters Using OSINT Techniques

Once a suspected fraudster is identified, OSINT analysts can begin gathering intelligence to uncover real identities, linked accounts, and financial transactions.

Key OSINT Techniques for Identifying Fraudsters

✓ **Domain & Website Analysis** – Investigating fake business websites, WHOIS records, and hosting details.

✓ **Social Media Tracking** – Identifying fraudsters by tracing personal connections, usernames, and social posts.

✓ **Email & Phone Number Lookup** – Checking fraudsters' contact details against data breaches and scam databases.

✓ **Cryptocurrency Address Investigation** – Analyzing Bitcoin, Ethereum, and other crypto wallets for suspicious transactions.

✓ **Dark Web & Underground Market Monitoring** – Searching for fraudsters selling stolen financial data or money laundering services.

✓ **Payment Platform & Money Flow Analysis** – Tracking PayPal, Venmo, CashApp, and other payment services for fraud indicators.

☐ **Useful OSINT Tools:**

- **ScamAdviser** – Analyzes trustworthiness of online shops and financial services.
- **HavelBeenPwned** – Checks if an email is linked to data breaches.
- **WHOIS Lookup** – Investigates domain registration information.
- **BitcoinWhosWho** – Identifies known fraudulent cryptocurrency wallets.
- **Sherlock** – Searches for usernames across multiple social media platforms.
- **OSINT Framework** – A collection of tools for fraud investigations.

🔎 **Example:**

An OSINT investigator discovered that a fake loan website used stock images for its "employees" and had a recently registered domain with hidden ownership, raising red flags.

Step 3: Connecting Fraudulent Accounts & Financial Networks

Fraudsters rarely operate in isolation. Many belong to larger fraud rings or organized networks, making link analysis a key OSINT strategy.

How to Link Financial Fraudsters Across Platforms:

✓ **Track Similar Usernames & Aliases** – Fraudsters often reuse variations of their usernames across multiple sites.

✓ **Analyze IP Addresses & Hosting Providers** – Identifying shared hosting or VPN usage can link multiple scam websites.

✓ **Monitor Affiliate Marketing & Referral Links** – Scammers often promote fraudulent schemes through social media influencers or referral programs.

✓ **Follow the Money Flow** – Identify linked bank accounts, crypto wallets, and financial transactions.

✓ **Reverse Image Search on Profile Pictures** – Fraudsters commonly use stolen or stock images.

Best Tools for Fraud Network Mapping:

- **Maltego** – Creates link analysis charts for fraud networks.
- **Spiderfoot** – Automated OSINT reconnaissance for fraud investigations.
- **Google Dorks** – Advanced Google search techniques to uncover hidden connections.
- **TLOxp & Skopenow** – People search engines used for fraud detection.

🔎 **Example:**

A group running a romance scam reused the same PayPal account and Bitcoin wallet across multiple fraud cases, allowing OSINT analysts to link multiple victims to the same perpetrators.

Step 4: Investigating Cryptocurrency Transactions & Laundering

Many fraudsters use cryptocurrency to move stolen funds anonymously, but OSINT can help track suspicious crypto transactions and wallet connections.

Techniques for Crypto Fraud Investigation:

✓ **Blockchain Analysis** – Tracking transactions on Bitcoin, Ethereum, and other public blockchains.

✓ **Wallet Address Clustering** – Identifying multiple addresses controlled by the same fraudster.

✓ **Transaction Timing & Patterns** – Examining how funds are moved across wallets.

✓ **Exchanges & Cash-Out Points** – Identifying where fraudsters convert crypto into real money.

Best Tools for Crypto Fraud Investigation:

- **Blockchain Explorer (BTC, ETH, etc.)** – Public transaction tracking.
- **CipherTrace** – Identifies illicit crypto transactions.
- **Chainalysis** – Advanced blockchain forensic tool.
- **Bitquery** – Tracks cross-chain transactions.

🔎 **Example:**

An OSINT analyst tracked a fraudster who stole funds via a fake NFT sale, following the crypto transactions to an exchange where the criminal attempted to cash out.

Step 5: Reporting Financial Fraud & Collaborating with Authorities

Once a fraudster is identified, investigators need to report their findings to relevant authorities or financial institutions for further action.

Best Practices for Fraud Reporting & Documentation:

✓ **Compile an OSINT Report** – Summarize findings with evidence, transaction links, and fraud patterns.

✓ **Report to Law Enforcement** – Submit fraud cases to FBI (IC3), Europol, or national cybercrime agencies.

✓ **Notify Affected Companies** – Banks, payment processors, and crypto exchanges can freeze fraudsters' assets.

✓ **Use Public Fraud Databases** – Report scams to websites like ScamWatch, FTC, and BBB Scam Tracker.

🔎 **Example:**

An OSINT analyst exposed a fake stock trading website, reporting it to Google Safe Browsing, IC3, and financial regulators, leading to its takedown.

Conclusion: Strengthening Fraud Investigations with OSINT

Financial fraudsters are becoming more sophisticated, but OSINT provides investigators with the tools to track, expose, and disrupt their operations.

✅ **Key Takeaways:**

✓ Understand different types of financial fraud schemes.

✓ Use OSINT techniques to trace fraudsters' digital footprints.

✓ Connect fraudulent accounts using usernames, IPs, and financial records.

✓ Investigate cryptocurrency fraud with blockchain analysis.

✓ Collaborate with authorities to take action against fraud networks.

By leveraging OSINT tools and investigative techniques, analysts can identify online financial fraudsters, prevent scams, and assist in bringing criminals to justice.

4.2 Tracking Money Laundering & Shell Companies

Introduction: The Challenge of Financial Secrecy

Money laundering is a critical component of organized crime, allowing criminals to disguise the origins of illicit funds and integrate them into the legitimate financial system. One of the most common tactics used in money laundering is the creation of shell companies—business entities that exist only on paper and are used to obscure financial transactions.

OSINT (Open-Source Intelligence) provides investigators with powerful tools and methodologies to track money laundering networks, uncover shell companies, and link fraudulent financial activities to criminal enterprises. This chapter explores the techniques and tools used to identify and investigate suspicious financial transactions, exposing the hidden connections between illicit actors.

Step 1: Understanding Money Laundering & Shell Companies

The Three Stages of Money Laundering

✓ **Placement** – Introducing illicit funds into the financial system (e.g., smurfing, cash deposits, gambling).
✓ **Layering** – Moving funds through complex transactions to obscure their origin (e.g., shell companies, offshore accounts).
✓ **Integration** – Using laundered money for legitimate investments (e.g., real estate, luxury goods, business ownership).

What Are Shell Companies?

A shell company is a business that has no physical presence, no real operations, and exists solely to move or conceal money. These companies are often used to:

✓ **Obscure ownership** – Hiding the true identity of beneficial owners.

✓ **Move illicit funds** – Facilitating fraud, corruption, and tax evasion.

✓ **Bypass regulations** – Avoiding anti-money laundering (AML) controls.

🔎 **Example:**

A criminal network laundered millions through a web of offshore shell companies registered in Panama and the British Virgin Islands, making it difficult for law enforcement to trace the funds.

Step 2: Identifying Suspicious Companies & Financial Networks

To track money laundering activities, OSINT investigators must analyze corporate records, financial transactions, and business relationships to identify patterns of deception.

OSINT Techniques for Investigating Shell Companies

✓ **Corporate Registry Searches** – Checking for missing information, nominee directors, and hidden ownership structures.

✓ **Address Analysis** – Identifying multiple companies registered at the same address (a sign of shell companies).

✓ **Beneficial Ownership Research** – Tracking who truly controls a company.

✓ **Tax Haven & Offshore Entity Checks** – Investigating companies registered in secrecy jurisdictions.

✓ **Transaction Flow Analysis** – Examining how money moves between related entities.

☐ **Useful OSINT Tools for Business & Company Investigations:**

- **OpenCorporates** – Global database of companies and directors.
- **Company House (UK), SEC (US), Europol EBR** – Official government business registries.
- **Offshore Leaks Database (ICIJ)** – Exposes offshore companies and beneficial owners.
- **LEI Lookup** – Identifies legal entities and corporate structures.
- **Google Dorks & WHOIS Lookup** – Uncover hidden corporate connections.

🔎 Example:

An investigator found that five companies in different countries were all registered at the same PO box in the Cayman Islands, with the same nominee director, indicating a likely shell company network.

Step 3: Following the Money – Transaction Tracking & Bank Transfers

Tracking the movement of illicit funds is a key step in uncovering money laundering. Criminals often move money through a complex network of bank accounts, offshore entities, and digital payment services.

How to Trace Suspicious Transactions:

✓ **Cross-Border Transfers** – Identifying frequent transfers between offshore jurisdictions.

✓ **Round-Tripping** – Detecting funds that return to their original source after multiple transfers.

✓ **Use of High-Risk Banks** – Checking if funds move through jurisdictions with weak AML regulations.

✓ **Fake Invoices & Trade-Based Laundering** – Investigating inflated contracts and overvalued goods.

☐ **OSINT Tools for Transaction Analysis & Money Flows:**

- **FinCEN Files (ICIJ)** – Database of suspicious financial activity reports.
- **SWIFT Transaction Analysis** – Monitoring international wire transfers.
- **Chainalysis & CipherTrace** – Tracking cryptocurrency money laundering.
- **TransparentTrade & ImportGenius** – Trade-based money laundering research.

🔎 Example:

A fraud investigation uncovered a fake import/export business that issued millions in fake invoices to move money between bank accounts in Dubai and Hong Kong.

Step 4: Exposing Hidden Beneficial Owners & Offshore Networks

Many shell companies and financial crime networks use nominee directors, offshore agents, and trust funds to hide the true owner of illicit funds. OSINT can help pierce these veils of secrecy.

How to Uncover Beneficial Owners:

✓ **Check Business Filings** – Identifying frequent name changes, missing records, or nominee shareholders.

✓ **Compare Leaks & Data Breaches** – Searching for leaked offshore documents (e.g., Panama Papers, Paradise Papers).

✓ **Follow Connections in Social Media & News** – Investigating individuals linked to suspicious businesses.

✓ **Use Reverse Image Search on Directors** – Finding reused photos across different fraudulent companies.

☐ **Best OSINT Tools for Beneficial Ownership Research:**

- **ICIJ Offshore Leaks Database** – Exposes hidden offshore entities.
- **Sayari Graph & Orbis** – Corporate intelligence platforms for ownership analysis.
- **LinkedIn & Social Media OSINT** – Identifies key business associates.
- **Sanctions & Watchlists (OFAC, Interpol)** – Checks if individuals are linked to financial crimes.

🔎 **Example:**

An OSINT investigator traced a suspected money launderer's shell companies to an anonymous trust in Liechtenstein, ultimately linking it back to a Russian oligarch under sanctions.

Step 5: Investigating Cryptocurrency & Digital Money Laundering

Many financial criminals now launder money through cryptocurrencies to avoid traditional banking regulations. OSINT can track crypto transactions, darknet wallets, and laundering services.

How to Track Crypto-Based Money Laundering:

✓ **Analyze Blockchain Transactions** – Identifying patterns of illicit transfers.

✓ **Look for Tumblers & Mixers** – Detecting money laundering through crypto blending services.

✓ **Monitor Dark Web Transactions** – Tracking illicit fund movements from underground markets.

✓ **Check Exchange Deposits & Withdrawals** – Following money through crypto-to-fiat conversions.

☐ **Best OSINT Tools for Crypto Money Laundering Investigations:**

- **Blockchain Explorer (BTC, ETH, etc.)** – Tracks cryptocurrency transactions.
- **Chainalysis & TRM Labs** – Advanced blockchain intelligence.
- **Elliptic & CipherTrace** – Crypto forensic tools for financial crime detection.

🔎 **Example:**

Investigators tracked drug cartel proceeds laundered through Bitcoin and cashed out via a Hong Kong-based exchange, leading to asset seizures.

Step 6: Collaborating with Authorities & Reporting Financial Crimes

Once OSINT findings confirm suspicious money flows and hidden financial networks, investigators must compile their evidence into a detailed financial intelligence report for law enforcement or regulatory agencies.

Best Practices for Reporting Money Laundering Cases:

✓ **Compile a Financial OSINT Report** – Include company ownership details, transaction links, and offshore accounts.

✓ **Submit to Regulatory Authorities** – FinCEN (US), FCA (UK), FATF, or Europol Financial Crimes Unit.

✓ **Report to Banks & Crypto Exchanges** – Alert financial institutions to fraudulent activities.

✓ **Use International AML Networks** – Collaborate with global anti-money laundering task forces.

🔎 **Example:**

An OSINT investigation led to the freezing of $50M in illicit funds after uncovering a network of shell companies linked to human trafficking profits.

Conclusion: OSINT as a Game-Changer in Financial Crime Investigations

By using OSINT to track money laundering, shell companies, and illicit financial networks, investigators can expose criminal enterprises and assist law enforcement in seizing assets and prosecuting offenders.

✅ **Key Takeaways:**

✓ Follow the money—transactions always leave a trail.

✓ Corporate records & offshore leaks can expose hidden owners.

✓ Cryptocurrency laundering is growing but can be tracked with OSINT tools.

✓ Collaboration with financial crime units is essential for stopping money laundering.

With the right OSINT techniques, financial criminals can no longer hide in the shadows.

4.3 Investigating Ponzi Schemes & Investment Fraud

Introduction: The Rise of Financial Scams

Ponzi schemes and investment fraud continue to be among the most prevalent financial crimes, defrauding victims of billions of dollars every year. These scams often lure victims with promises of high returns, low risk, and exclusive investment opportunities. Using OSINT (Open-Source Intelligence), investigators can identify fraudulent investment schemes, track suspicious financial activities, and uncover the individuals behind these scams.

In this chapter, we will explore how Ponzi schemes operate, the red flags of investment fraud, and the OSINT techniques used to expose financial criminals before they vanish with investors' money.

Step 1: Understanding Ponzi Schemes & Investment Fraud

What Is a Ponzi Scheme?

A Ponzi scheme is a fraudulent investment operation where returns to earlier investors are paid using new investors' money, rather than from legitimate business profits. Eventually, the scheme collapses when it can no longer recruit new victims.

🔎 Key Characteristics of a Ponzi Scheme:

✓ **Guaranteed high returns** – Unrealistic profit promises with little or no risk.

✓ **Consistent earnings** – Profits appear stable, even during economic downturns.

✓ **Complex or secretive investment strategies** – Vague or confusing explanations of how the business generates profits.

✓ **Recruitment of new investors** – Heavy reliance on referrals and recruitment bonuses.

✓ **Difficulty withdrawing funds** – Delays or restrictions when investors try to cash out.

Types of Investment Fraud Beyond Ponzi Schemes:

✓ **Pyramid Schemes** – Similar to Ponzi schemes, but require direct recruitment of new investors.

✓ **Pump-and-Dump Scams** – Fraudsters inflate stock prices with misleading promotions and then sell off shares.

✓ **Crypto Investment Fraud** – Fake cryptocurrency projects promising massive returns.

✓ **Fake Hedge Funds & Private Equity Scams** – Bogus investment firms with fabricated performance records.

🔎 Example:

Bernie Madoff's Ponzi scheme defrauded investors of $65 billion, making it one of the largest financial frauds in history.

Step 2: Identifying Red Flags of Ponzi Schemes Using OSINT

Before a Ponzi scheme collapses, there are often warning signs that investigators can detect using OSINT techniques.

Common OSINT-Based Red Flags:

✓ **Company website & online presence analysis** – Fake investment firms often have newly registered domains, vague "About Us" pages, and no verifiable history.

✓ **Social media promotions** – Many scams aggressively market on Twitter, Facebook, LinkedIn, and Telegram, often using fake testimonials.

✓ **Google Dorking for hidden information** – Searching for investor complaints, regulatory warnings, or past fraud connections.

✓ **Whois Lookup & Domain Age Checks** – Identifying websites registered recently or with hidden ownership.

✓ **Negative News Search & Lawsuit Records** – Searching for past fraud cases involving key executives.

✓ **Regulatory Warnings & Licensing Checks** – Verifying whether the investment firm is registered with SEC, FCA, or FINRA.

☐ **Useful OSINT Tools:**

- **EDGAR (SEC Filings Database)** – Checks US investment firms for financial disclosures.
- **FINRA BrokerCheck** – Verifies if a broker or investment firm is legitimate.
- **Offshore Leaks Database** – Identifies companies linked to offshore tax havens.

Google Dorking Queries:

- **"Investment scam site:reddit.com"** (Checks forums for fraud discussions)
- **"Ponzi scheme + [Company Name]"** (Finds fraud accusations)
- **"site:sec.gov [Company Name]"** (Checks for SEC warnings)

🔎 **Example:**

An OSINT analyst discovered that a crypto Ponzi scheme was using paid actors for fake video testimonials, leading to its exposure before a major collapse.

Step 3: Investigating the Operators Behind Ponzi Schemes

Many Ponzi scheme operators hide their identities using fake names, shell companies, and offshore accounts. OSINT can help unmask these individuals by tracing their digital footprints.

How to Track Investment Fraud Operators:

✓ **Reverse Image Search on CEOs & Executives** – Fake LinkedIn profiles often use stolen stock images.

✓ **Cross-Referencing Names & Aliases** – Checking if individuals have changed names or have multiple identities.

✓ **Social Media Analysis** – Identifying fraudulent investment promoters and their networks.

✓ **Checking Past Business Records** – Verifying if company executives were involved in previous scams.

✓ **Tracking Online Reviews & Complaints** – Many investors report scams on forums like Trustpilot, BBB, and Ripoff Report.

☐ **Best OSINT Tools for People Investigations:**

- **Pipl & Spokeo** – Uncover social media and email connections.
- **Wayback Machine** – View past versions of company websites to check inconsistencies.
- **LinkedIn & Twitter Investigations** – Identify scam promoters and their recruitment networks.
- **Court Records & Bankruptcy Filings** – Check for past legal issues.

🔎 **Example:**

Investigators uncovered that an investment firm CEO had changed his name twice after previous fraud convictions, exposing the scam.

Step 4: Following the Money – Tracking Investment Fraud Transactions

Ponzi schemes often move investor money through shell companies, offshore accounts, and cryptocurrencies to evade detection. OSINT techniques can help trace suspicious transactions and recover lost funds.

How to Trace Ponzi Scheme Funds:

✓ **Examining Public Financial Filings** – Checking for inconsistencies in reported earnings.

✓ **Tracking Shell Companies & Offshore Accounts** – Investigating suspicious business connections.

✓ **Cryptocurrency Wallet Analysis** – Checking if investor funds are moved to crypto mixers and offshore exchanges.

✓ **Monitoring High-Value Purchases** – Ponzi operators often buy luxury homes, cars, and artwork to launder money.

⬜ **Best OSINT Tools for Financial Tracking:**

- **Chainalysis & Blockchain Explorer** – Follows cryptocurrency transactions.
- **OpenCorporates & Orbis** – Identifies shell companies.
- **Luxury Asset Databases** – Tracks real estate, yachts, and private jets owned by fraudsters.

🔎 **Example:**

An investigator traced Ponzi scheme funds from a fraudulent forex trading platform to offshore accounts in Belize, leading to asset seizures.

Step 5: Reporting Investment Fraud & Working with Authorities

Once an OSINT investigation confirms investment fraud, the next step is reporting the findings to financial regulators and law enforcement agencies.

Best Practices for Reporting Investment Scams:

✓ **Compile a Detailed OSINT Report** – Include fraudulent claims, financial links, and key individuals.

✓ **Submit to Regulatory Bodies** – SEC (US), FCA (UK), ASIC (Australia), or Interpol's financial crime unit.

✓ **Work with Journalists & Consumer Advocacy Groups** – Raising public awareness of investment fraud.

✓ **Alert Financial Institutions** – Requesting account freezes for known fraudsters.

🔎 **Example:**

An OSINT-driven investigation led to the arrest of a Ponzi scheme operator who defrauded investors of $200M, thanks to early detection by financial analysts.

Conclusion: Using OSINT to Stop Ponzi Schemes & Investment Fraud

With financial scams becoming more sophisticated, OSINT is an essential tool for exposing fraudulent schemes before they escalate. By monitoring online activities, analyzing business records, and tracking suspicious transactions, investigators can protect investors, assist regulators, and disrupt financial crime networks.

✅ **Key Takeaways:**

✔ Ponzi schemes often collapse when recruitment slows—OSINT can detect early warning signs.

✔ Fake investment firms leave digital footprints—domain history, social media, and regulatory filings can reveal fraud.

✔ Following the money trail—OSINT tools can track illicit financial movements through shell companies and crypto wallets.

✔ Collaboration is key—sharing intelligence with financial regulators leads to arrests and asset recoveries.

By leveraging OSINT techniques, investigators can expose investment fraudsters before they disappear with victims' money.

4.4 Detecting Payment & E-Commerce Scams

Introduction: The Rise of Digital Payment Fraud

As online transactions become the norm, payment fraud and e-commerce scams have surged, costing consumers and businesses billions of dollars annually. Fraudsters exploit digital payment systems, online marketplaces, and social media platforms to steal money, commit identity theft, and deceive unsuspecting victims.

Open-Source Intelligence (OSINT) plays a critical role in detecting, tracking, and mitigating these scams. By analyzing digital footprints, payment records, and scam patterns, investigators can identify fraudulent sellers, detect stolen payment credentials, and prevent further financial losses.

Step 1: Understanding Common Payment & E-Commerce Scams

Payment and e-commerce fraud comes in various forms, with scammers continuously evolving their tactics. Below are some of the most common methods criminals use:

1 Fake Online Stores & Dropshipping Scams

✔ Fraudulent websites advertise heavily on social media, selling non-existent or low-quality products.

✔ Often, these sites use stolen product images and claim unrealistic discounts.

✔ Once victims make a purchase, the seller disappears, stops responding, or ships counterfeit goods.

2 Credit Card Fraud & Stolen Payment Credentials

✔ Scammers steal credit card details through data breaches, phishing, and dark web markets.

✔ Fraudsters then purchase goods or services using compromised payment information.

✔ Some create fake accounts on e-commerce platforms and conduct "card testing" to verify stolen credentials.

3 Peer-to-Peer (P2P) Payment Scams

✔ Fraudsters trick victims into sending money via Venmo, Cash App, Zelle, or PayPal.

✔ Once the money is sent, it's nearly impossible to recover—especially with "friends and family" transactions.

✔ Examples include fake ticket sales, rental deposit scams, and puppy scams.

4️⃣ Marketplace & Auction Fraud

✓ Scammers use platforms like Facebook Marketplace, eBay, and Craigslist to list fake or stolen goods.

✓ Some use "overpayment scams", where they send extra money and demand a refund before the initial payment clears.

✓ Others run "non-delivery scams", taking payment and never shipping the product.

5️⃣ Chargeback & Refund Fraud

✓ Fraudsters purchase goods and file chargeback claims, falsely stating the item wasn't received.

✓ Some abuse refund policies by ordering expensive items and returning cheap knock-offs.

🔎 Example:

An OSINT investigator uncovered a network of fake luxury watch sellers who used Instagram ads to lure victims into making payments via untraceable cryptocurrency transactions.

Step 2: OSINT Techniques for Detecting Payment & E-Commerce Fraud

1️⃣ Website & Domain Investigations

☐ **Tools:**

- **Whois Lookup** – Checks domain registration details for suspicious ownership.
- **Wayback Machine** – Views past versions of scam websites that frequently change names.
- **ScamAdviser & Fake Website Detectors** – Evaluates trust scores of online stores.

- "site:[suspectdomain].com" + "scam" OR "fraud" OR "complaints" (Finds complaints about an e-commerce site)
- "Whois domain lookup [suspect domain]" (Identifies recently registered scam websites)

2️⃣ Analyzing Payment & Transaction Patterns

☐ **Techniques:**

✓ Checking if a merchant has multiple chargebacks, refund claims, or customer complaints.

✓ Monitoring digital wallet activity for suspicious fund transfers.

✓ Tracking cryptocurrency transactions used for illicit purchases.

☐ **Tools:**

- **Bitcoin Explorer & Blockchain Analysis** – Tracks fraudulent crypto payments.
- **PayPal & Venmo Fraud Checkers** – Identifies suspicious seller patterns.

3️⃣ Social Media & Marketplace Investigations

☐ **Techniques:**

✓ Reverse image searches on product photos to detect stolen content.

✓ Tracking usernames, email addresses, and phone numbers linked to past scams.

✓ Cross-referencing seller profiles across multiple platforms.

☐ **Tools:**

- **Google Reverse Image Search & TinEye** – Checks if product photos are stolen.
- **Facebook & Instagram Lookup** – Identifies marketplace scammers.
- **Scamwatch Databases** – Tracks fraud reports from victims.

🔍 **Example OSINT Query:**

- "site:reddit.com [seller name] scam" (Finds complaints about a suspicious merchant)
- "Reverse image search + [product photo]" (Detects stolen images used in scams)

Step 3: Investigating Fake Online Stores & Fraudulent Sellers

How to Spot a Fake E-Commerce Store Using OSINT

✓ **Recently registered domains** – Many scam stores are less than 6 months old.

✓ **No physical address or customer support** – Fraudulent sites often lack contact information.

✓ **Generic or copied product descriptions** – Scammers copy listings from legitimate retailers.

✓ **Unrealistic discounts** – If a deal looks too good to be true, it probably is.

☐ **Best OSINT Tools for E-Commerce Investigations:**

- **Google Transparency Report** – Identifies unsafe websites.
- **ScamDoc & Trustpilot** – Checks store reputations.
- **Reverse WHOIS Lookup** – Finds other scam sites linked to the same owner.

🔎 **Example:**

An OSINT investigator found that a fake sneaker store was registered in China under multiple names, linking it to a network of counterfeit goods sellers.

Step 4: Identifying & Tracking Payment Fraud Networks

Fraudulent payment schemes often involve multiple accounts, stolen identities, and money laundering tactics. OSINT can help uncover networks of scammers operating across different platforms.

How to Track Fraud Networks:

✓ Connecting multiple scam websites through WHOIS data & IP addresses.

✓ Analyzing social media ads promoting suspicious online stores.

✓ Tracking Bitcoin & crypto transactions used in payment fraud.

✓ Identifying recurring patterns in fake customer reviews & complaints.

☐ **Best OSINT Tools for Payment Fraud Investigations:**

- **Maltego & SpiderFoot** – Maps fraud networks & linked accounts.
- **HavelBeenPwned** – Checks if email addresses are linked to past fraud.
- **Bitcoin Explorer & Chainalysis** – Investigates cryptocurrency transactions used in scams.

🔎 **Example:**

Investigators traced a large-scale PayPal refund fraud ring using OSINT, leading to the seizure of $3 million in stolen funds.

Step 5: Reporting & Preventing Payment Scams

Once fraud is identified, OSINT investigators can report scam merchants, warn consumers, and assist law enforcement in shutting down fraudulent operations.

How to Report E-Commerce & Payment Scams:

✓ Report to platforms like eBay, Amazon, PayPal, and Facebook Marketplace.

✓ Submit complaints to fraud agencies like the FBI's IC3 (USA), Action Fraud (UK), and Europol.

✓ Warn the public through social media and scam reporting websites.

🔎 **Example:**

A payment fraud OSINT team helped dismantle a major eBay scam, where fraudsters were selling non-existent gaming consoles, resulting in multiple arrests.

Conclusion: OSINT as a Weapon Against Payment Scams

With digital fraud on the rise, OSINT is essential for detecting payment scams, tracking fraudulent sellers, and exposing e-commerce criminals. By analyzing domain data, financial transactions, and social media activity, investigators can identify scam networks before they cause more harm.

✓ Key Takeaways:

✓ Scammers frequently change websites—tracking domain history helps uncover fraud.

✓ Reverse image searches expose stolen product listings used by fake sellers.

✓ Social media analysis identifies fraudulent e-commerce promoters.

✓ Blockchain tracking helps follow money trails in crypto payment fraud.

By leveraging OSINT techniques, law enforcement, businesses, and consumers can stay ahead of scammers and make online transactions safer.

4.5 OSINT Tools for Analyzing Financial Transactions

Introduction: The Role of OSINT in Financial Investigations

Financial transactions leave digital footprints, and Open-Source Intelligence (OSINT) tools help investigators track, analyze, and uncover suspicious financial activities. Whether it's money laundering, fraud, terrorist financing, or illicit cryptocurrency transactions, OSINT provides essential capabilities for identifying patterns, tracing funds, and connecting financial data points.

This chapter explores key OSINT tools and techniques for analyzing banking transactions, cryptocurrency flows, shell companies, and financial fraud networks.

Step 1: Tracking Traditional Financial Transactions

1️ Bank Account & Wire Transfer Investigations

Although bank transactions are generally protected by privacy laws, OSINT tools can still provide useful intelligence.

☐ Key OSINT Methods:

✓ Monitoring leaked financial databases for exposed transaction data.

✓ Analyzing public financial records, SEC filings, and regulatory reports.

✓ Using corporate registries to track business accounts and shell companies.

✓ Cross-referencing bank account holders with legal cases or fraud complaints.

🔎 **Best OSINT Tools:**

- **OpenCorporates** – Investigates bank-linked shell companies.
- **SEC EDGAR Database** – Tracks financial disclosures of registered entities.
- **Leaks & Breach Databases (e.g., HaveIBeenPwned, DeHashed)** – Finds exposed financial credentials.

📌 **Example:**

An OSINT investigator used SEC filings and leaked financial reports to uncover a Ponzi scheme involving fraudulent hedge fund investments.

Step 2: Cryptocurrency & Blockchain Investigations

2️ Tracing Bitcoin & Crypto Transactions

Cryptocurrency transactions are pseudo-anonymous, but OSINT tools can track wallet addresses, transaction flows, and dark web payments.

☐ Key OSINT Methods:

✓ Tracking Bitcoin transactions using blockchain explorers.

✓ Identifying crypto wallets linked to ransomware payments.

✓ Mapping crypto exchange accounts tied to illicit transactions.

✓ Analyzing Ethereum smart contracts & DeFi transactions.

🔎 **Best OSINT Tools:**

- **Blockchain.com Explorer** – Searches Bitcoin and Ethereum transactions.
- **Chainalysis & CipherTrace** – Investigates money laundering in cryptocurrency.

- **Elliptic** – Identifies illicit transactions & dark web crypto payments.
- **WalletExplorer** – Unmasks crypto wallets linked to known addresses.

📌 **Example:**

Investigators used Chainalysis to track Bitcoin ransom payments linked to a cybercrime syndicate laundering money through crypto tumblers.

Step 3: Shell Companies & Money Laundering Investigations

3️⃣ Identifying Shell Companies & Front Businesses

Criminals use shell companies, offshore accounts, and fake corporations to hide illicit financial activities. OSINT tools help uncover these hidden connections.

🔲 **Key OSINT Methods:**

✔ Using corporate registries to track shell companies & business owners.

✔ Mapping financial links between fraudulent enterprises.

✔ Analyzing real estate records to detect money laundering purchases.

🔍 **Best OSINT Tools:**

- **OpenCorporates & Orbis** – Tracks global business registrations.
- **Offshore Leaks Database (ICIJ)** – Investigates offshore tax havens & shell firms.
- **LuxLeaks & Panama Papers** – Exposes hidden assets of criminals & corrupt officials.

📌 **Example:**

A journalist used the Panama Papers leak to uncover money laundering by a political leader, who funneled stolen funds through offshore companies.

Step 4: Analyzing Payment Networks & Fraud Rings

4️⃣ Tracking Financial Fraud & Payment Scams

Fraud networks use stolen credit cards, fake invoices, and online payment scams to move illicit money. OSINT tools can detect patterns of suspicious transactions.

☐ **Key OSINT Methods:**

✓ Analyzing payment networks & transaction metadata.

✓ Detecting fake e-commerce stores laundering money.

✓ Tracking fund movements between scam operators.

🔎 **Best OSINT Tools:**

- **Maltego** – Maps payment fraud networks.
- **ScamAdviser** – Detects fake merchant websites.
- **PayPal Transaction Checker** – Analyzes suspicious PayPal transactions.

📌 **Example:**

An investigator used Maltego to map a multi-million-dollar credit card fraud ring, linking fake e-commerce websites to stolen payment credentials.

Step 5: Financial Data Leak Investigations

5☐ Using OSINT to Analyze Leaked Financial Records

Dark web markets and hacker forums often sell stolen banking credentials, credit card details, and financial data. OSINT tools can monitor these leaks to identify compromised accounts and fraud operations.

☐ **Key OSINT Methods:**

✓ Searching dark web forums for leaked banking data.

✓ Monitoring breach databases for exposed financial credentials.

✓ Analyzing ransomware attacks targeting financial institutions.

🔎 **Best OSINT Tools:**

- **IntelX & DeHashed** – Finds leaked financial records.

- **BreachForums & Dark Web Search Engines** – Identifies compromised banking data.
- **SpiderFoot** – Automates deep web searches for financial leaks.

📌 **Example:**

OSINT analysts tracked a dark web hacker selling thousands of stolen PayPal accounts, leading to an international fraud investigation.

Step 6: Investigating Terrorist Financing & Sanctions Violations

6⬜ OSINT in Counter-Terrorism & Sanctions Monitoring

Financial OSINT helps detect illicit transactions funding terrorism, organized crime, and sanctioned entities.

⬜ **Key OSINT Methods:**

✔ Identifying crypto transactions linked to terrorist organizations.

✔ Monitoring bank accounts flagged for sanctions violations.

✔ Cross-referencing suspicious donations to extremist groups.

🔎 **Best OSINT Tools:**

- **World-Check & OFAC Sanctions List** – Flags entities involved in financial crimes.
- **TRM Labs & Elliptic** – Tracks crypto transactions linked to terrorist groups.
- **FinCEN Files (ICIJ)** – Exposes global money laundering networks.

📌 **Example:**

Investigators used OFAC sanctions databases to track money laundering by a sanctioned state actor using cryptocurrency.

Conclusion: OSINT's Power in Financial Investigations

OSINT is an invaluable asset in financial crime investigations, enabling analysts to track money flows, detect fraud networks, and expose hidden assets. By leveraging corporate records, blockchain forensics, and financial leak databases, investigators can connect financial dots and dismantle illicit networks.

☑ **Key Takeaways:**

✓ OSINT tools help track traditional and cryptocurrency transactions.

✓ Financial leaks & data breaches expose fraudulent financial activities.

✓ Shell companies and offshore firms often hide illicit wealth.

✓ Dark web markets sell stolen banking credentials & payment data.

By mastering these OSINT techniques, investigators can follow the money, uncover fraud, and bring financial criminals to justice.

4.6 Case Study: Investigating a Large-Scale Online Fraud

Introduction: The Growing Threat of Online Financial Fraud

In an era where digital transactions dominate, online fraud has become one of the most lucrative criminal enterprises. Fraudsters exploit vulnerabilities in e-commerce, banking, and cryptocurrency systems to conduct large-scale financial crimes, stealing billions annually.

This case study explores how OSINT techniques and tools were used to investigate a major online fraud operation involving fake e-commerce stores, stolen payment credentials, and cryptocurrency laundering.

The Fraud Operation: How It Worked

A multi-national fraud syndicate created hundreds of fake online stores advertising high-demand products, such as electronics, luxury items, and fashion brands. Victims would make payments, but never receive their orders.

Key Components of the Scam:

✓ **Fake E-Commerce Websites** – Designed to look like real online stores with professional branding.

✓ **Stolen Credit Cards & Payment Data** – Used to process fraudulent transactions.

✓ **Money Laundering Through Cryptocurrency** – Funds were converted into Bitcoin to evade detection.

✓ **Social Media Ads & Phishing Campaigns** – Attracted victims with fake promotions.

Step 1: Identifying the Fraudulent Websites

OSINT Investigation Strategy:

🔍 Domain Analysis:

- Investigators conducted WHOIS lookups and found that multiple scam websites were registered under the same anonymous hosting provider.
- Many domains were less than six months old, a common red flag for scam sites.

☐ OSINT Tools Used:

- **Whois Lookup** – Identified domain registration details.
- **Wayback Machine** – Tracked previous versions of the fraudulent sites.
- **ScamAdviser** – Verified suspicious website trust scores.

📌 Findings:

✓ Over 150 fake stores were linked to a single fraud network operating from Eastern Europe.

✓ The domains were frequently changed every few weeks to avoid detection.

Step 2: Tracking Payment Processing & Financial Trails

Analyzing Fraudulent Transactions:

💳 The scam websites primarily accepted payments through:

- Compromised credit cards obtained from the dark web.
- Cryptocurrency payments, making it difficult to track fund movements.

🔎 Key OSINT Techniques Used:

✓ Cross-referencing credit card transactions with leaked financial databases.

✓ Blockchain forensics to trace cryptocurrency payments.

✓ Monitoring refund fraud patterns through online complaints.

☐ **OSINT Tools Used:**

- **Blockchain Explorer** – Tracked Bitcoin payments used by fraudsters.
- **Elliptic & Chainalysis** – Identified money laundering through crypto tumblers.
- **DeHashed & HavelBeenPwned** – Searched for leaked payment credentials used in the scam.

📌 **Findings:**

✓ The criminals laundered funds through multiple Bitcoin wallets, transferring money through exchanges in Russia and Hong Kong.

✓ Stolen credit cards were being used for "card testing" on small transactions before making large fraudulent purchases.

Step 3: Investigating the Operators Behind the Fraud

Unmasking the Scammers:

🔍 **Social Media & Digital Footprint Analysis:**

✓ Investigators used reverse image searches on profile pictures linked to fake seller accounts.

✓ Fake store operators were advertising their scam sites on Facebook, Instagram, and Telegram.

✓ Some fraudsters reused the same email addresses and usernames across multiple platforms.

☐ **OSINT Tools Used:**

- **Maltego** – Mapped connections between fraudulent accounts.
- **Google Reverse Image Search & TinEye** – Traced fake store profile pictures.
- **UserRecon & WhatsMyName** – Cross-referenced usernames on various platforms.

📌 Findings:

✓ The scammers operated under multiple aliases, but OSINT linked them to a criminal network in Ukraine.

✓ Some fraudsters were previously involved in phishing scams and ransomware attacks.

Step 4: Uncovering Money Laundering Methods

How the Fraudsters Hid Their Profits:

💰 The criminals converted stolen funds into:

✓ **Cryptocurrency (Bitcoin & Monero)** – Harder to trace.

✓ **Luxury goods & real estate purchases** – Money laundering through high-value assets.

✓ **Fake online services** – Generating "legitimate" revenue through fabricated invoices.

🔎 Key OSINT Techniques Used:

✓ Blockchain transaction tracking to follow Bitcoin transfers.

✓ Examining shell companies registered under fraudulent identities.

✓ Cross-referencing financial transactions with leaked offshore banking records.

☐ OSINT Tools Used:

- **Panama Papers & Offshore Leaks Database** – Identified shell companies.
- **Bitcoin Explorer** – Tracked stolen funds through cryptocurrency exchanges.
- **Google Earth & OpenCorporates** – Investigated real estate transactions linked to the fraud.

📌 Findings:

✓ The syndicate laundered over $20 million through a network of offshore bank accounts and crypto wallets.

✓ Funds were eventually transferred to high-end real estate investments in Dubai.

Step 5: Law Enforcement Collaboration & Takedown

Reporting & Coordinating the Crackdown

🔍 How Investigators Worked with Authorities:

✓ OSINT findings were shared with INTERPOL, Europol, and local financial crime units.

✓ Blockchain analysis helped seize fraud-linked cryptocurrency wallets.

✓ Domain registrars and hosting providers were notified to shut down the scam websites.

📌 Final Outcome:

✓ Authorities arrested multiple individuals involved in the fraud operation.

✓ Over $5 million in stolen cryptocurrency was recovered.

✓ International law enforcement shut down 120+ scam websites.

Key Takeaways: How OSINT Can Expose Online Fraud

✅ Fake e-commerce stores and scam websites are often part of large criminal networks.

✅ Tracking digital footprints and payment trails can reveal the operators behind fraud schemes.

✅ Blockchain forensics is a powerful tool for tracing illicit cryptocurrency transactions.

✅ Social media analysis helps connect fraudulent sellers across multiple platforms.

✅ Collaboration with law enforcement and financial institutions is crucial in taking down large-scale fraud rings.

Conclusion: OSINT as a Game-Changer in Financial Crime Investigations

This case study highlights how OSINT techniques, digital forensics, and financial intelligence were successfully used to dismantle a multi-million-dollar fraud operation.

By leveraging domain analysis, social media tracking, blockchain forensics, and financial OSINT tools, investigators uncovered the fraudsters' network, traced their money laundering schemes, and facilitated their arrests.

As online fraud continues to evolve, OSINT remains a critical tool for exposing financial criminals and protecting consumers from digital scams.

5. Geolocation OSINT for Missing Persons Cases

In this chapter, we explore the use of geolocation-based OSINT techniques in solving missing persons cases. In an age where digital footprints are left behind in almost every interaction, investigators can leverage geolocation data from social media, mobile devices, and online platforms to trace a person's last known movements and uncover vital clues. We will discuss how OSINT tools help map out locations, analyze patterns of activity, and cross-reference data to create a more comprehensive search strategy. By highlighting real-life examples, this chapter demonstrates how geolocation intelligence is transforming the search efforts, increasing the chances of locating missing individuals more quickly and efficiently.

5.1 The Role of OSINT in Missing Persons Investigations

Introduction: How OSINT Aids in Finding the Missing

Every year, thousands of people go missing worldwide—whether due to abductions, trafficking, criminal activity, or voluntary disappearances. Law enforcement, private investigators, and concerned families often struggle to gather leads quickly enough to locate missing individuals. Open-Source Intelligence (OSINT) has become an essential tool in these cases, offering real-time data collection, geolocation analysis, and social media tracking to aid investigations.

By leveraging publicly available information, OSINT investigators can trace digital footprints, analyze last-known locations, monitor online activity, and uncover potential sightings. This chapter explores the role of OSINT in missing persons cases and the techniques used to bring people home.

Step 1: Collecting Initial Intelligence

The first phase of a missing persons investigation involves gathering as much baseline intelligence as possible. This includes:

✓ Last known location (physical or digital).

✓ Recent social media activity (posts, messages, location check-ins).

✓ Known contacts and recent communications.

✓ Digital assets (phone data, emails, cloud storage).

OSINT Techniques for Initial Data Collection:

☐ **Social Media Scraping** – Searching for new activity, last posts, tagged locations.
☐ **Metadata Extraction** – Analyzing timestamps and GPS data from images or videos.
☐ **Public Records & Databases** – Checking legal documents, recent purchases, or financial transactions.

🔎 **Best OSINT Tools:**

- **Facebook & Instagram Search** – Finds recent activity and possible contacts.
- **ExifTool & FotoForensics** – Extracts metadata from images to determine where they were taken.
- **Pipl & Spokeo** – Checks public records for identity verification.

📌 **Example**: A missing teenager was found after investigators analyzed metadata from a recent selfie she sent to a friend. The GPS coordinates revealed her exact location.

Step 2: Tracking Social Media & Online Activity

Many missing persons cases involve individuals who still have access to their devices and accounts, providing investigators with crucial online signals.

Key Social Media OSINT Methods:

✓ Monitoring recent logins and location tags.

✓ Analyzing new friend requests or messages.

✓ Tracking aliases and alternate profiles.

🔎 **Best OSINT Tools:**

- **ShadowDragon SocialNet** – Maps social media connections.
- **TweetDeck & Social Bearing** – Analyzes Twitter geotags and activity.
- **WhatsMyName** – Finds accounts linked to a username across platforms.

📌 **Example**: A woman who disappeared after a road trip was located in a different state after OSINT analysts found her new Instagram account under a different name, linked to a local business.

Step 3: Using Geolocation & Image Analysis

1️⃣ Geolocation from Photos & Videos

Images posted online often contain hidden metadata or recognizable landmarks that can reveal a missing person's location.

🔲 **Techniques Used:**

✔ **Reverse Image Search** – Checks if a person has appeared in recent photos.

✔ **Google Earth & Street View** – Matches landmarks in images to real-world locations.

✔ **YouTube Data Viewer** – Extracts metadata from uploaded videos.

🔍 **Best OSINT Tools:**

- **Google Lens & TinEye** – Reverse image search for clues.
- **EXIF.tools** – Extracts GPS coordinates from photos.
- **Mapillary** – Crowdsourced street-level images for location matching.

📌 **Example**: Investigators found a missing woman after identifying a unique bridge in the background of a social media video, leading them to a city she was last seen in.

2️⃣ Finding Patterns in Digital Footprints

Even when a missing person is not actively posting online, OSINT can track their movements through digital traces, including:

✔ Ride-sharing apps (Uber, Lyft) and travel bookings.

✔ Forum activity and classified ads.

✔ Dark web searches (for trafficking or exploitation cases).

🔍 **Best OSINT Tools:**

- **FlightAware & MarineTraffic** – Tracks air and sea travel.
- **CheckUsernames** – Finds alternate accounts on forums.
- **DarkTracer** – Searches for personal data on the dark web.

📌 **Example**: A missing journalist was found after investigators tracked his Airbnb stays and cross-referenced his last booking with local CCTV footage.

Step 4: Leveraging Public & Government Databases

3️⃣ Searching Law Enforcement & Government Resources

Many missing persons cases benefit from cross-referencing official databases and public reports, including:

✔ Police reports & missing person registries.

✔ Hospital and morgue records.

✔ License plate recognition systems.

🔍 **Best OSINT Tools:**

- **NamUs & Interpol Missing Persons Database** – Lists missing individuals worldwide.
- **LEO Database Search** – Checks law enforcement records (when accessible).
- **ALPR Systems (Automatic License Plate Recognition)** – Tracks vehicle movement.

📌 **Example**: A missing elderly man with Alzheimer's was located after his license plate was detected by a city's automated traffic camera system.

Step 5: Identifying Human Trafficking or Criminal Involvement

4️⃣ OSINT for High-Risk Missing Persons Cases

When a missing person is believed to be a victim of trafficking, abduction, or foul play, OSINT can assist by:

✔ Monitoring escort ads & suspicious online job postings.

✔ Tracking phone numbers linked to exploitation networks.

✔ Using dark web forums to find mentions of the missing person.

🔎 **Best OSINT Tools:**

- **TraffickCam** – Identifies hotel rooms where victims were last seen.
- **PhoneInfoga & TrueCaller** – Traces phone numbers linked to scams or trafficking.
- **OSINT Combine Dark Web Search** – Finds mentions of missing persons in underground forums.

📌 **Example**: A missing teenager was recovered after OSINT analysts linked her phone number to escort ads in multiple cities, leading to a police rescue operation.

Challenges & Ethical Considerations in OSINT Missing Person Cases

While OSINT is a powerful tool, investigators must navigate ethical and legal challenges when searching for missing individuals:

⚠ **Privacy Laws** – Accessing certain data may violate privacy policies.
⚠ **False Positives** – Misidentification can waste resources and cause distress.
⚠ **Data Sensitivity** – Releasing OSINT findings publicly can endanger the missing person.

✔ **Best Practices:**

✔ Work closely with law enforcement & trusted organizations.

✔ Verify all information before acting on leads.

✔ Avoid accessing restricted or illegal data sources.

Conclusion: OSINT's Power in Finding the Missing

Open-Source Intelligence has transformed missing persons investigations, providing law enforcement and civilian searchers with critical digital tools to track footprints, analyze geolocation data, and uncover new leads.

Key Takeaways:

✓ Social media & online activity provide valuable clues.

✓ Geolocation techniques can pinpoint last-known locations.

✓ Financial transactions and travel data can reveal movement patterns.

✓ Dark web searches help locate victims of trafficking & exploitation.

By combining OSINT with law enforcement cooperation and responsible investigation techniques, more missing individuals can be found and reunited with their families.

5.2 Tracking Last-Known Digital Locations

Introduction: The Importance of Digital Location Data

In missing persons investigations, time is critical. One of the most valuable pieces of intelligence is the last-known location of the missing individual. In the digital age, people leave behind numerous electronic traces—whether through social media check-ins, GPS-enabled apps, messaging metadata, or financial transactions. These digital footprints can provide investigators with crucial information about where a person was last seen, their potential movements, and possible points of contact.

This chapter explores the methods and tools used to track a missing person's last-known digital location through publicly available data, OSINT techniques, and real-time monitoring strategies.

Step 1: Identifying Key Digital Location Sources

A missing person may leave location data in multiple online sources. Investigators can use OSINT to track these data points to reconstruct their movements.

Common Sources of Digital Location Data:

✓ **Social Media Activity** – Location tags, geotagged posts, live-streaming data.

✓ **Messaging Apps & Metadata** – IP logs, device information, time stamps.

✓ **Mobile Apps & GPS Services** – Rideshare history, fitness tracking, travel bookings.

✓ **Financial Transactions** – ATM withdrawals, credit card purchases, cryptocurrency movements.

📌 **Example**: A missing woman was located after OSINT analysts found a recent Instagram story where she tagged a local coffee shop, providing investigators with a time-stamped geolocation.

Step 2: Analyzing Social Media & Online Activity

Many social media platforms automatically collect and store location data, even when users don't explicitly share it. Investigators can scrape and analyze this data to determine a missing person's last-known location.

Key Social Media OSINT Techniques:

🔍 **Checking Geotagged Posts** – Photos and videos often include embedded latitude & longitude coordinates.
🔍 **Searching for Mentions & Tags** – Friends may tag the missing person in a location.
🔍 **Analyzing Live Streams & Story Features** – Apps like Instagram and TikTok track where live content is broadcasted.

☐ **Best OSINT Tools for Social Media Tracking:**

- **Instagram Location Search** – Finds public posts tagged at specific places.
- **TweetDeck & Social Bearing** – Analyzes geotagged Twitter posts.
- **Facebook Graph Search (Advanced Search Tools)** – Finds check-ins and location-based activity.
- **YouTube Data Viewer** – Extracts metadata from video uploads.

📌 **Example**: A missing student was found after investigators used TweetDeck to locate his last geotagged tweet, showing he had checked in at a train station.

Step 3: Extracting Metadata from Images & Videos

Many digital files, such as photos and videos, contain hidden metadata that can reveal when and where they were taken. This is especially useful when a missing person has sent images to friends or posted them online.

How to Extract Metadata:

✓ **EXIF Data Analysis** – Photos taken on mobile devices often contain GPS coordinates in their metadata.

✓ **Reverse Image Search** – Locating where and when an image was previously used.

✓ **Object & Landmark Recognition** – Identifying locations based on background details in images.

☐ **Best OSINT Tools for Metadata Extraction:**

- **EXIF.tools & FotoForensics** – Extracts GPS data from images.
- **Google Lens & TinEye** – Reverse image search to find where a picture appears online.
- **Mapillary & Google Earth** – Matches objects in photos to real-world locations.

📌 **Example**: Investigators recovered a selfie sent via WhatsApp from a missing teenager. Using EXIF.tools, they extracted the exact GPS coordinates, leading authorities to a remote motel where she was found.

Step 4: Leveraging Mobile & GPS Data

Most modern smartphones constantly transmit location data through various apps and services. Even if a missing person is not posting online, investigators may still be able to track their last movements through mobile device forensics.

Sources of Mobile Location Data:

📍 **Google Location History** – If enabled, Google saves past locations from a device.
📍 **Rideshare & Transportation Apps** – Uber, Lyft, and taxi apps log ride locations.
📍 **Fitness & Navigation Apps** – Apps like Strava and Google Maps store route data.
📍 **Wi-Fi & Cell Tower Data** – Some data may be retrievable via legal requests.

☐ **Best OSINT Tools for Mobile Tracking:**

- **Google Timeline & Takeout** – Extracts Google location history if credentials are available.
- **Uber & Lyft Receipts** – Investigators can check ride history for last-known drop-off points.

- **Strava Heatmap & OpenStreetMap** – Tracks recent activity routes from fitness apps.

📌 **Example**: A missing hiker was located after OSINT analysts found his last Strava GPS route, leading rescue teams directly to his location.

Step 5: Analyzing Financial Transactions & Travel Records

Banking activity and financial records can provide clues about a missing person's last whereabouts. Even cash withdrawals, airline tickets, and hotel bookings can be indicators of their movements.

Key OSINT Techniques for Financial & Travel Tracking:

💰 **Checking Bank Transactions** – Credit card purchases and ATM withdrawals leave timestamps.
💰 **Analyzing Cryptocurrency Movements** – Bitcoin and Monero transactions can be traced.
💰 **Looking at Hotel & Travel Bookings** – Flight records and hotel stays may show movement patterns.

☐ **Best OSINT Tools for Financial & Travel Tracking:**

- **FlightAware & MarineTraffic** – Tracks flights and ship movements.
- **Blockchain Explorer & Chainalysis** – Monitors cryptocurrency payments.
- **CheckMyTrip & PNR Locator** – Searches for airline ticket bookings.

📌 **Example**: A missing businessman was found after investigators tracked his last credit card transaction, revealing he had checked into a hotel under an alias.

Step 6: Correlating Data to Establish Movement Patterns

Once various location data points have been gathered, OSINT investigators must analyze them collectively to establish:

✓ Last confirmed location (digital or physical).

✓ Direction of travel (based on timestamps & transaction history).

✓ Potential high-risk areas (crime hotspots, human trafficking routes, etc.).

Best Practices for Data Correlation:

☑ Cross-check timestamps from multiple sources.

☑ Look for patterns—frequent locations, travel routes, or check-ins.

☑ Use visual mapping tools to plot movement trends.

☐ **Best OSINT Tools for Mapping & Analysis:**

- **Maltego** – Creates relationship graphs between data points.
- **Google Earth & ArcGIS** – Maps movement patterns.
- **Hunchly** – Helps organize OSINT findings for investigation reports.

📌 **Example**: A missing teenage girl was found after investigators mapped her last-known Instagram check-in, Uber ride logs, and ATM withdrawal history, pinpointing her next likely location.

Challenges & Ethical Considerations

While OSINT is invaluable in tracking missing persons, investigators must navigate ethical and legal boundaries when gathering data.

⚠ **Privacy Concerns** – Unauthorized access to private accounts is illegal.

⚠ **Data Accuracy** – False positives can mislead investigations.

⚠ **Legal Compliance** – Some data may only be accessed through law enforcement requests.

☑ **Best Practices:**

✓ Always verify geolocation data from multiple sources.

✓ Use publicly available and legally accessible data only.

✓ Work in collaboration with law enforcement & family members.

Conclusion: OSINT's Critical Role in Digital Location Tracking

The ability to track last-known digital locations is one of the most powerful OSINT applications in missing persons cases. By leveraging social media, GPS data, financial transactions, and online activity, investigators can reconstruct movements, uncover new leads, and increase the chances of a successful recovery.

Key Takeaways:

✓ Social media & metadata provide timestamped location clues.

✓ GPS-enabled apps and rideshare history can reveal movement patterns.

✓ Bank transactions & hotel bookings leave digital trails.

✓ Cross-referencing multiple data points increases accuracy.

By combining these OSINT techniques with law enforcement collaboration, missing persons investigations can be conducted more efficiently—helping reunite families and save lives.

5.3 Using Social Media Check-ins & Geotagged Content

Introduction: The Power of Location Data in OSINT

In the digital age, social media activity often provides critical clues in missing persons cases. Many individuals unknowingly share their locations through check-ins, geotagged posts, live streams, and metadata embedded in images or videos. OSINT investigators can leverage this data to track a missing person's last-known whereabouts, movement patterns, and potential contacts.

This chapter explores the techniques, tools, and real-world case applications of social media location tracking to aid in missing persons investigations.

Step 1: Understanding Social Media Check-ins & Geotags

Most major social media platforms allow users to check in at locations or attach geotags to their posts. These features provide time-stamped geographic data, which can be used to reconstruct a person's movements before they disappeared.

Types of Location-Based Data on Social Media:

🔎 **Check-ins** – Users voluntarily mark their presence at a location (e.g., "Checked in at Starbucks").

🔎 **Geotagged Posts** – Photos, videos, and status updates may include GPS coordinates.

🔎 **Live Streams & Stories** – Real-time content may reveal immediate location clues.

🔎 **Tagged Locations by Friends** – Other users may tag a missing person in a location.

📌 **Example**: A missing college student was found after an OSINT investigator discovered a Facebook check-in at a nightclub, indicating the last place she was seen.

Step 2: Extracting Location Data from Social Media Platforms

Each social media platform provides different levels of location data. Investigators must understand how to search for, extract, and analyze this information effectively.

Popular Platforms & Their Location Features:

◆ **Facebook & Instagram**

✓ Users can check in at specific locations.

✓ Posts, reels, and stories may contain geotags.

✓ Friends can tag others in location-based posts.

◆ **Twitter (X)**

✓ Some tweets are geotagged with city or exact GPS coordinates.

✓ Users may share their location in their bio or tweets.

◆ **TikTok & Snapchat**

✓ Public posts may have embedded location data.

✓ Snap Maps show real-time location of active users.

◆ **YouTube & Live Streaming Platforms**

✓ Some videos contain location metadata.

✓ Live streams often display the broadcaster's location.

📌 **Example**: A missing teenager was located after investigators found a Snapchat post tagged at a shopping mall, showing she was alive hours after last contact.

Step 3: Searching for Geotagged Content Across Platforms

Methods for Finding Geotagged Data:

🔍 Using Built-In Social Media Search Features

✓ Search for places or locations in Facebook and Instagram.

✓ Use Twitter Advanced Search with geolocation filters.

✓ Look for location-specific hashtags (e.g., #NYC, #TimesSquare).

🔍 Using OSINT Geolocation Search Tools

✓ **Instagram Location Search** – Finds public posts at specific locations.

✓ **TweetDeck & Social Bearing** – Identifies geotagged tweets.

✓ **Wikimapia & Geofeedia** – Maps public geotagged posts from various platforms.

📌 **Example**: A missing woman's last sighting was confirmed when investigators found an Instagram post geotagged at a park, uploaded the evening of her disappearance.

Step 4: Extracting GPS Coordinates from Images & Videos

Even when users don't explicitly share their locations, photos and videos often contain hidden metadata that can be extracted for clues.

EXIF Data: The Hidden GPS in Photos

✓ Exchangeable Image File Format (EXIF) metadata often includes GPS coordinates of where a picture was taken.

✓ If a missing person has sent photos via WhatsApp, email, or posted online, investigators can extract this data to determine their location.

How to Extract EXIF Data:

☐ **Tools for Metadata Extraction:**

- **EXIF.tools & Jeffrey's EXIF Viewer** – Extracts GPS data from images.
- **FotoForensics** – Reveals hidden metadata in images.
- **Google Lens & TinEye** – Performs reverse image searches to find related locations.

📌 **Example**: A kidnapped child was rescued after police analyzed a selfie posted online, extracting GPS coordinates that led them to an abandoned warehouse.

Step 5: Analyzing Live Streams & Real-Time Content

Live streaming platforms like TikTok, Instagram Live, YouTube Live, and Twitch can reveal real-time location details of a missing person.

Key OSINT Techniques for Live Stream Analysis:

✓ Look for visible landmarks, signs, or storefronts in the video background.

✓ Identify street names, billboards, or recognizable buildings.

✓ Use Google Street View or Mapillary to match visual elements to real-world locations.

📌 **Example**: A missing influencer was found when investigators recognized a neon sign in her TikTok live stream, matching it to a hotel in Los Angeles using Google Street View.

Step 6: Cross-Referencing Location Data with Other OSINT Sources

Combining Multiple OSINT Techniques:

✅ **Social Media Check-ins + EXIF Data from Photos** = Verified Last-Known Location.

✅ **Twitter Geotags + Google Maps Street View** = Identifying Nearby Landmarks.

✅ **Live Stream Analysis + FlightAware (Travel Records)** = Tracking Possible Destinations.

Example Case:

A missing teenager was found after investigators combined:

✓ Her last Facebook check-in at a shopping mall.

✓ A Twitter post with a geotag near a gas station.

✓ EXIF data from an Instagram picture revealing GPS coordinates.

Together, these clues narrowed down her location to a 2-block radius, leading to her safe recovery.

Challenges & Ethical Considerations

Limitations of Social Media Location Data:

⚠ Privacy Settings: Some users disable location tracking.
⚠ False or Misleading Geotags: People may spoof locations or use VPNs.
⚠ Deleted Posts: Critical data may be removed before investigators can analyze it.

Ethical & Legal Considerations:

✓ Always use publicly available data—never hack or illegally access accounts.

✓ Verify multiple sources before taking action on geotagged information.

✓ Work with law enforcement when handling sensitive location data.

Conclusion: Leveraging Social Media for Missing Persons OSINT

Social media check-ins and geotagged content provide invaluable clues in tracking missing persons. By analyzing posts, extracting metadata, and cross-referencing location data, OSINT investigators can reconstruct a subject's movements and identify their last-known location.

Key Takeaways:

✓ Social media posts, check-ins, and geotags can reveal last-known locations.

✓ EXIF metadata from images provides hidden GPS coordinates.

✓ Live streams and videos can contain visual clues to real-world locations.

✓ Cross-referencing social media data with OSINT tools increases accuracy.

By combining these techniques with law enforcement collaboration, OSINT analysts can significantly enhance the success of missing persons investigations.

5.4 Satellite & Street View Analysis for Leads

Introduction: The Power of Geospatial OSINT in Investigations

When traditional investigative methods hit a dead end, geospatial intelligence (GEOINT) techniques—such as satellite imagery and street-level mapping—can provide crucial insights. By analyzing aerial views, road networks, and real-world surroundings, OSINT investigators can develop new leads in missing persons cases, fugitive tracking, and criminal investigations.

This chapter explores how to use satellite imagery, Google Street View, and other mapping tools to track movements, identify locations, and generate actionable intelligence.

Step 1: Understanding Satellite & Street View OSINT

What Is Satellite & Street View Analysis?

☐ **Satellite Imagery** – Provides top-down aerial views of locations, showing buildings, roads, and terrain.
🚗 **Street View** – Offers on-the-ground perspectives, helping investigators recognize businesses, landmarks, vehicles, and foot traffic patterns.

Key Uses in OSINT Investigations:

✅ Identifying last-known locations of missing persons.

✅ Analyzing travel routes and escape paths.

✅ Matching backgrounds in images/videos to real-world locations.

✅ Pinpointing safe houses, hideouts, or suspicious activities.

📌 **Example**: A missing woman's location was confirmed when OSINT investigators matched the background of her Instagram photo to a unique street view landmark using Google Maps.

Step 2: Using Satellite Imagery for Investigations

Finding & Analyzing Satellite Data

🔍 **Google Earth Pro** – Provides high-resolution, historical satellite imagery to track changes over time.
🔍 **Sentinel Hub & NASA Worldview** – Offers real-time satellite imagery for active investigations.
🔍 **Zoom Earth & Bing Maps** – Alternative sources for detailed aerial views.

How to Analyze Satellite Imagery for Leads:

✔ **Look for unusual activity** – Recently disturbed ground, abandoned vehicles, or new structures may be relevant.
✔ **Compare historical images** – Identify changes in a suspect's property, new routes, or movement patterns.
✔ **Cross-reference locations** – Match satellite views with social media check-ins or cellphone pings.

📌 **Example**: A human trafficking case was cracked when investigators found a hidden compound in a remote area, visible only through Google Earth's satellite imagery.

Step 3: Leveraging Google Street View for OSINT

Why Street View Is a Powerful Tool

Unlike satellite images, Street View provides ground-level perspectives, allowing investigators to:

☐ Confirm a suspect's presence at a location based on landmarks.
☐ Identify possible surveillance cameras in the area.
☐ Reconstruct travel routes using road layouts.

🔎 Verify addresses from social media posts, emails, or online ads.

How to Use Google Street View for Investigations:

🔎 **Matching Backgrounds in Images & Videos**

- Compare social media photos to Street View images.
- Identify storefronts, graffiti, or unique objects to pinpoint locations.

🔎 **Checking the Surroundings of a Crime Scene or Last-Known Location**

- Look for entry/exit points, alleys, or hidden paths.
- Identify transportation hubs (bus stops, train stations, parking lots).

🔎 **Verifying Witness or Suspect Statements**

- Confirm if a reported location exists or matches descriptions.
- Check distances between key locations to detect inconsistencies.

📌 **Example**: A fugitive was tracked down when OSINT analysts matched his social media selfie's background to a hotel entrance visible on Google Street View.

Step 4: Cross-Referencing Mapping Data with OSINT Sources

To strengthen an investigation, Street View and satellite imagery should be combined with other OSINT methods, such as:

✅ **Social Media Analysis** – Compare geotagged posts with satellite views to verify locations.
✅ **EXIF Data Extraction** – Use GPS metadata from images to find exact map coordinates.
✅ **Public Records Search** – Identify property owners, businesses, or rental locations.

📌 **Example**: A missing teenager was located when investigators cross-referenced her last Instagram check-in with a satellite image of an abandoned warehouse, later confirmed through Street View.

Step 5: Advanced Geolocation Techniques for Investigators

Reverse Image Geolocation

If a suspect posts a photo with no location tags, OSINT analysts can:

🔍 Use Google Reverse Image Search or TinEye to find similar images.

🔍 Compare skyline silhouettes, building shapes, or street signs using Street View.

🔍 Cross-check with Google Earth Pro to confirm satellite imagery of the same location.

📌 **Example**: A missing hiker was found when OSINT experts matched a rock formation in her last Instagram photo to a satellite image of a national park.

Step 6: Legal & Ethical Considerations in Geospatial OSINT

Limitations of Satellite & Street View Analysis:

⚠ **Delayed Imagery** – Satellite images may be outdated (weeks or months old).

⚠ **Limited Coverage** – Some areas lack Street View access.

⚠ **Privacy Concerns** – Certain locations may be blurred or restricted.

Ethical Best Practices:

✓ Use only publicly available data – No unauthorized access to private systems.

✓ Confirm findings with multiple sources – Avoid false leads.

✓ Collaborate with law enforcement when necessary.

Conclusion: Enhancing OSINT Investigations with Satellite & Street View Data

By leveraging satellite imagery and Street View, OSINT investigators can identify last-known locations, track movements, and generate new leads in missing persons cases.

Key Takeaways:

✓ Satellite imagery helps analyze large-scale locations & terrain.

✓ Street View allows on-the-ground verification of places & landmarks.

✓ Cross-referencing mapping data with social media, EXIF, and public records strengthens investigations.

✓ Ethical considerations must be followed to protect privacy & legal boundaries.

With these tools, OSINT analysts can significantly improve their ability to locate missing persons, track criminals, and provide intelligence for law enforcement.

5.5 OSINT Collaboration with Families & NGOs

Introduction: The Role of Families & NGOs in OSINT Investigations

In missing persons cases, law enforcement agencies are often limited by jurisdictional constraints, bureaucracy, and resource limitations. This is where families, advocacy groups, and non-governmental organizations (NGOs) play a crucial role. By working together with OSINT investigators, these groups can gather, verify, and share critical information that may lead to locating a missing person.

This chapter explores how OSINT analysts can collaborate with families and NGOs, providing guidance on best practices, communication strategies, and ethical considerations in digital investigations.

Step 1: Understanding the Role of Families & NGOs in OSINT

Why Families & NGOs Matter in Investigations

✓ **Immediate Access to Personal Information** – Families can provide photos, social media accounts, personal habits, and contacts.
✓ **Crowdsourced Intelligence** – NGOs often have networks of volunteers who can assist in OSINT efforts.
✓ **Media & Awareness Campaigns** – Social media campaigns, press releases, and missing person alerts can generate public engagement and tips.
✓ **Extended Search Capabilities** – Unlike law enforcement, NGOs can continue searching indefinitely, even when cases go cold.

📌 **Example**: In a high-profile missing persons case, an NGO partnered with OSINT experts to analyze a victim's digital footprint and identified a key suspect through social media interactions, leading to an arrest.

Step 2: Establishing Effective Collaboration in OSINT Investigations

For OSINT analysts to work effectively with families and NGOs, clear roles and responsibilities should be established.

Best Practices for OSINT Collaboration:

◆ **Clear Communication** – Set expectations with families about what OSINT can and cannot do.

◆ **Data Organization** – Create a centralized database with all relevant details (e.g., last-known locations, online accounts, contacts).

◆ **Verification Protocols** – Cross-check any tips received before acting on them.

◆ **Secure Data Sharing** – Use encrypted communication tools when handling sensitive information.

📌 **Example**: An OSINT team helped a family organize all digital clues (emails, messages, social media posts) into a structured timeline, which later pinpointed a suspect's location.

Step 3: Utilizing Social Media for Public Awareness & OSINT

Social media is one of the most powerful tools in missing persons investigations. Families and NGOs can use platforms like Facebook, Twitter, Instagram, and TikTok to spread awareness and collect digital clues.

How to Leverage Social Media for OSINT Investigations:

🔊 **Creating Digital Awareness Campaigns**

✓ Share missing persons posters with last-known information.

✓ Use hashtags to increase reach (e.g., #FindJohnDoe, #MissingAlert).

✓ Engage with local communities & influencers to spread the word.

☐ **Monitoring Digital Clues**

✓ Check comments & direct messages for potential leads.

✓ Analyze social media interactions (who was the person in contact with?).

✓ Use OSINT tools to track geotagged posts near last-known locations.

📌 **Example**: A missing teen was found when a TikTok video surfaced showing her in a mall. OSINT investigators geolocated the video, leading to her rescue.

Step 4: Crowdsourced OSINT Investigations

How NGOs & Volunteers Contribute to OSINT:

☐ **Digital Volunteers** – Open-source communities (like Trace Labs) conduct crowdsourced missing persons searches.
☐ **Amateur Investigators** – Online forums (e.g., Websleuths, Reddit) often discuss unsolved cases.
📢 **Public Tip Lines** – Families and NGOs can set up secure reporting systems for anonymous tips.

⚠ **Caution**: Crowdsourced efforts must be managed carefully to avoid misinformation, privacy violations, or interference with official investigations.

📌 **Example**: A group of digital volunteers analyzed CCTV footage & social media check-ins to help locate a missing person who had crossed into another country.

Step 5: Ethical & Legal Considerations in OSINT Collaboration

Key Ethical Considerations:

✅ **Respect Privacy** – Do not publish sensitive personal data online.
✅ **Verify Before Sharing** – False information can mislead investigations.
✅ **Avoid Interfering with Law Enforcement** – Coordinate efforts where possible.
✅ **Obtain Consent** – Families should approve any public awareness campaign.

Legal Limitations to Keep in Mind:

⚖ **Data Protection Laws** – Ensure compliance with GDPR, CCPA, and other privacy laws.
⚖ **No Unauthorized Access** – OSINT should be based on publicly available data only.
⚖ **Avoid Defamation** – Wrongly accusing someone can lead to legal consequences.

📌 **Example**: An OSINT team worked with an NGO to ensure that victim details were only shared on verified platforms, preventing the spread of misinformation.

Conclusion: Strengthening OSINT Collaboration for Missing Persons Cases

By working closely with families, NGOs, and digital volunteers, OSINT investigators can expand their reach, analyze more data, and generate new leads in missing persons cases.

Key Takeaways:

✔ Families & NGOs provide critical data & long-term support.

✔ Social media campaigns help spread awareness & collect tips.

✔ Crowdsourced OSINT efforts can enhance search efforts but must be managed carefully.

✔ Ethical & legal considerations are essential in protecting privacy & ensuring accuracy.

With the right collaboration, OSINT investigations become significantly more powerful, increasing the chances of finding missing individuals and solving cases effectively.

5.6 Case Study: How OSINT Helped Locate a Missing Person

Introduction: The Power of OSINT in Missing Persons Investigations

When a person goes missing, every second counts. Traditional law enforcement methods, while effective, can be slow due to bureaucracy, jurisdictional limitations, and resource constraints. In contrast, Open-Source Intelligence (OSINT) allows investigators to quickly analyze digital footprints, track geolocation data, and uncover leads that may otherwise go unnoticed.

This case study details how OSINT techniques, including social media monitoring, geolocation analysis, and digital forensics, helped locate a missing 19-year-old college student.

Case Background: The Disappearance of Emma Carter

Initial Report & Last-Known Movements

Emma Carter, a 19-year-old college student, was last seen leaving a coffee shop near her university campus on a Friday evening at 8:30 PM. Her roommates reported her missing when she failed to return home and missed a scheduled morning shift at her part-time job.

Key Initial Findings:

✓ Her phone was turned off at 9:15 PM, approximately 45 minutes after she left the coffee shop.

✓ Her last known location was near a public bus stop, but no immediate witnesses could confirm if she boarded a bus.

✓ Social media activity stopped abruptly, with no new posts or messages after the time of disappearance.

✓ No signs of forced entry or struggle were found at her home or near the last-known location.

Family and friends launched a public social media campaign with missing person flyers and contacted law enforcement. However, with no leads emerging in the first 48 hours, OSINT specialists were asked to assist.

Step 1: Analyzing Emma's Digital Footprint

Social Media Analysis

The OSINT team began by retrieving data from Emma's social media profiles.

🔍 Recent Activity:

✓ Her last Instagram story showed her inside the coffee shop, timestamped at 8:20 PM.

✓ A Snapchat location check-in placed her near the bus stop at 8:45 PM, indicating she had likely left the coffee shop.

✓ Friends reported that Emma had been messaging someone new on Instagram before she disappeared.

Username & Contact Analysis

OSINT investigators scraped her social media accounts to identify:

✓ Any unknown or suspicious contacts in her recent interactions.

✓ Username correlations across platforms to determine if the person she was messaging had other online identities.

📌 **Finding**: Emma's Instagram messages showed she had been talking to an unknown person named "J.D.", who had a private account with limited followers.

Step 2: Geolocation Analysis & Digital Clues

Reverse Image Geolocation

Using OSINT image analysis tools, investigators examined:

✓ Background elements from Emma's last social media posts.

✓ Any potential street signs, buildings, or unique landmarks.

📌 Key Breakthrough: A blurred street sign in her last Snapchat story was enhanced and identified as a bus stop near an industrial area, 3 miles from her university.

Tracking Publicly Available Surveillance Data

✓ OSINT specialists checked public CCTV cameras in the area.

✓ No public bus camera footage was found, but a gas station nearby had security cameras.

✓ Investigators cross-referenced Google Street View and identified a nearby alleyway where a vehicle had been parked during the time of disappearance.

Step 3: Identifying the Suspect Using OSINT

Tracing "J.D." – The Unknown Online Contact

Investigators cross-checked the username "J.D." across multiple platforms using:

✓ Username lookup tools (e.g., WhatsMyName, Namechk).

✓ Reverse email & phone number searches (from previous social media leaks).

✓ Dark web & forum monitoring to check if the alias had been used before.

📌 **Key Finding**: The username was linked to a secondary Facebook account, revealing the full name of a 25-year-old male named Jason Delgado, who had a prior record for harassment and stalking.

Discovering the Connection

✓ Jason Delgado had previously attended the same college but dropped out two years earlier.

✓ He had commented on Emma's public Instagram posts months before her disappearance.

✓ Using OSINT, investigators found an old Reddit post where he discussed stalking an ex-girlfriend and using fake social media accounts to interact with her.

🚨 At this stage, law enforcement was alerted, and Jason Delgado was flagged as a person of interest.

Step 4: Locating Emma Using OSINT & Law Enforcement Collaboration

Financial & Digital Transaction Tracking

✓ Investigators monitored recent banking transactions linked to Emma's account.

✓ A small food purchase was made at a gas station ATM near the suspected location.

✓ Surveillance footage confirmed Emma was seen entering a vehicle matching Delgado's car.

Final Breakthrough: Mobile OSINT & Location Tracking

✓ Delgado's known phone number was used in an OSINT mobile tracking tool, revealing a last pinged location near an abandoned warehouse.

✓ The location was cross-checked with satellite imagery using Google Earth and Bing Maps.

☐ Police conducted a raid at the warehouse and found Emma inside—alive but restrained. Delgado was arrested at the scene.

Lessons Learned: OSINT's Impact in Missing Persons Cases

Key OSINT Techniques Used in This Investigation:

✓ **Social Media Footprint Analysis** – Revealed last interactions & suspicious contacts.

✓ **Geolocation OSINT** – Identified her last-known location via Snapchat & background elements.

✓ **Username Correlation & Identity Matching** – Exposed the suspect's real identity & history of stalking.

✓ **Publicly Available CCTV & Street View Analysis** – Helped map potential abduction sites.

✓ **Financial OSINT & Mobile Tracking** – Pinpointed suspicious transactions & the suspect's final location.

Conclusion: The Future of OSINT in Missing Persons Cases

This case highlights how OSINT tools and techniques can provide crucial intelligence that accelerates missing persons investigations.

Key Takeaways:

✓ OSINT fills the gaps when traditional investigations slow down.

✓ Social media & geolocation data are powerful tools for real-time tracking.

✓ Username analysis can reveal hidden identities & criminal behavior.

✔ OSINT collaboration with law enforcement, families, and NGOs enhances success rates.

🚨 OSINT is not just an investigative tool—it's a lifeline. By leveraging digital footprints, geolocation data, and social media intelligence, we can bring missing persons home and ensure justice is served.

6. Criminal Networks & Organized Crime Intelligence

In this chapter, we delve into the role of OSINT in uncovering and dismantling criminal networks and organized crime syndicates. The digital age has provided new opportunities for criminal organizations to operate covertly, but it has also created a wealth of open-source information that can be exploited to track their activities. By analyzing digital trails, such as communication patterns, financial transactions, and social media connections, OSINT tools enable investigators to map out complex criminal networks. Through case studies and practical strategies, this chapter shows how OSINT aids in identifying key figures, understanding organizational structures, and ultimately disrupting criminal operations on a global scale.

6.1 Identifying & Mapping Criminal Organizations

Introduction: Understanding Criminal Networks Through OSINT

Organized crime operates in complex, decentralized structures, making traditional investigative techniques challenging when trying to dismantle these networks. However, Open-Source Intelligence (OSINT) provides powerful tools to map, analyze, and track criminal organizations. By leveraging public records, social media, financial transactions, and deep/dark web monitoring, investigators can uncover hidden connections between individuals, businesses, and illicit activities.

This chapter explores how OSINT can be used to identify and map criminal organizations, detailing techniques such as network analysis, relationship mapping, and digital footprint tracking to expose organized crime groups, cartels, cybercriminal rings, and trafficking networks.

Step 1: Identifying Key Criminal Entities & Structure

Organized crime groups are not structured like traditional businesses; they function as loose networks with hierarchical or decentralized nodes. To effectively map their structure, OSINT investigators must first identify key players, their roles, and their communication channels.

Common Criminal Organization Structures:

- **Hierarchical** – Mafia-style groups with leaders, enforcers, and lower-level operatives.
- **Cell-Based** – Terrorist or trafficking organizations that operate in compartmentalized cells to avoid detection.
- **Networked** – Cybercriminal and fraud rings where individuals collaborate based on skills rather than rank.

Key OSINT Techniques for Identifying Criminal Networks:

✓ **Social Media Monitoring** – Detecting known affiliates, coded language, and group interactions.

✓ **Public Records & Leaks** – Identifying criminal ties through business ownerships, financial statements, and past arrests.

✓ **Forum & Dark Web Analysis** – Finding discussions, transactions, and recruitment efforts in hidden spaces.

✓ **Alias & Username Tracking** – Connecting criminals across multiple platforms using OSINT tools.

📌 **Example**: A drug cartel's WhatsApp groups and Telegram channels were monitored, revealing a network of suppliers and distributors, which helped authorities disrupt its operations.

Step 2: Network Mapping & Relationship Analysis

Once key figures in a criminal organization are identified, the next step is mapping their relationships to understand who influences whom.

How OSINT Helps Build Criminal Network Maps:

📌 **Social Graph Analysis** – Mapping direct and indirect connections between members.
📌 **Financial OSINT** – Tracking shared assets, money transfers, and shell companies.
📌 **Geospatial Analysis** – Identifying meeting locations, trafficking routes, and operational zones.

Tools for Criminal Network Mapping:

🔍 **Maltego** – Visualization of complex relationships between people, companies, and digital traces.

🔍 **Linkurious** – Graph analytics for uncovering hidden connections in large datasets.

🔍 **SpiderFoot** – Automates data collection from various OSINT sources to track digital footprints.

📌 **Example**: Investigators used Maltego to map a human trafficking ring, identifying connections between escort services, fake job postings, and overseas recruiters.

Step 3: Tracking Digital Footprints & Communication Patterns

Key Digital Traces Criminals Leave Behind:

✓ **Social Media Posts & Interactions** – Criminals often post coded messages, gang signs, or recruitment efforts.

✓ **Email & Phone Number Correlations** – One exposed email can be linked to multiple fraudulent businesses or transactions.

✓ **Forum Activity & Dark Web Profiles** – Cybercriminals and drug traffickers use marketplaces to sell illicit goods.

📌 **Example**: A darknet arms dealer was identified through a reused email address, linking their profile to a legitimate shipping company that was moving illegal weapons.

Step 4: Case Study – Mapping an International Drug Cartel Using OSINT

Background:

A South American drug cartel was suspected of smuggling narcotics into Europe through legitimate business fronts. Law enforcement needed OSINT-based intelligence to map their network.

How OSINT Exposed the Organization:

- **Public Company Registries** – Identified shell companies tied to cartel members.
- **Maritime Shipping Logs** – Tracked suspicious cargo ships linked to their logistics network.
- **Social Media & Messaging Apps** – Analyzed encrypted Telegram groups where shipments were coordinated.

- **Financial Transactions** – Cross-referenced Bitcoin wallet addresses used for laundering drug money.

Outcome:

◆ The OSINT investigation uncovered direct links between cartel leaders, financial operators, and distributors.

◆ Law enforcement seized shipments worth $500 million and arrested key cartel members.

Step 5: Challenges in Mapping Criminal Organizations Using OSINT

While OSINT is a powerful tool, there are challenges in tracking and mapping organized crime:

⚠ **Data Overload** – Large datasets require automated tools for analysis.

⚠ **Privacy Laws & Ethical Boundaries** – Investigators must comply with GDPR, CCPA, and other privacy laws.

⚠ **Anonymization & Encryption** – Criminals use VPNs, burner phones, and encrypted messaging apps to evade detection.

⚠ **False Information & Misinformation** – Organized crime groups spread disinformation to mislead investigators.

📌 **Solution**: OSINT professionals must verify sources, collaborate with law enforcement, and use advanced analytical tools to separate legitimate intelligence from false leads.

Conclusion: The Future of OSINT in Criminal Intelligence

By leveraging OSINT, law enforcement agencies, private investigators, and intelligence analysts can expose, track, and dismantle criminal organizations more efficiently. The ability to map connections, track digital footprints, and analyze financial flows provides a clearer picture of how these groups operate.

Key Takeaways:

✓ OSINT helps identify criminal networks and key players.

✓ Network mapping tools like Maltego reveal hidden relationships.

✓ Digital footprints expose communications, locations, and illicit activities.

✓ Challenges such as encryption, privacy laws, and misinformation must be addressed carefully.

With continuous advancements in OSINT tools and techniques, the ability to combat organized crime is stronger than ever.

6.2 Tracking Drug Trafficking Networks with OSINT

Introduction: The Role of OSINT in Drug Trafficking Investigations

Drug trafficking is one of the most complex and profitable criminal enterprises, spanning across international borders, digital marketplaces, and underground networks. Traditional law enforcement methods, such as informants, undercover operations, and controlled buys, remain essential. However, Open-Source Intelligence (OSINT) has become a game-changer in mapping drug supply chains, identifying key players, and tracking illicit financial transactions.

This chapter explores how OSINT tools and techniques can be used to track drug trafficking networks, from monitoring social media and dark web drug markets to analyzing financial transactions and geospatial data.

Step 1: Identifying Drug Trafficking Networks

Drug cartels and organized traffickers do not operate in isolation. Their supply chains involve producers, transporters, distributors, money launderers, and street-level dealers.

OSINT Techniques for Identifying Drug Networks:

✓ **Social Media Intelligence (SOCMINT)** – Dealers and traffickers advertise drugs on social media platforms using coded language, emojis, and hashtags.

✓ **Dark Web Marketplaces** – Drug sales occur on hidden sites like Tor marketplaces, often with cryptocurrency transactions.

✓ **Deep Web & Forum Monitoring** – Traffickers recruit couriers and exchange smuggling techniques in underground forums.

✓ **Public Business Records & Shell Companies** – Drug networks often use legitimate businesses to launder money and disguise supply chains.

📌 **Example**: A Telegram group used emoji codes (💊 for pills, 🚀 for fast delivery) to sell drugs in multiple countries. OSINT tracking helped law enforcement infiltrate and shut down the operation.

Step 2: Social Media & Messaging App Monitoring

How Drug Dealers Use Social Media

Drug dealers and trafficking organizations increasingly use social media platforms such as:

✓ **Instagram, Snapchat, TikTok, and Twitter** – Dealers post stories with disappearing messages, emojis, and slang to advertise drugs.

✓ **WhatsApp & Telegram** – Encrypted channels organize deliveries and recruit customers.

✓ **Facebook Marketplace & Craigslist** – Code words are used to sell drugs disguised as everyday items.

OSINT Tools for Social Media Analysis

🔍 **Hoaxy & Botometer** – Detect automated drug-selling accounts.
🔍 **Social Bearing & Echosec** – Map geo-tagged drug advertisements.
🔍 **Hashtag & Emoji Tracking** – Monitor drug-related slang and symbols (e.g., 💊 for pills, 🌿 for marijuana, ❄️ for cocaine).

📌 **Case Study**: An OSINT team tracked fentanyl sales in the U.S. by monitoring Snapchat usernames linked to drug sales. The investigation led to multiple arrests of street-level dealers.

Step 3: Dark Web & Crypto Transactions in Drug Trafficking

How the Dark Web Facilitates Drug Sales

Drug traffickers use dark web markets (e.g., AlphaBay, White House Market) to sell substances anonymously. Payments are typically made via cryptocurrencies like Bitcoin and Monero to evade tracking.

OSINT Techniques for Dark Web Monitoring

✔ **Dark Web Crawlers** – Search for listings on hidden markets.

✔ **Cryptocurrency Transaction Analysis** – Track suspicious transactions through blockchain analysis tools.

✔ **Vendor & Buyer Reviews** – Drug buyers leave feedback and transaction histories, which can be analyzed for intelligence.

📌 **Example**: OSINT analysts tracked Bitcoin transactions from a darknet fentanyl vendor and identified laundering accounts used by the network. Law enforcement seized $10 million in illicit funds.

Step 4: Geospatial Intelligence (GEOINT) in Drug Smuggling Routes

Drug cartels rely on specific smuggling routes across borders, highways, and maritime shipping lanes. OSINT can map these routes and predict future trafficking patterns.

How OSINT Helps Track Smuggling Routes

✔ **Satellite Imagery & Google Earth** – Identify clandestine airstrips, remote drug labs, and border crossings.

✔ **Maritime Tracking (AIS Data)** – Monitor suspicious cargo ships and "ghost" vessels that disable tracking near drug-smuggling regions.

✔ **Drone & UAV Footage** – Detect illegal activities in remote areas where drugs are stored or transported.

📌 **Case Study**: Using Google Earth and satellite images, OSINT specialists discovered hidden airstrips in Central America used by a cartel. This intelligence helped authorities intercept drug shipments worth millions.

Step 5: Financial OSINT & Money Laundering Investigations

Drug trafficking generates billions in illicit profits, which are laundered through fake businesses, real estate, and crypto transactions. OSINT tools help track financial patterns and expose money laundering schemes.

Common Money Laundering Methods Used by Drug Cartels:

✓ **Shell Companies & Front Businesses** – Restaurants, casinos, and nightclubs hide drug money in legal revenue streams.

✓ **Cryptocurrency Mixing Services** – Criminals use "tumblers" to obfuscate Bitcoin transactions.

✓ **Luxury Asset Purchases** – Expensive cars, jewelry, and real estate store drug money in assets.

OSINT Tools for Financial Investigation

🔍 **OpenCorporates & Company Registries** – Identify shell companies linked to drug profits.

🔍 **Blockchain Analysis (Chainalysis, CipherTrace)** – Track crypto transactions linked to illegal drug sales.

🔍 **SAR (Suspicious Activity Reports) Analysis** – Monitor banks & financial transactions flagged for money laundering.

📌 **Example**: Investigators used blockchain analysis to track Bitcoin payments from a darknet drug vendor to real estate purchases in Miami. This intelligence led to multiple asset seizures.

Step 6: Case Study – Exposing an International Cocaine Smuggling Ring

Background:

An OSINT task force was assigned to investigate a cocaine trafficking operation suspected of using shipping containers to transport drugs from South America to Europe.

How OSINT Helped Uncover the Network:

- **Maritime OSINT** – AIS (Automatic Identification System) data identified a pattern of suspicious container ships stopping at unregistered ports.
- **Social Media Intelligence** – Traffickers coordinated shipments via Instagram and WhatsApp, using coded messages.
- **Business Registry Analysis** – Shell companies in Panama and Spain were traced to cartel members.
- **Dark Web Transactions** – Bitcoin payments were linked to large-scale drug orders.

Outcome:

☐ Authorities seized 5 tons of cocaine hidden in cargo containers, and 14 suspects were arrested.

Challenges & Limitations in OSINT Drug Trafficking Investigations

While OSINT is highly effective, there are challenges:

⚠ **Encrypted Messaging** – Apps like Signal and Telegram use end-to-end encryption.
⚠ **Dark Web Anonymity** – Dealers use VPNs & Tor to hide identities.
⚠ **Rapidly Changing Slang** – Drug dealers frequently change hashtags & emoji codes.
⚠ **Legal & Ethical Issues** – OSINT must comply with privacy laws & avoid illegal surveillance.

📌 **Solution**: Law enforcement must combine OSINT with traditional investigations, undercover work, and legal subpoenas to gather admissible evidence.

Conclusion: OSINT's Growing Role in Disrupting Drug Networks

Drug trafficking remains one of the biggest global criminal threats, but OSINT provides powerful tools to track and dismantle these networks.

Key Takeaways:

✓ Social media & dark web monitoring expose trafficking operations.

✓ Cryptocurrency tracking uncovers drug money laundering schemes.

✓ Geospatial OSINT maps drug smuggling routes.

✓ Business & financial OSINT reveals shell companies tied to cartels.

🏛 With continuous advancements in OSINT tools, authorities can stay ahead of traffickers and dismantle drug networks faster than ever.

6.3 Investigating Gangs & Street Crime Networks

Introduction: The Role of OSINT in Gang & Street Crime Investigations

Gang-related crime is a persistent challenge for law enforcement worldwide, involving drug trafficking, violent crimes, human trafficking, and illicit financial activities. These networks operate in local communities and extend into online spaces, using social media, encrypted messaging apps, and deep web forums to communicate, recruit members, and conduct illegal activities.

Open-Source Intelligence (OSINT) plays a critical role in tracking gang activities, identifying key members, mapping their networks, and predicting future crimes. By analyzing digital footprints, geotagged posts, and financial transactions, OSINT investigators can connect physical street crime to digital evidence, leading to more effective gang suppression strategies.

Step 1: Identifying Gang Members & Affiliates

Gang members often publicly display their affiliations through social media posts, tattoos, clothing, hand signs, and graffiti. OSINT can help verify gang membership and uncover hidden connections within their networks.

Indicators of Gang Affiliation:

- **Social Media Profiles** – Gang members often use specific colors, symbols, numbers, or acronyms in their usernames and bios.
- **Hand Signs & Tattoos** – Photos and videos on Instagram, TikTok, and Facebook may show gang hand signs or tattoos that indicate affiliation.
- **Graffiti & Street Tags** – Gangs use graffiti to mark territories, communicate messages, and issue threats to rivals.
- **Hashtags & Emojis** – Gangs develop coded language using emojis and hashtags to discuss crimes without drawing attention.

OSINT Tools for Gang Identification:

- **PimEyes & Face Recognition Tools** – Analyze gang tattoos & symbols from images.
- **Social Media Trackers (Echosec, Babel Street)** – Monitor gang-related hashtags & mentions.
- **Google Reverse Image Search** – Track graffiti tags & gang insignias in different locations.

Example: Investigators used Instagram and Snapchat OSINT to track a Chicago gang's recruitment of minors, leading to the arrest of multiple leaders.

Step 2: Mapping Gang Territories & Rivalries

How OSINT Helps Detect Gang Activity in Specific Areas:

- **Geotagged Posts & Check-ins** – Gang members often post photos or live stream from their controlled territories.
- **Crime Heat Maps** – Open crime databases like SpotCrime and CrimeMapping reveal patterns of gang violence.
- **Google Street View & Public Surveillance Feeds** – Analyze graffiti tags and gathering spots in gang-controlled areas.

Tools for Mapping Gang Networks:

- **ArcGIS & QGIS** – Map gang-related crime clusters.
- **GeoSocial Footprint & Echosec** – Analyze social media check-ins in gang territories.
- **LexisNexis Crime Data** – Access historical crime reports linked to gang violence.

Case Study: OSINT analysts tracked an LA-based gang's expansion into new territories by analyzing Snapchat videos tagged with gang symbols, helping law enforcement anticipate violent clashes.

Step 3: Tracking Gang Communications & Recruitment

Gangs recruit new members through social media, music videos, gaming platforms, and private messaging apps. OSINT techniques can monitor and disrupt these recruitment strategies.

Key Gang Recruitment Tactics Online:

- **Music & Drill Rap Videos** – Some gangs use rap videos to glorify violence, call out rivals, and recruit new members.
- **Video Game Chats (GTA, Call of Duty)** – Gang members communicate and recruit via in-game chat features.
- **Encrypted Messaging (WhatsApp, Telegram, Signal)** – Gangs coordinate drug deals and attacks using private channels.

- **Threats & Challenges on Social Media** – Rivals provoke each other on Facebook, Instagram, and TikTok, often leading to real-world violence.

OSINT Tools for Tracking Gang Communications:

- **TikTok & YouTube Monitoring** – Scan gang-related rap videos for threats & coded messages.
- **Discord & Gaming Platform OSINT (Fauxpersky, DeSnake)** – Identify gang recruitment in gaming communities.
- **Telegram & Dark Web Crawlers** – Track drug sales & trafficking discussions.

Example: In the UK, OSINT investigations into drill rap lyrics and YouTube comments led police to uncover planned gang retaliations, preventing multiple shootings.

Step 4: Financial OSINT & Tracking Gang-Related Transactions

Gangs fund their operations through drug sales, weapons trafficking, extortion, and fraud schemes. OSINT investigators can follow digital financial footprints to uncover these illicit activities.

How Gangs Move & Launder Money:

- **Cash App, Venmo, & Cryptocurrency** – Gang members use peer-to-peer payment apps and crypto to transfer illegal funds.
- **Prepaid Debit Cards** – Used to pay for drugs, weapons, and bribes without linking back to real identities.
- **Front Businesses** – Gangs launder money through nightclubs, barbershops, and car washes.

OSINT Tools for Financial Tracking:

- **Blockchain Analysis (Chainalysis, CipherTrace)** – Track crypto transactions linked to drug sales.
- **OpenCorporates & Business Registries** – Identify gang-linked front businesses.
- **Cash App & PayPal Transaction Monitoring** – OSINT tools can analyze suspicious payment patterns.

Example: Investigators tracked Bitcoin transactions from a gang's darknet drug sales, linking them to real estate purchases in Miami, leading to asset seizures.

Step 5: Case Study – Dismantling a Violent Street Gang Using OSINT

Background:

A notorious gang in New York was responsible for a string of shootings, drug trafficking, and online fraud schemes. Law enforcement leveraged OSINT to map their structure and operations.

How OSINT Exposed the Gang Network:

- **Social Media Analysis** – Instagram posts revealed rival tensions and upcoming planned attacks.
- **Geotagging & Surveillance** – Snapchat videos helped detect meeting locations and track members' movements.
- **Financial Tracking** – Cryptocurrency transactions led to hidden assets used for laundering drug money.
- **Dark Web Monitoring** – The gang used fake IDs & fraudulent credit cards, traced through darknet forums.

Outcome:

Law enforcement arrested over 30 gang members, seized $2 million in drugs & weapons, and prevented multiple violent retaliations.

Step 6: Challenges in OSINT Gang Investigations

While OSINT is highly effective, it presents challenges in gang investigations:

- **Encrypted Messaging** – Many gangs use end-to-end encrypted apps, making interception difficult.
- **Evolving Slang & Codes** – Gangs frequently change their terminology to avoid detection.
- **Fake Accounts & Misinformation** – Gang members use burner accounts and fake names.
- **Legal & Privacy Issues** – Investigators must ensure OSINT data is collected ethically and legally.

Solution: OSINT should be combined with traditional surveillance, confidential informants, and forensic analysis for maximum effectiveness.

Conclusion: OSINT's Growing Role in Combating Gang Crime

OSINT provides powerful tools to track gang activities, disrupt recruitment, and map criminal networks. With continuous advancements in AI-driven analytics and social media monitoring, investigators can stay ahead of evolving gang tactics.

Key Takeaways:

- Social media analysis reveals gang recruitment & rivalries.
- Geospatial OSINT helps track gang territories.
- Financial tracking uncovers money laundering & illicit transactions.
- Dark web monitoring exposes weapons & drug sales.

With proactive OSINT strategies, law enforcement can dismantle street crime networks and prevent violent crimes before they happen.

6.4 Money Laundering & Financial Crime Connections

Introduction: The Role of OSINT in Uncovering Financial Crime

Money laundering is the lifeblood of organized crime, allowing gangs, cartels, and criminal enterprises to clean illicit funds obtained from drug trafficking, fraud, human trafficking, extortion, and other illegal activities. By disguising the origins of dirty money and integrating it into the legitimate financial system, criminals can fund operations, bribe officials, and evade law enforcement.

Open-Source Intelligence (OSINT) plays a critical role in detecting suspicious financial transactions, identifying shell companies, tracking cryptocurrency flows, and exposing hidden assets. By leveraging public databases, blockchain analysis tools, leaked financial records, and social media intelligence, OSINT investigators can connect criminal networks to financial activities and dismantle their operations.

Step 1: Understanding the Money Laundering Process

Money laundering typically occurs in three stages, all of which can be analyzed using OSINT techniques:

1. Placement – Injecting illegal money into the financial system

- Cash-based businesses (restaurants, nightclubs, casinos)
- Prepaid debit cards, gift cards, and digital payment platforms
- Cryptocurrency purchases & anonymous wallets

2. Layering – Concealing the origin of illicit funds

- Multiple bank transfers between offshore accounts
- Shell companies & fake business transactions
- Converting assets into high-value items (luxury cars, real estate, art)

3. Integration – Making laundered money appear legitimate

- Investment in legitimate businesses
- Real estate acquisitions through intermediaries
- Donations to charities controlled by criminals

Example: A Mexican drug cartel laundered millions by purchasing Bitcoin, funneling it through shell companies, and reinvesting in legitimate real estate. OSINT investigators tracked their crypto transactions and linked them to cartel leaders.

Step 2: Identifying Shell Companies & Front Businesses

Criminal organizations often hide illicit funds behind fake businesses and offshore entities. OSINT can help uncover these fraudulent companies by analyzing:

- Public business registries (OpenCorporates, SEC filings, company databases)
- LinkedIn profiles & social media activity of business owners
- Leaked financial data (Panama Papers, Paradise Papers)
- Connections between multiple shell companies

Red Flags for Criminal Front Companies:

- Unusually high revenue with minimal operations
- Frequent ownership changes & complex structures
- Similar business names registered in different countries
- Lack of online presence or real customers

Example: OSINT analysts uncovered a Colombian drug cartel's front company, which operated as a real estate investment firm in Miami. By cross-referencing property records and social media posts, investigators linked the business to known traffickers.

Step 3: Tracking Cryptocurrency & Dark Web Transactions

Criminals increasingly use cryptocurrency to launder money due to its pseudo-anonymity and decentralized nature. However, OSINT techniques can trace crypto transactions and connect wallets to real identities.

OSINT Tools for Cryptocurrency Tracking:

- **Chainalysis & CipherTrace** – Track Bitcoin & Ethereum transactions
- **WalletExplorer & Blockchain.com** – Identify wallet owners & transaction histories
- **Dark Web Crawlers** – Monitor illicit marketplaces & crypto-based laundering services

How Criminals Use Crypto for Money Laundering:

- **Bitcoin ATMs & peer-to-peer exchanges** – Convert cash to crypto anonymously
- **Mixing/Tumbling Services** – Obscure transaction trails by pooling funds
- **NFT & Digital Art Purchases** – Buy & sell digital assets to move money undetected

Example: An OSINT investigation into a dark web marketplace revealed that drug traffickers used Monero (XMR) transactions to launder millions. By analyzing blockchain transaction patterns, law enforcement uncovered real-world identities linked to crypto wallets.

Step 4: Analyzing High-Value Asset Purchases

Criminals often launder money by buying luxury assets that can later be sold for clean cash. OSINT techniques can track suspicious purchases in:

- Real estate (luxury apartments, vacation homes)
- High-end cars & private jets
- Expensive jewelry & artwork

OSINT Techniques for Asset Tracking:

- **Real Estate Databases (Zillow, Realtor, Land Registry records)** – Identify properties owned by criminals

- **Aircraft & Yacht Registries** – Track luxury vehicles linked to money launderers
- **Auction & Sales Websites (Sotheby's, Christie's)** – Find suspicious high-value purchases

Example: Investigators used OSINT to track real estate transactions in London, exposing a Russian oligarch laundering billions through luxury apartments.

Step 5: Case Study – Exposing an International Money Laundering Operation

Background:

An international criminal network was laundering drug proceeds through cryptocurrency, offshore accounts, and luxury assets.

How OSINT Exposed the Network:

- **Shell Company Analysis** – Cross-referenced business registries & leaked financial records to find front companies.
- **Blockchain Tracking** – Monitored crypto transactions from darknet drug sales to real-world accounts.
- **Luxury Asset Investigations** – Identified real estate purchases in Dubai & Switzerland linked to cartel members.
- **Social Media & Leaked Data** – Analyzed high-profile criminals' Instagram posts showing luxury lifestyles inconsistent with declared income.

Outcome:

Law enforcement seized over $500 million in assets, shut down multiple shell companies, and arrested key money launderers.

Step 6: Overcoming Challenges in Financial Crime OSINT

While OSINT is powerful in tracking money laundering, investigators face several challenges:

- **Complex Ownership Structures** – Criminals use offshore firms, nominee directors, and layered transactions.
- **Anonymity in Cryptocurrencies** – Some cryptocurrencies, like Monero & Zcash, offer enhanced privacy features.

- **Legal & Compliance Barriers** – Investigating international financial crimes requires coordination across jurisdictions.
- **Data Overload** – Large-scale financial data requires AI-driven analytics to detect patterns.

Solution: OSINT investigators should combine blockchain forensics, financial intelligence, and corporate registry analysis to connect financial transactions to criminal organizations.

Conclusion: The Power of OSINT in Exposing Financial Crime

Money laundering fuels drug trafficking, terrorism, human trafficking, and fraud. OSINT provides law enforcement with the digital tools to track illicit transactions, uncover hidden assets, and dismantle organized crime networks.

Key Takeaways:

- Shell company analysis reveals criminal financial networks.
- Cryptocurrency tracking exposes illicit fund transfers.
- Luxury asset monitoring connects criminals to real estate & high-value goods.
- Blockchain forensics & dark web OSINT are crucial for modern financial crime investigations.

By leveraging OSINT, investigators can stay ahead of financial criminals and disrupt illicit money flows before they fuel further crimes.

6.5 OSINT for Investigating Human Smuggling & Trafficking

Introduction: The Role of OSINT in Combatting Human Trafficking

Human smuggling and trafficking are multi-billion-dollar criminal enterprises that exploit vulnerable populations worldwide. Organized crime networks facilitate illegal border crossings, forced labor, sexual exploitation, and child trafficking using a mix of covert communication channels, encrypted messaging apps, and online recruitment platforms.

Open-Source Intelligence (OSINT) plays a critical role in uncovering trafficking networks, tracking smuggling routes, identifying perpetrators, and rescuing victims. By analyzing social media activity, darknet forums, classified ads, and financial transactions, investigators can map out trafficking rings, disrupt their operations, and assist law enforcement in prosecuting traffickers.

Step 1: Understanding the Difference Between Human Smuggling & Trafficking

Human Smuggling – A paid service where individuals are illegally transported across borders. Smuggled individuals are not necessarily victims unless they face coercion, exploitation, or abuse.

Human Trafficking – The forced exploitation of individuals for sex work, labor, or organ harvesting. Victims may be trafficked across or within national borders through deception, coercion, or threats.

Key Indicators of Trafficking Networks:

- Frequent advertisements for "escort services" with vague or coded language
- Social media profiles showing young individuals in suspicious circumstances
- Multiple victims using the same phone number, address, or recruiter
- Hotels, motels, and short-term rentals used as trafficking hubs

Example: An OSINT investigation uncovered a trafficking ring using fake job postings on Facebook to lure victims into forced labor. Investigators linked multiple accounts to a single recruiter operating across Southeast Asia.

Step 2: Identifying Traffickers & Smuggling Routes

Traffickers use social media, online marketplaces, and encrypted messaging apps to communicate and recruit victims. OSINT can help identify:

- **Recruitment Ads** – Posts offering too-good-to-be-true job opportunities (e.g., modeling, travel, babysitting)
- **Fake Travel Agencies** – Websites that offer "visa assistance" and "relocation services"
- **Dark Web Activity** – Human trafficking forums, cryptocurrency payments for illicit services
- **Border Crossings & Safe Houses** – Identifying frequent travel patterns & temporary accommodations

OSINT Methods for Tracking Smuggling Networks:

- **Social Media Analysis** – Monitor Facebook, Instagram, TikTok, and Telegram for suspicious job offers
- **Classified Ads Investigations** – Scrape platforms like Craigslist, Backpage, or adult service websites
- **Dark Web Monitoring** – Use Tor search engines to identify hidden trafficking forums
- **Financial Tracking** – Follow money transfers to known traffickers

Example: Investigators used OSINT to map a human smuggling route from Libya to Italy, identifying social media recruiters and encrypted Telegram groups coordinating illegal crossings.

Step 3: Tracking Victims Using OSINT Techniques

Victims of trafficking often leave digital traces that can help locate and rescue them.

Sources for Finding Trafficked Individuals:

- **Missing Persons Databases** – Cross-referencing with online escort advertisements
- **Hotel & Rental Listings** – Searching for frequent bookings linked to trafficking suspects
- **Social Media Footprints** – Identifying coded distress messages or geotagged photos
- **Facial Recognition & Reverse Image Search** – Analyzing victim images in escort ads

Tools for Finding Trafficking Victims:

- **Google Reverse Image Search, PimEyes** – Identify victim images in different ads
- **Maltego & Link Analysis Software** – Connect social media profiles to traffickers
- **Geo-OSINT Tools** – Use Google Earth, Sentinel Hub, and social media check-ins to pinpoint victim locations

Example: Investigators rescued a teenager trafficked for online sex work by tracking her Instagram posts geotagged to multiple motels in Texas.

Step 4: Investigating Online Trafficking Marketplaces

Many trafficking operations rely on escort websites, classified ads, and encrypted platforms to advertise victims. OSINT can help track where and how victims are being exploited.

- **Escort & Adult Service Websites** – Analyzing ads on SugarDaddy, OnlyFans, SkiptheGames, and similar sites
- **Coded Language & Emojis** – Traffickers use hidden messages (e.g., "fresh," "new to town," "donations accepted")
- **Tracking Phone Numbers & Emails** – Reverse searching contact details linked to multiple ads

Red Flags in Online Advertisements:

- Vague or misleading job descriptions
- Repeated use of the same images, phone numbers, or phrases
- High-pressure offers, immediate cash payments, or travel promises

Example: OSINT analysts uncovered a trafficking ring using Instagram to advertise escort services. Investigators matched usernames, hashtags, and geolocation data to identify both victims and recruiters.

Step 5: Dark Web Intelligence on Human Trafficking

The dark web is a major hub for human trafficking activities, with forums dedicated to illicit labor, sex trafficking, and even organ trade. OSINT experts use specialized tools to monitor and infiltrate these networks.

Common Dark Web Marketplaces for Trafficking:

- Encrypted forums & private Telegram channels
- Tor-based trafficking platforms (e.g., hidden marketplaces)
- Bitcoin payments for illegal services

Dark Web OSINT Techniques:

- Tracking Bitcoin transactions using Chainalysis & CipherTrace
- Monitoring known trafficking forums via Tor search engines
- Using fake identities to gather intelligence on trafficker operations

Example: Investigators used blockchain forensics to track Bitcoin payments linked to a dark web child trafficking ring, leading to multiple arrests.

Step 6: Case Study – Dismantling a Human Trafficking Network

Background:

A transnational human trafficking network was exploiting women from Eastern Europe, luring them with fake modeling jobs and forcing them into sex work in major U.S. cities.

OSINT Investigation Process:

- **Social Media & Classified Ads** – Analysts scraped escort advertisements, identifying repeated phrases and contact numbers.
- **Reverse Image Searches** – Photos from escort ads matched missing persons reports.
- **Financial Transactions** – Money was funneled through cryptocurrency wallets & offshore accounts.
- **Dark Web Monitoring** – Investigators identified online trafficker discussions regarding victim transportation.

Outcome:

Law enforcement arrested 14 traffickers, freed over 50 victims, and shut down multiple escort websites linked to the operation.

Step 7: Challenges & Ethical Considerations in Trafficking OSINT

- **Encryption & Privacy Barriers** – Traffickers use encrypted apps like Signal & ProtonMail
- **Legal & Ethical Issues** – Investigators must follow legal guidelines for OSINT collection
- **False Positives** – Incorrect identification can endanger innocent people

Best Practices for Ethical OSINT Investigations:

- Work alongside law enforcement & NGOs
- Verify all intelligence before acting
- Respect victim privacy and avoid exposing sensitive information

Conclusion: How OSINT is Reshaping Human Trafficking Investigations

Human smuggling and trafficking are complex global crimes, but OSINT provides powerful tools to uncover perpetrators, track victims, and dismantle networks. By using social media analysis, dark web monitoring, blockchain forensics, and geolocation intelligence, investigators can proactively combat human trafficking and save lives.

With OSINT, we can expose the hidden world of human trafficking and bring justice to its victims.

6.6 Case Study: Mapping an Organized Crime Syndicate

Introduction: The Power of OSINT in Organized Crime Investigations

Organized crime syndicates operate through complex networks of individuals, businesses, and illicit financial transactions. These groups engage in a wide range of illegal activities, including drug trafficking, human smuggling, money laundering, cybercrime, and weapons trafficking. Unlike isolated criminals, syndicates function like corporations, with hierarchies, logistics, and covert communication systems.

Using Open-Source Intelligence (OSINT), investigators can map out these networks, identify key players, track financial transactions, and expose criminal connections. This case study demonstrates how OSINT was used to uncover and dismantle an international organized crime syndicate involved in drug trafficking and financial fraud.

Background: The Crime Syndicate and Its Operations

Authorities received intelligence about a sophisticated crime syndicate operating across multiple countries. The group was involved in:

✓ **Drug trafficking** – Smuggling narcotics through container shipments and private couriers

✓ **Money laundering** – Using offshore accounts, cryptocurrency, and shell companies

✓ **Cybercrime** – Engaging in credit card fraud, phishing scams, and identity theft

✓ **Human trafficking** – Exploiting individuals through forced labor and illegal immigration services

The challenge was identifying the syndicate's structure, key members, financial flows, and criminal activities without direct access to classified law enforcement databases. OSINT played a critical role in mapping the organization.

Step 1: Identifying Key Players Through Social Media & Business Records

The investigation began by searching social media platforms, business registries, and financial records to identify individuals potentially linked to the syndicate.

✓ **Social Media Profiles** – Investigators analyzed Instagram, Facebook, and LinkedIn accounts of suspected members

✓ **Company Registrations** – Cross-referenced corporate ownership records in multiple jurisdictions

✓ **Public Leaks & Data Breaches** – Examined leaked documents containing financial transactions, emails, and phone numbers

Key Findings:

📌 A suspected crime boss posted images of luxury cars, private jets, and trips to known trafficking hubs

📌 Multiple shell companies registered under the same addresses were linked to drug trade profits

📌 Leaked financial documents revealed unusual cryptocurrency transfers to known darknet markets

🔎 **OSINT Insight**: Criminals often use legitimate businesses as fronts for money laundering. Investigators found that a "construction company" in Dubai was actually a drug cartel's money-laundering hub.

Step 2: Mapping the Syndicate's Communication Network

Using OSINT-based link analysis tools like Maltego, investigators mapped relationships between individuals, companies, and criminal activities.

✓ **Telegram & WhatsApp Groups** – Monitored encrypted chat groups where smuggling logistics were discussed

✓ **Dark Web Forums** – Found cybercrime services offered by syndicate members

✓ **Call Detail Records (CDRs) Leaks** – Connected known traffickers through shared contact numbers

Network Mapping Insights:

📌 A logistics manager in Spain was connected to drug shipment coordinators in Latin America

📌 A fake charity organization in Eastern Europe was actually trafficking women into the sex trade

📌 A Bitcoin wallet tied to ransomware payments was linked to a money laundering operation in Hong Kong

💷 **OSINT Insight**: By analyzing Telegram usernames, email addresses, and IP logs, investigators found that multiple accounts were operated by the same individuals under different aliases.

Step 3: Following the Money – Uncovering Laundered Funds

Organized crime syndicates rely on layered financial transactions to obscure illicit money. OSINT tools helped track:

✓ **Cryptocurrency Transactions** – Using blockchain forensics (Chainalysis, CipherTrace) to track Bitcoin and Monero transactions

✓ **Luxury Asset Purchases** – Identifying real estate, exotic cars, and art used to launder money

✓ **Bank Leaks & Offshore Accounts** – Examining leaked banking data from the Panama Papers and Paradise Papers

Key Findings:

📌 A drug cartel leader purchased multimillion-dollar apartments in London and Dubai through offshore shell companies

📌 Syndicate members used gift cards and prepaid debit cards to move illicit funds without banking oversight

📌 A Bitcoin tumbling service was used to obfuscate ransom payments from cyber fraud

OSINT Insight: By cross-referencing blockchain transactions with known darknet wallet addresses, investigators identified a major money laundering operation funneling millions into cryptocurrencies.

Step 4: Unraveling the Drug Trafficking Routes

Using geospatial OSINT and satellite imagery, investigators uncovered drug trafficking routes used by the syndicate.

✓ **Ship & Flight Tracking** – Monitored maritime routes and flight paths of suspicious cargo shipments
✓ **Satellite & Street View Analysis** – Identified stash houses and transit hubs in rural areas
✓ **Border Surveillance Data Leaks** – Examined illegal border crossings through leaked government data

Drug Smuggling Patterns Discovered:

📌 Cocaine shipments disguised as fruit exports were routed from Colombia to ports in Spain and the Netherlands
📌 Dark web marketplaces were selling fentanyl shipped from China to North America using fake pharmaceutical companies
📌 A motorcycle gang in Canada was acting as a distribution arm for a European heroin ring

OSINT Insight: By tracking shipping container movements and monitoring darknet forums for buyer reviews, investigators discovered which routes were most frequently used for drug smuggling.

Step 5: Linking the Syndicate to Corrupt Officials & Fraudulent Activities

Organized crime groups often bribe officials to protect their operations. OSINT investigations revealed:

✓ **Political Donations & Lobbying** – Syndicate leaders funneled millions into political campaigns to gain protection

✓ **Fake Charities & NGOs** – Used as money laundering fronts to conceal illicit transactions

✓ **Leaked Documents & Whistleblower Reports** – Revealed government officials aiding trafficking operations

🏛 **OSINT Insight**: A high-ranking customs official in South America was caught facilitating drug shipments through fake export licenses.

Final Outcome: The Dismantling of the Crime Syndicate

☐ **Law enforcement agencies used OSINT findings to:**

✅ Arrest 23 high-ranking members of the crime syndicate

✅ Seize $120 million in assets, including real estate, luxury cars, and offshore accounts

✅ Shut down multiple darknet marketplaces used for cyber fraud and drug distribution

✅ Rescue over 50 human trafficking victims from forced labor and sexual exploitation

Key Takeaways from This OSINT Investigation:

✓ Social Media & Business Registries helped identify crime bosses and their financial interests

✓ Network Analysis & Dark Web Monitoring exposed how different branches of the syndicate operated

✓ Blockchain Forensics & Bank Leaks tracked illicit funds across multiple jurisdictions

✓ Satellite Imagery & Shipment Tracking uncovered drug smuggling routes

Conclusion: The Future of OSINT in Organized Crime Investigations

OSINT has revolutionized the fight against organized crime, offering real-time intelligence, financial tracking, and digital surveillance capabilities. By leveraging social media analysis, blockchain forensics, and geospatial intelligence, investigators can map, track, and dismantle complex criminal networks.

🔍 With OSINT, law enforcement can expose the hidden operations of crime syndicates and bring them to justice.

7. Investigating Scams & Online Fraud Rings

This chapter focuses on the critical use of OSINT in investigating scams and online fraud rings, which have become increasingly sophisticated in the digital era. From phishing schemes to fake e-commerce sites, fraudsters exploit the anonymity of the internet to deceive and exploit unsuspecting victims. We will examine how OSINT techniques can uncover fraudulent activities by tracing digital footprints, analyzing communication patterns, and identifying connections between different fraudulent entities. Through real-world examples, this chapter illustrates how investigators use OSINT to expose scams, disrupt online fraud rings, and protect individuals and organizations from falling prey to cybercriminals.

7.1 Identifying & Tracking Online Scammers

Introduction: The Rise of Online Scams

The internet has become a global marketplace, but it has also become a breeding ground for scammers who exploit unsuspecting victims. From investment fraud and romance scams to phishing attacks and fake e-commerce stores, cybercriminals use deception, anonymity, and digital tools to steal money, identities, and sensitive information.

Using Open-Source Intelligence (OSINT), investigators can identify, track, and expose online scammers, helping law enforcement and victims recover losses. This chapter explores key OSINT techniques for detecting and monitoring scam operations.

Step 1: Recognizing Common Online Scams

Scammers operate in many different ways, but most schemes follow recognizable patterns. Some of the most prevalent scams include:

✓ **Romance Scams** – Fraudsters pretend to be interested in a romantic relationship, gaining trust before requesting money

✓ **Investment & Crypto Scams** – Fake investment firms promise high returns on Bitcoin or stocks but steal deposits

✓ **Phishing & Impersonation** – Scammers pose as banks, tech support, or government agencies to steal credentials

✔ **E-Commerce & Marketplace Fraud** – Fake online stores take payments but never deliver products

✔ **Ransomware & Extortion** – Cybercriminals threaten to leak personal data unless a ransom is paid

📖 **OSINT Insight**: Many scams recycle the same website templates, email formats, and fake testimonials, making it easier to track their activities.

Step 2: OSINT Techniques for Identifying Scammers

To unmask scammers, investigators rely on digital footprints, domain intelligence, social media monitoring, and financial tracking.

1️⃣ Reverse Image & Video Search

🔍 **Scammers often steal profile pictures from real people. Use:**

✔ Google Reverse Image Search

✔ Yandex & TinEye for deeper searches

✔ InVID to analyze videos for manipulation

Example: A romance scammer's profile photo matched a stock image of a male model found on multiple scam reports.

2️⃣ Analyzing Email Headers & IP Addresses

📧 **Emails from scammers often reveal key metadata, such as:**

✔ IP addresses (unless spoofed)

✔ Mail server origins (using MXToolbox)

✔ Fraudulent domain registrations

Example: A phishing email pretending to be from PayPal actually originated from a Russian web host linked to past scam reports.

3️⃣ Domain & Website Analysis

☐ **Many scams use fake websites. Investigators can check:**

✓ **WHOIS Lookup (Who.is, ICANN WHOIS)** – Reveals registration details & hosting providers
✓ **Wayback Machine (Archive.org)** – Tracks website changes over time
✓ **SSL Certificates & Server Data (Shodan, Censys)** – Identifies associated IPs & related sites

Example: A fraudulent investment website claimed to be a 10-year-old company, but WHOIS data showed it was registered only 2 months ago.

4️⃣ Tracking Social Media & Forum Activity

📱 **Many scammers promote their schemes on social media. OSINT tools help track:**

✓ Usernames across platforms (using Namechk, WhatsMyName)

✓ Scammer posts in forums & Telegram groups

✓ Linked accounts & followers for connections

Example: A fake Instagram "crypto trader" also had accounts on Reddit & Telegram, where they used similar usernames to lure victims.

Step 3: Linking Scammers to Larger Fraud Networks

Scammers rarely work alone—they operate in networks, often using:

✓ Multiple fake websites with similar layouts

✓ Shared phone numbers, emails, and bank accounts

✓ Cryptocurrency wallets to launder stolen funds

1️⃣ Analyzing Bitcoin & Crypto Transactions

💰 Many scammers ask for payments in Bitcoin, Ethereum, or USDT. Investigators can track these using:

✓ **Blockchain Explorers** (Blockchain.com, Etherscan, Chainalysis)

✓ **Dark Web Market Monitoring** (to check if funds are cashed out)

Example: A Ponzi scheme scammed victims of $5 million in Bitcoin. Blockchain analysis showed the funds were funneled into an exchange in Eastern Europe.

2️⃣ Identifying Shared Digital Infrastructure

🔗 Many scam sites use the same hosting services, templates, and ad campaigns. Investigators can:

✓ Compare HTML code & website templates

✓ Look for duplicate contact details

✓ Check IP addresses & shared hosting providers

Example: A fake forex trading site had the same phone number as another scam site, linking them to a larger fraud network.

Step 4: Reporting & Taking Action Against Scammers

Once a scammer's identity is uncovered, investigators can:

✓ Report fraud websites to hosting providers (AbuseIPDB, ScamAdviser)

✓ Submit financial fraud cases to authorities (FTC, Europol, FBI IC3)

✓ Warn the public through scam forums & social media

🏛 **Case Example**: A fake Amazon seller scammed dozens of customers. OSINT tracking revealed they operated 12 other fake stores, leading to their PayPal account being frozen.

Conclusion: OSINT as a Weapon Against Online Scams

OSINT empowers investigators to track, expose, and report scammers before they harm more victims. By combining domain research, blockchain analysis, social media tracking, and scam pattern recognition, OSINT practitioners can disrupt online fraud networks and assist law enforcement.

🚨 With OSINT, online scammers can no longer hide.

7.2 Investigating Romance Scams & Social Engineering Fraud

Introduction: The Emotional Manipulation Behind Online Scams

Romance scams and social engineering fraud rely on psychological manipulation to exploit victims emotionally and financially. Scammers create fake identities, build trust, and then fabricate emergencies or investment opportunities to extract money. These fraudsters often operate from cybercrime rings, using scripted conversations and stolen images to deceive multiple victims simultaneously.

Using Open-Source Intelligence (OSINT), investigators can identify, track, and expose romance scammers by analyzing their digital footprints, social media activity, financial transactions, and fake identities.

Step 1: Understanding How Romance Scams Work

Romance scammers often follow a pattern of deception:

Common Tactics Used in Romance Scams

✓ **Fake Profiles** – Scammers steal photos from models, military personnel, or professionals

✓ **Rapid Emotional Bonding** – They express strong love and commitment within days or weeks

✓ **Excuses to Avoid Meeting** – They claim to be in the military, working overseas, or on a secret mission

✓ **Fake Emergencies** – They request money for medical bills, legal fees, or travel expenses

✓ **Investment Scams** – They persuade victims to invest in fake cryptocurrency or business ventures

📖 **Example**: A scammer impersonating a U.S. Army officer convinced victims on Facebook to send money for a "classified mission." OSINT tools later revealed the same images were used in multiple scam reports.

Step 2: Identifying Fake Identities & Stolen Photos

Scammers often recycle the same profile pictures, usernames, and email addresses across multiple platforms. OSINT tools help verify their authenticity.

1️ **Reverse Image Search**

☐ Many romance scammers use stolen images from social media or stock photography websites. Use:

✓ Google Reverse Image Search

✓ Yandex & TinEye for broader searches

✓ PimEyes for facial recognition tracking

📖 **Example**: A scammer pretending to be a wealthy businessman was using a stock image of an Italian model found in multiple scam databases.

2️ **Social Media & Username Analysis**

🔍 Scammers often create fake social media accounts with minimal activity. Investigators can check:

✓ Username history across platforms (Namechk, WhatsMyName)

✓ Friends list & activity patterns (real users vs. bot accounts)

✓ Posts & comments to spot inconsistencies

📖 **Example**: A romance scammer claimed to be a London-based doctor but had friends only from West Africa, revealing inconsistencies in their backstory.

3️⃣ Email & Phone Number Verification

✉️ Scammers use disposable emails and VoIP phone numbers. Tools like:

✔ ScamWarners & RomanceScam.com (to check reported scammers)

✔ HaveIBeenPwned (to see if their email was in a breach)

✔ Phone number lookup services (TrueCaller, Sync.me)

🔍 **Example**: A scammer using a Gmail account with a fake doctor profile had their email flagged in multiple fraud databases.

Step 3: Investigating Social Engineering Fraud

Social engineering fraud goes beyond romance scams, involving:

✔ **Tech Support Scams** – Fake calls/emails from "Microsoft" or "Apple" demanding remote access

✔ **CEO Fraud** – Impersonating executives to trick employees into wiring money

✔ **Government & IRS Scams** – Fake officials threaten victims with legal action unless they pay immediately

✔ **Lottery & Inheritance Scams** – Victims are told they "won" money but must pay fees to claim it

1️⃣ Identifying Phishing Websites & Fake Companies

🕵️ Fraudsters create fake investment platforms and impersonate real companies. OSINT can uncover:

✔ Domain registration details (Whois Lookup, ICANN WHOIS)

✔ Website history & changes (Wayback Machine)

✔ IP tracking & hosting provider details (Shodan, Censys)

🏦 **Example**: A fake crypto trading platform promised 500% returns but was registered only two weeks ago with a hidden owner.

2️⃣ Following the Money – Tracking Transactions

💰 Scammers launder stolen funds through:

✓ Cryptocurrency wallets (Blockchain explorers like Etherscan, Chainalysis)

✓ Fake bank accounts & money mule networks

✓ Gift cards & prepaid debit cards

🏦 **Example**: A romance scam victim sent Bitcoin to a scammer, whose wallet was linked to a known darknet exchange.

Step 4: Unmasking & Reporting Scammers

Once a scammer is identified, investigators can:

✓ Report fake profiles on social media (Facebook, Instagram, LinkedIn)

✓ Submit fraud cases to authorities (FBI IC3, Europol, FTC)

✓ Expose scammers through public forums (ScamWarners, ScamSurvivors)

🏦 **Case Study**: A romance scammer operating 30 fake profiles was exposed when OSINT tools linked their email address to multiple fraud reports across different dating platforms.

Conclusion: Fighting Romance Scams with OSINT

Romance scams and social engineering fraud rely on psychological deception and digital manipulation. By using OSINT techniques such as reverse image searches, social media monitoring, email analysis, and financial tracking, investigators can unmask scammers, prevent fraud, and protect victims.

🏦 With OSINT, romance scammers can no longer hide behind fake identities.

7.3 Phishing Campaigns & Email Scam Investigations

Introduction: The Growing Threat of Phishing Attacks

Phishing is one of the most common cybercrime tactics, used by scammers to steal login credentials, financial data, and personal information. These scams typically involve fraudulent emails, fake websites, and social engineering to trick victims into revealing sensitive details.

Law enforcement, cybersecurity professionals, and OSINT investigators rely on Open-Source Intelligence (OSINT) to analyze phishing emails, track scam infrastructure, and uncover criminal networks behind these attacks.

Step 1: Identifying Common Phishing Campaigns

Phishing scams often follow predictable patterns. Some of the most widespread phishing campaigns include:

✓ **Credential Theft** – Fake login pages for banks, social media, or corporate portals

✓ **Financial Fraud** – Emails pretending to be PayPal, Amazon, or banks requesting urgent payments

✓ **Ransomware & Malware Distribution** – Malicious attachments disguised as invoices or security alerts

✓ **Government & IRS Scams** – Fake emails from tax agencies or law enforcement demanding fines

✓ **Tech Support & Impersonation** – Emails pretending to be Microsoft, Apple, or Google requesting remote access

🏛 **Example**: A phishing email pretending to be from Netflix asked users to "verify" their account by entering their credit card details on a fake login page.

Step 2: Investigating Phishing Emails with OSINT

Phishing emails contain clues that help investigators trace their origin. Key OSINT techniques include analyzing email headers, domain registrations, and scam infrastructure.

1️⃣ Extracting Email Headers & Metadata

✉️ **Email headers contain technical details that reveal:**

✓ Sender's IP address & mail server

✓ Fake "From" addresses (email spoofing)

✓ Metadata showing email relay paths

🔍 **Tools for Email Header Analysis:**

✓ **Google Admin Toolbox** (MessageHeader)

✓ **MXToolbox** (Email Header Analyzer)

✓ **IPinfo & AbuseIPDB** (for IP tracking)

🔎 **Example**: A phishing email claiming to be from Amazon had an IP address originating from a server in Nigeria, unrelated to Amazon's actual infrastructure.

2️⃣ Analyzing Phishing Links & Fake Websites

☐ Many phishing emails include fraudulent links leading to fake websites that mimic legitimate brands. OSINT tools can verify:

✓ **Domain registration details** (Whois Lookup, ICANN WHOIS)

✓ **Website security certificates & hosting data** (Shodan, Censys)

✓ **Past versions of the website** (Wayback Machine, URLScan.io)

🔍 **Tools for URL & Domain Analysis:**

✓ **VirusTotal** (to check if a link is flagged as malicious)

✓ **URLScan.io** (to analyze phishing websites)

✓ **PhishTank** (to see if a phishing site is already reported)

🚨 **Example**: A fake banking website used a domain similar to "BankofAmerica" but registered in Russia, exposing it as a scam.

3️⃣ Investigating Malicious Attachments & Payloads

💼 Many phishing emails contain infected attachments that install malware or ransomware. OSINT tools can analyze and deconstruct these files safely.

🔍 **Tools for File & Malware Analysis:**

✓ **VirusTotal** (for malware detection)

✓ **Hybrid Analysis** (sandboxing malicious files)

✓ **Any.Run** (interactive malware analysis)

🚨 **Example**: An email attachment claiming to be an "urgent invoice" contained a macro that downloaded spyware, flagged as malware in VirusTotal.

Step 3: Tracing Phishing Campaigns to Criminal Networks

Phishing attacks are rarely isolated—they are often part of larger cybercrime operations. Investigators can map connections between phishing campaigns by tracking:

✓ Repeated use of the same hosting services & IP addresses

✓ Identical email templates & scam techniques across multiple campaigns

✓ Crypto wallets & payment accounts linked to fraud

1️⃣ Finding Connections Between Phishing Domains

🔍 Many phishing websites share infrastructure, allowing investigators to track:

✓ Shared hosting providers & registrars

✓ Linked email addresses in WHOIS data

✓ Common phishing kits & templates

🔎 **Example**: A fake PayPal login page hosted on the same server as multiple other phishing sites, indicating a coordinated scam operation.

2️⃣ Tracking Bitcoin & Payment Details

💰 Some phishing scams demand Bitcoin payments or wire transfers. Investigators can:

✓ Analyze blockchain transactions (Etherscan, Blockchain.com)
✓ Monitor scam reports on forums (ScamWarners, Reddit)

🔎 **Example**: A phishing scam demanding Bitcoin payments for a fake tax debt was linked to previous cryptocurrency fraud schemes.

Step 4: Reporting & Mitigating Phishing Attacks

Once a phishing scam is identified, investigators can take action by:

✓ Reporting phishing websites to domain registrars & hosting providers
✓ Submitting phishing emails to cybersecurity firms (PhishTank, Spamhaus)
✓ Informing affected organizations & law enforcement (FBI IC3, Europol)

🔎 **Case Study**: A phishing campaign targeting bank customers was taken down after investigators linked multiple fraudulent login pages to the same hosting provider, leading to domain suspension.

Conclusion: Using OSINT to Stop Phishing Scams

Phishing attacks continue to evolve, but OSINT techniques allow investigators to analyze, track, and disrupt scam operations. By leveraging email metadata, domain intelligence, malware analysis, and financial tracking, investigators can expose cybercriminals and protect victims from fraud.

🔎 With OSINT, phishing campaigns can no longer remain hidden.

7.4 Tracking Fake E-Commerce Sites & Online Stores

Introduction: The Rise of Fake Online Stores

With the growth of e-commerce, cybercriminals have exploited online shopping platforms to create fraudulent websites that steal money, personal data, or financial details from unsuspecting consumers. Fake e-commerce sites often sell counterfeit products, never deliver goods, or act as phishing platforms to collect credit card information.

Using Open-Source Intelligence (OSINT), investigators can identify, track, and expose fake online stores by analyzing domain registrations, website infrastructure, payment methods, and customer complaints.

Step 1: Identifying Red Flags of Fake E-Commerce Sites

Many fraudulent online stores look professional, making it difficult for consumers to differentiate between legitimate businesses and scams. However, there are key warning signs that investigators can look for:

✓ **Unrealistically Low Prices** – Fraudulent stores advertise luxury goods at huge discounts

✓ **Limited or Fake Contact Information** – Many scam websites lack a real address or phone number

✓ **Recently Registered Domains** – Scammers frequently create new websites to avoid detection

✓ **Stock Images & Copied Content** – Fake stores steal photos and descriptions from legitimate retailers

✓ **Suspicious Payment Methods** – Many fraudulent sites accept only wire transfers, cryptocurrency, or gift cards

✓ **Fake Customer Reviews** – Scam sites fabricate positive reviews to appear trustworthy

🏛 **Example**: A website claiming to sell high-end sneakers at 90% off had a recently registered domain, no contact details, and only accepted Bitcoin, signaling a scam.

Step 2: Investigating Fake E-Commerce Websites with OSINT

Once a suspicious website is identified, investigators can use OSINT techniques to gather evidence and track the individuals behind the scam.

1⃞ Analyzing Domain Registration & Website History

⃞ Most scam websites use recently registered domains with hidden ownership details. OSINT tools can uncover:

✓ Domain registration details (Whois Lookup, ICANN WHOIS)

✓ Hosting provider & IP address (Shodan, Censys, ViewDNS.info)

✓ Past versions of the website (Wayback Machine, URLScan.io)

🔍 OSINT Tools for Domain Analysis:

✓ Whois Lookup (to check registration details)

✓ Wayback Machine (to see historical versions of the site)

✓ DomainTools (for tracking domain activity)

📷 **Example**: A fake electronics store had a domain registered only one month ago, with the owner's details hidden behind a privacy protection service, indicating a possible scam.

2⃞ Checking for Cloned or Stolen Website Content

Many fake stores copy product descriptions, images, and layouts from legitimate retailers. Investigators can:

✓ Use Google Reverse Image Search to find stolen product images

✓ Compare website text with original sellers using plagiarism checkers

✓ Look for identical page layouts & themes across multiple scam sites

📷 **Example**: A counterfeit watch retailer had the exact same product images and descriptions as a legitimate brand but with a different domain name and cheaper prices.

3⃞ Tracking Payment Methods & Financial Transactions

💰 Fake e-commerce sites often use untraceable payment methods, but OSINT can help track:

✔ Cryptocurrency wallets linked to fraud (Etherscan, Blockchain Explorer)

✔ Merchant accounts and bank details (BIN lookup, card fraud reports)

✔ Payment processors used in previous scams

🔍 **OSINT Tools for Financial Tracking:**

✔ **Etherscan** (to check cryptocurrency transactions)

✔ **ScamAdviser** (to see if a store is blacklisted)

✔ **Binlist.net** (to verify credit card issuer details)

📖 **Example**: A fraudulent clothing store only accepted payments via Western Union and Bitcoin, both common scam indicators.

Step 3: Investigating Customer Complaints & Scam Reports

Victims of fake e-commerce scams often report their experiences online. OSINT researchers can collect intelligence from:

✔ Scam-reporting websites (ScamAdviser, Trustpilot, Reddit, BBB, FTC)

✔ Social media discussions exposing fraud sites

✔ Dark web forums selling fake store templates

🔍 **OSINT Tools for Scam Research:**

✔ **ScamAdviser & Trustpilot** (to check store reviews)

✔ **Reddit & Twitter** (to find scam discussions)

✔ **Fraud databases** (Better Business Bureau, FBI IC3 reports)

📖 **Example**: A supposed "high-end jewelry store" had dozens of complaints on Trustpilot from customers who never received their orders.

Step 4: Tracing the Operators Behind Fake Stores

Scammers running fake e-commerce sites often use multiple domains, fake identities, and different platforms to continue their operations. OSINT methods can help unmask these fraudsters.

✓ Tracking multiple domains registered with the same email/IP

✓ Investigating connections between fake stores using identical layouts

✓ Analyzing social media profiles linked to scam operations

🔍 OSINT Tools for Investigating Scammers:

✓ **Reverse WHOIS** (to find other domains by the same owner)

✓ **Namechk & WhatsMyName** (to check username reuse)

✓ **Facebook & LinkedIn** (to find linked profiles)

📢 **Example**: A fraudster running multiple fake clothing stores used the same email address across six different scam websites, exposing their network.

Step 5: Reporting & Shutting Down Fake Online Stores

Once a fraudulent store is identified, investigators can:

✓ Report fake websites to hosting providers & domain registrars

✓ Submit scam details to consumer protection agencies (FTC, Europol, FBI IC3)

✓ Help victims recover funds by reporting fraudulent transactions

📢 **Case Study**: A fake electronics store selling PlayStation consoles at 70% off was taken down after OSINT analysts linked its email address to previous scams, leading to the domain being suspended.

Conclusion: Stopping Fake E-Commerce Scams with OSINT

Fake online stores continue to evolve, but OSINT provides investigators with powerful tools to analyze, track, and expose e-commerce fraud. By leveraging domain intelligence, website analysis, payment tracking, and scam reporting, investigators can identify fake stores, prevent financial losses, and protect online shoppers.

🚨 With OSINT, fraudulent e-commerce sites can no longer remain hidden.

7.5 Dark Web Fraud Markets & Identity Theft Rings

Introduction: The Underground Economy of Cybercrime

The dark web serves as a hidden marketplace where cybercriminals engage in illicit activities, including financial fraud, identity theft, and the sale of stolen data. Fraud markets on the dark web offer everything from compromised credit card details and counterfeit IDs to hacked bank accounts and personal information.

Using Open-Source Intelligence (OSINT), investigators can monitor, track, and infiltrate these underground networks to expose criminals, disrupt fraud operations, and prevent financial crimes.

Step 1: Understanding Dark Web Fraud Markets

Dark web fraud markets operate on Tor (The Onion Router) and I2P (Invisible Internet Project), providing criminals with anonymity. These marketplaces function similarly to legitimate e-commerce sites, featuring:

✓ **Vendor Listings** – Sellers offer stolen identities, credit card dumps, and hacking tools

✓ **Escrow Services** – Transactions are secured with cryptocurrency payments

✓ **Customer Reviews & Ratings** – Buyers leave feedback on stolen data quality

✓ **Discussion Forums** – Fraudsters share tips, tactics, and resources

🚨 **Example**: A dark web forum advertised "fullz" (complete identity packages) containing a victim's name, Social Security number, address, date of birth, and banking details for just $50 in Bitcoin.

Step 2: Investigating Identity Theft Rings with OSINT

OSINT techniques help investigators track stolen data, analyze dark web activities, and identify cybercriminals.

1️ Tracking Leaked Personal Data & Stolen Identities

🔍 **Data breaches expose millions of personal records, which are often sold on dark web markets. OSINT tools can:**

✓ Search for compromised credentials (Have I Been Pwned, DeHashed, WeLeakInfo)

✓ Monitor deep web forums for mentions of stolen identities

✓ Identify patterns in leaked data (Pastebin, BreachForums, IntelX)

🔍 **OSINT Tools for Data Leak Investigations:**

✓ **Have I Been Pwned** (to check compromised emails)

✓ **DeHashed** (for leaked passwords & personal data)

✓ **LeakLooker** (for searching exposed databases)

🚨 **Example**: A breach of a major retailer led to thousands of stolen customer credit cards appearing on dark web marketplaces.

2️ Analyzing Dark Web Marketplace Listings

OSINT investigators can monitor dark web markets to:

✓ Track listings of stolen financial data & fake documents

✓ Identify recurring vendors selling fraudulent materials

✓ Analyze cryptocurrency wallets used for payments

🔍 **OSINT Tools for Dark Web Analysis:**

✓ **Tor Browser** (to access dark web marketplaces)

✓ **DarkOwl** (for monitoring cybercriminal forums)

✓ **Blockchain Explorer** (to track Bitcoin transactions)

📖 **Example**: A dark web vendor was selling phishing kits & fake passports with instructions on committing financial fraud.

3️⃣ Investigating Cryptocurrency Transactions

💰 Most fraud transactions on the dark web are conducted in Bitcoin (BTC), Monero (XMR), and Ethereum (ETH). OSINT tools help investigators:

✓ Track payments made to fraud vendors

✓ Analyze wallet addresses linked to previous scams

✓ Identify laundering patterns used by criminals

🔍 OSINT Tools for Crypto Investigations:

✓ **Etherscan & Blockchain Explorer** (for Bitcoin & Ethereum tracking)

✓ **CipherTrace & Chainalysis** (for advanced crypto analytics)

✓ **BitcoinAbuse** (to report fraud-linked wallets)

📖 **Example**: A fraudster selling stolen PayPal accounts was linked to a Bitcoin wallet that had received over $200,000 from other scams.

Step 3: Uncovering Dark Web Fraud Networks

Cybercriminals operating in fraud markets reuse usernames, email addresses, and aliases across different platforms, allowing OSINT investigators to make connections.

✓ Finding shared usernames across forums & markets

✓ Analyzing writing styles & digital fingerprints

✓ Connecting dark web vendors to real-world identities

🔍 OSINT Tools for Tracking Dark Web Identities:

✓ **WhatsMyName & Namechk** (to find reused usernames)

✓ **IntelX & Ahmia** (to search dark web content)

✓ **Spiderfoot & Maltego** (for network mapping)

🔍 **Example**: A seller offering fake driver's licenses was found using the same alias on a cybersecurity forum, revealing more details about their operations.

Step 4: Law Enforcement & Intelligence Collaboration

Once fraud markets and identity theft rings are identified, OSINT investigators can:

✓ Report dark web fraud vendors to cybersecurity agencies (Europol, FBI IC3, FTC)

✓ Track large-scale identity theft rings & organized cybercrime groups

✓ Collaborate with financial institutions to prevent fraudulent transactions

🔍 **Case Study**: A law enforcement task force infiltrated a dark web fraud market, leading to the arrest of several identity thieves and the shutdown of the platform.

Conclusion: Fighting Dark Web Fraud with OSINT

Dark web fraud markets continue to expand, but OSINT tools allow investigators to track, analyze, and disrupt identity theft operations. By leveraging data breach monitoring, dark web tracking, cryptocurrency analysis, and identity tracing, investigators can expose cybercriminals and protect victims from financial fraud.

🔍 With OSINT, dark web fraud networks can no longer remain hidden.

7.6 Case Study: Uncovering a Global Fraud Network

Introduction: A Deep Web of Financial Crime

In 2023, an international cybercrime investigation uncovered a massive global fraud network operating across multiple continents. The criminals behind this network engaged in identity theft, credit card fraud, money laundering, and e-commerce scams, siphoning millions of dollars from victims worldwide.

Leveraging Open-Source Intelligence (OSINT), investigators tracked the digital footprints of key operators, analyzed their financial transactions, and linked fraudulent activities across various platforms. This case study demonstrates how OSINT techniques played a critical role in dismantling one of the largest online fraud operations in recent years.

Phase 1: Identifying the Fraud Network

The investigation began when multiple financial institutions reported a sharp increase in fraudulent transactions linked to stolen credit card data. Victims' personal and banking details were appearing on dark web markets, leading investigators to suspect an organized cybercriminal syndicate.

Key OSINT Findings:

✓ Thousands of compromised credit card numbers were found for sale on dark web marketplaces.

✓ Several fraudulent e-commerce stores were acting as fronts for laundering stolen funds.

✓ Social media profiles & chat groups were used to recruit money mules to transfer illicit earnings.

✓ Cryptocurrency wallets linked to scam operations showed large-scale Bitcoin laundering activities.

Q OSINT Tools Used:

✓ Have I Been Pwned & DeHashed (to check leaked credentials)

✓ DarkOwl & IntelX (to track dark web discussions)

✓ Etherscan & Chainalysis (to analyze Bitcoin transactions)

Breakthrough: Investigators identified a recurring username appearing on multiple fraud forums and cryptocurrency wallets, linking a single cybercriminal to numerous illegal activities.

Phase 2: Mapping the Fraud Operations

As investigators delved deeper, they mapped out a structured criminal network, with different teams handling stolen data collection, financial fraud execution, and money laundering.

Criminal Network Structure:

1️ **Data Breach Specialists** – Stole personal information & sold it on the dark web.

2️ **Fraudulent E-Commerce Operators** – Created fake online stores to process stolen card payments.

3️ **Money Mules & Launderers** – Moved funds through shell companies, cryptocurrency, and offshore accounts.

Key OSINT Techniques Used:

✓ Cross-referencing domain registrations (to connect multiple scam websites).

✓ Tracking fake e-commerce reviews & social media ads (to find victims).

✓ Analyzing blockchain transactions (to follow the flow of illicit funds).

🔍 OSINT Tools Used:

✓ **Whois Lookup & DomainTools** (to identify linked scam websites)

✓ **Trustpilot & ScamAdviser** (to analyze customer complaints)

✓ **Blockchain Explorer & CipherTrace** (to track cryptocurrency payments)

Breakthrough: A fraudulent luxury goods website, previously flagged as a scam, was found reusing the same cryptocurrency payment address across multiple fraudulent domains—exposing connections between different scam operations.

Phase 3: Unmasking the Key Suspects

By tracking usernames, emails, and reused credentials, investigators identified the individuals operating the fraud network. Many cybercriminals unknowingly left digital traces, such as:

✓ Using the same aliases across multiple forums and platforms.

✓ Revealing real-world IP addresses by accident when logging into non-secure accounts.

✓ Posting identifiable photos and information on social media.

🔍 **OSINT Tools Used:**

✓ Namechk & WhatsMyName (to track username reuse).

✓ Maltego & Spiderfoot (to map social connections).

✓ Ahmia & Tor Analysis Tools (to monitor dark web activity).

🚔 **Breakthrough**: One of the fraud ring's top operators used the same email address for both his dark web vendor account and a social media profile, allowing law enforcement to confirm his real identity.

Phase 4: Law Enforcement Action & Network Takedown

Armed with OSINT intelligence, international law enforcement agencies coordinated a series of raids across multiple countries, leading to:

✓ The arrest of 12 key fraud operators, including the group's leader.

✓ The seizure of over $15 million in cryptocurrency and bank assets.

✓ The takedown of 30+ fraudulent websites & dark web markets.

🚔 **Final Outcome**: The entire global fraud network was dismantled, preventing further financial losses for victims and businesses worldwide.

Conclusion: The Power of OSINT in Cybercrime Investigations

This case study highlights how OSINT played a pivotal role in exposing and dismantling a global fraud network. By using domain analysis, cryptocurrency tracking, dark web monitoring, and social media intelligence, investigators were able to:

✔ Identify the fraud ring's digital footprint.

✔ Map connections between scam websites, vendors, and financial transactions.

✔ Uncover key individuals behind the operation.

✔ Assist law enforcement in taking down a global cybercrime syndicate.

🚨 With OSINT, cybercriminals can no longer hide behind anonymity.

8. Dark Web & Human Trafficking Investigations

In this chapter, we explore the dark web's role in facilitating illegal activities, particularly in human trafficking, and how OSINT can be a powerful tool in combating this grave crime. The dark web provides a hidden space where traffickers exploit vulnerable individuals and engage in illicit trade, making it difficult for authorities to trace their activities. We will examine the techniques used to navigate the dark web, analyze hidden communications, and track illicit transactions to uncover trafficking networks. By combining OSINT with traditional investigative methods, this chapter demonstrates how digital intelligence can play a crucial role in rescuing victims and dismantling human trafficking operations.

8.1 The Role of the Dark Web in Human Trafficking

Introduction: The Dark Web as a Criminal Marketplace

Human trafficking is one of the most heinous crimes, affecting millions of victims worldwide. While some trafficking operations occur in plain sight through social media and classified ads, a significant portion is hidden deep within the dark web—a concealed part of the internet that requires specialized tools like Tor (The Onion Router) to access.

The dark web provides anonymity for criminals, making it a hub for illegal marketplaces, hidden forums, and encrypted communications used to facilitate human trafficking. OSINT (Open-Source Intelligence) plays a critical role in monitoring, investigating, and disrupting these underground operations.

How Human Traffickers Use the Dark Web

1⃣ Online Marketplaces for Human Exploitation

✓ Sex trafficking rings advertise victims on hidden dark web forums and illicit marketplaces.

✓ Traffickers use cryptocurrency payments (Bitcoin, Monero) to remain anonymous.

✓ Victims' services are often disguised as escort ads, job offers, or adult entertainment.

🔍 **Example**: In a major investigation, law enforcement uncovered a dark web forum where traffickers auctioned off kidnapped individuals to the highest bidder.

2️⃣ Encrypted Communications & Recruitment

✓ Traffickers use end-to-end encrypted messaging apps (Wickr, Signal, Telegram) to coordinate operations.

✓ Recruitment happens through dark web chat rooms, where criminals groom victims under false pretenses.

✓ Live-streamed trafficking content is sometimes sold in underground networks.

🔍 **Example**: A child trafficking network was discovered using dark web forums to communicate with buyers, hiding behind PGP-encrypted messages.

3️⃣ Selling Fake Documents for Trafficking

✓ The dark web offers forged passports, visas, and fake IDs for smuggling victims across borders.

✓ Criminals launder illicit profits through cryptocurrency exchanges to avoid detection.

🔍 **Example**: A dark web vendor sold thousands of fake identity documents, some used to smuggle victims into foreign countries.

How OSINT Helps Investigate Human Trafficking on the Dark Web

1️⃣ Monitoring Dark Web Marketplaces & Forums

✓ DarkOwl, Ahmia, and Tor Search Engines help track illegal content.

✓ OSINT analysts infiltrate forums to identify trafficker networks.

✓ Maltego and Spiderfoot map relationships between traffickers.

🔍 **Example**: A hidden forum discussing human trafficking was linked to known criminal networks through shared usernames and cryptocurrency addresses.

2️⃣ Cryptocurrency Transaction Tracking

✓ Blockchain analysis tools (CipherTrace, Chainalysis, Etherscan) track payments made to traffickers.

✓ Investigators follow the money trail to uncover real-world operators.

🔍 **Example**: Law enforcement followed Bitcoin transactions from a dark web trafficking ring to a real-world bank account, leading to arrests.

3️⃣ Identifying Victims & Missing Persons

✓ OSINT analysts compare dark web images to social media photos to identify victims.

✓ Reverse image search tools like Google Lens & PimEyes help match faces.

✓ Geo-location analysis of dark web content helps pinpoint trafficking hubs.

🔍 **Example**: A missing teenager's photo was found on a dark web site, leading to her rescue in another country.

Conclusion: Fighting Human Trafficking with OSINT

The dark web enables traffickers to operate in secrecy, but OSINT provides investigators with the tools to track them down. By monitoring hidden marketplaces, tracing cryptocurrency transactions, and identifying victims, OSINT analysts play a critical role in combating human trafficking.

📹 No trafficker can remain hidden forever when OSINT is watching.

8.2 Identifying & Investigating Online Trafficking Networks

Introduction: The Digital Trail of Human Trafficking

Human trafficking networks have adapted to the digital age, using the internet, social media, encrypted messaging apps, and the dark web to coordinate their operations.

These networks exploit online anonymity to recruit, advertise, and sell victims, making detection challenging. However, OSINT (Open-Source Intelligence) provides powerful techniques to identify, track, and disrupt these operations.

This chapter explores key OSINT methodologies used to investigate trafficking networks, from identifying digital footprints to mapping criminal connections across platforms.

1️⃣ Recognizing Online Trafficking Indicators

Traffickers leave behind digital clues, often hidden within coded language, online ads, and suspicious transactions. Investigators must learn to recognize these patterns.

Common Digital Signs of Human Trafficking:

✔ Escort advertisements using vague or suggestive language.

✔ Social media profiles of potential victims showing sudden changes in behavior or travel.

✔ Frequent postings with different locations, suggesting movement across regions.

✔ Use of specific emojis or codewords (e.g., 🌀🔻🍭, meaning "underage" in trafficking ads).

✔ High-priced services with vague descriptions, often requesting cryptocurrency payments.

🔍 **Example**: An OSINT analyst identified a trafficking victim by cross-referencing an Instagram profile with escort listings, revealing she was being moved across different states.

2️⃣ Tracking Trafficking Networks on Social Media

Social media is a primary recruitment tool for traffickers. They target vulnerable individuals through fake job offers, modeling contracts, or fake friendships, then lure them into exploitation.

OSINT Techniques for Social Media Investigations:

✔ Username cross-checking across platforms using tools like WhatsMyName & Namechk.

✓ Reverse image searches (Google Lens, PimEyes) to link social media photos to escort ads.

✓ Hashtag monitoring (e.g., #newgirl, #available, #travelgirl) to track suspicious activities.

✓ Following digital relationships to map traffickers and their victims.

🔍 **Example**: A missing teen was found after OSINT analysts tracked her last Instagram check-in to a suspicious account advertising escort services.

3️⃣ Investigating Dark Web Trafficking Networks

The dark web hosts illegal trafficking marketplaces, where traffickers communicate anonymously and sell victims for forced labor, prostitution, and exploitation.

OSINT Techniques for Dark Web Investigations:

✓ Dark web monitoring tools (Ahmia, DarkOwl) to search for trafficking forums.

✓ Analyzing cryptocurrency transactions (Chainalysis, Etherscan) to track illegal payments.

✓ Monitoring Tor-based messaging services for trafficking discussions.

✓ Matching dark web images with known missing persons using AI-driven facial recognition.

🔍 **Example**: Investigators linked a Bitcoin wallet used for dark web trafficking to a suspect's social media account, leading to arrests.

4️⃣ Mapping Human Trafficking Networks with OSINT

To dismantle a trafficking ring, investigators must map connections between traffickers, victims, and their digital infrastructure.

OSINT Mapping Techniques:

✓ Link analysis (Maltego, Spiderfoot) to connect traffickers across platforms.

✓ Phone number & email tracing (DeHashed, Scylla) to uncover linked accounts.

✓ Domain analysis (Whois lookup, DomainTools) to track escort websites and shell companies.

✓ Financial tracking to expose money laundering operations.

🔍 **Example**: A trafficking network was exposed after multiple escort sites were traced back to the same domain registration and bank account.

5️⃣ Case Study: Uncovering a Global Trafficking Network

Investigators used OSINT to track a global sex trafficking operation that moved victims between multiple countries. By analyzing escort listings, cryptocurrency payments, and dark web discussions, law enforcement:

✓ Identified the traffickers' online infrastructure.

✓ Mapped connections between fake businesses and real-world criminals.

✓ Tracked victims' movements using geotagged content.

✓ Collaborated with international law enforcement to shut down the network.

🔒 **Outcome**: Over 50 traffickers arrested, 100+ victims rescued, and $10 million in assets seized.

Conclusion: The Power of OSINT in Fighting Human Trafficking

OSINT enables investigators to unmask traffickers, trace illicit networks, and rescue victims by analyzing their digital footprints. By monitoring social media, tracking financial transactions, and mapping criminal connections, OSINT plays a crucial role in disrupting human trafficking networks worldwide.

🔒 With OSINT, no trafficker can hide forever.

8.3 Monitoring Escort & Classified Ad Websites for Leads

Introduction: The Digital Marketplace for Human Trafficking

Escort and classified ad websites are often exploited by human traffickers to advertise victims under the guise of legal adult services. These platforms allow traffickers to recruit, advertise, and communicate with buyers while maintaining a veil of anonymity. OSINT (Open-Source Intelligence) techniques can help investigators analyze these listings, identify victims, and track traffickers through digital breadcrumbs.

This chapter explores how OSINT professionals and law enforcement can monitor, analyze, and investigate escort and classified ad sites to uncover trafficking networks.

1 Understanding How Escort & Classified Ads Facilitate Trafficking

Many escort and classified ad sites host both legitimate and illegal listings, making it crucial to differentiate between consensual work and trafficking victims.

Common Red Flags in Trafficking-Related Ads:

✔ Overly vague or coded language (e.g., "new in town," "young & fresh," "no experience needed").

✔ Frequent movement across cities (suggesting victim relocation).

✔ Multiple ads with similar wording & photos posted under different names.

✔ Excessive pricing or demand for cryptocurrency payments.

✔ Visible signs of coercion (ads that sound scripted or posted by a third party).

🔍 **Example**: A trafficking victim was identified when OSINT analysts matched her missing persons report with an escort ad using a reverse image search.

2 OSINT Techniques for Escort & Classified Ad Monitoring

Investigators can use a combination of manual searches, automated tools, and pattern recognition to monitor these websites.

OSINT Tools & Methods:

✓ Reverse image searches (Google Lens, PimEyes, TinEye) to check if escort photos match missing persons reports.

✓ Phone number lookups (WhoCalledMe, PhoneInfoga) to trace contact details.

✓ Username cross-referencing (WhatsMyName, Namechk) to link escort profiles to social media.

✓ Web scrapers & monitoring tools (Hunchly, Scrapy) to collect and analyze bulk ad data.

✓ Metadata analysis to extract location and device details from images.

🔍 **Example**: Investigators tracked a trafficker's movements by linking their escort ads across different cities over time.

3️⃣ Case Study: Tracking a Human Trafficker Through Escort Ads

An OSINT task force monitored a series of escort ads that repeatedly used the same contact number and ad format across multiple states. By:

✓ Cross-referencing phone numbers and email addresses from ads.

✓ Using geolocation analysis on photos to find hotel locations.

✓ Linking social media accounts associated with ad posters.

✓ Tracking cryptocurrency payments made through encrypted transactions.

⚖ **Outcome**: Law enforcement arrested the trafficker, rescued multiple victims, and shut down the trafficking ring.

4️⃣ Challenges & Ethical Considerations in Escort Ad Monitoring

While OSINT is powerful, investigators must navigate legal, ethical, and privacy challenges when monitoring escort ads.

Key Challenges:

✓ Distinguishing voluntary work from trafficking victims.

✓ Ensuring data collection complies with privacy laws.

✓ Avoiding victim re-exploitation by mishandling evidence.

✓ Overcoming site takedowns and changing domains used by traffickers.

🔍 **Solution**: Collaboration with law enforcement and NGOs ensures ethical investigations while protecting victims.

Conclusion: OSINT's Role in Fighting Human Trafficking via Escort Ads

Escort and classified ad websites are a key front for human trafficking, but OSINT allows investigators to uncover hidden networks, identify victims, and track traffickers. By combining digital forensics, social media analysis, and financial tracking, law enforcement can disrupt trafficking rings and rescue victims.

🚨 No trafficker is truly anonymous in the digital age. OSINT ensures they leave a trail.

8.4 Cryptocurrency & Financial Tracking in Trafficking Cases

Introduction: The Financial Trail of Human Trafficking

Human trafficking is a multi-billion-dollar industry, and financial transactions play a crucial role in its operations. While traffickers once relied on cash transactions, they now increasingly use cryptocurrency, prepaid cards, and online payment systems to move and launder money anonymously. However, OSINT (Open-Source Intelligence) and blockchain analysis tools provide investigators with methods to track, trace, and disrupt these financial flows.

This chapter explores how cryptocurrency and financial tracking techniques are used in trafficking investigations to expose networks and bring traffickers to justice.

1️ How Human Traffickers Use Cryptocurrency & Financial Systems

Traffickers exploit both traditional banking systems and cryptocurrencies to conceal their earnings. Understanding their financial tactics is key to dismantling these networks.

Common Financial Tactics in Human Trafficking:

✓ Use of cryptocurrency payments (Bitcoin, Monero, USDT) for escort ads and dark web transactions.

✓ Money laundering through prepaid cards, gift cards, and shell companies.

✓ Frequent cash deposits & withdrawals to avoid detection.

✓ Use of peer-to-peer (P2P) transactions and crypto mixing services to erase financial trails.

✓ International money transfers through unregulated exchanges or hawala networks.

🔍 **Example**: A trafficking ring was exposed when investigators tracked Bitcoin payments from escort ad listings to a major trafficking operation.

2️ OSINT Techniques for Cryptocurrency Tracking in Trafficking Cases

Cryptocurrencies are pseudonymous, but transactions are recorded on public blockchains, allowing investigators to trace financial movements.

Key OSINT Tools & Techniques for Crypto Investigations:

✓ Blockchain Explorers (Etherscan, Blockchain.com) to track transactions.

✓ Crypto wallet tracing (Chainalysis, CipherTrace) to link wallets to real-world users.

✓ Transaction clustering analysis (Elliptic, Crystal Blockchain) to identify patterns.

✓ Dark web financial tracking to monitor illicit transactions.

✓ Monitoring crypto-to-fiat exchange points to identify traffickers cashing out their earnings.

🔍 **Example**: Law enforcement traced Monero transactions from a dark web human trafficking forum to a centralized exchange, where the trafficker converted it to fiat and withdrew funds, leading to an arrest.

3️ Investigating Money Laundering & Shell Companies

Traffickers often launder money through fake businesses, cash-intensive enterprises, and online payment services. OSINT techniques can help detect suspicious financial activity.

Methods to Uncover Money Laundering Operations:

✔ Corporate record searches (OpenCorporates, Company House) to find shell companies.

✔ Bank account analysis for unusual transactions and structuring.

✔ Tracing prepaid cards & digital wallets linked to illicit activity.

✔ Cross-referencing multiple accounts to identify money mules.

🔍 **Example**: A trafficking organization was uncovered when OSINT analysts found multiple escort websites tied to the same PayPal and Stripe accounts, linking back to a shell company.

4️ Case Study: Using OSINT to Track a Crypto-Funded Trafficking Operation

Investigators identified a trafficking network operating through a dark web marketplace where victims were being auctioned for Bitcoin. By:

✔ Tracing Bitcoin transactions from the marketplace to known crypto exchanges.

✔ Identifying linked wallet addresses and their IP locations.

✔ Following the money trail to a real-world bank account used by the trafficker.

✔ Coordinating with law enforcement to seize assets and arrest key suspects.

🚨 **Outcome**: The operation led to the rescue of 15 victims, the arrest of multiple traffickers, and the seizure of millions in cryptocurrency.

5️ Challenges & Future Trends in Financial Tracking

Despite the effectiveness of OSINT in financial investigations, traffickers are constantly evolving their tactics to avoid detection.

Key Challenges:

✔ Use of privacy coins like Monero and Zcash, which obscure transaction history.

✓ Emerging use of DeFi (Decentralized Finance) platforms for money laundering.

✓ Cross-border financial movements that require global cooperation.

🔍 **Solution**: Advancing OSINT tools and blockchain analysis capabilities will be critical to staying ahead of traffickers.

Conclusion: Following the Money to Stop Human Trafficking

Cryptocurrency and financial tracking are powerful OSINT tools in human trafficking investigations. By analyzing blockchain transactions, monitoring payment flows, and uncovering laundering networks, investigators can disrupt trafficking operations, recover illicit funds, and rescue victims.

🏛 Traffickers may hide in the shadows, but their money leaves a trail. OSINT ensures they can't escape justice.

8.5 Collaborating with NGOs & Law Enforcement Agencies

Introduction: The Power of Multi-Agency Collaboration

Fighting human trafficking requires a coordinated effort between law enforcement agencies, NGOs (non-governmental organizations), intelligence analysts, and private sector partners. Each entity brings unique expertise—law enforcement has the authority to investigate and arrest, while NGOs provide victim support, intelligence gathering, and advocacy. When these groups collaborate, OSINT (Open-Source Intelligence) investigations become more effective, leading to more rescued victims and dismantled trafficking networks.

This chapter explores how OSINT professionals, NGOs, and law enforcement agencies can work together to enhance human trafficking investigations.

1️⃣ The Role of NGOs in Human Trafficking Investigations

NGOs play a crucial role in identifying, tracking, and reporting human trafficking cases, often working in partnership with OSINT analysts.

Key Contributions of NGOs:

✔ Victim identification & support: NGOs interact directly with survivors, helping law enforcement understand trafficking patterns.

✔ Data collection & OSINT investigations: Many NGOs monitor escort ads, dark web forums, and social media to identify trafficking networks.

✔ Raising awareness & training: NGOs provide specialized training to law enforcement on trafficking trends and OSINT tools.

✔ International collaboration: Many NGOs operate across borders, providing intelligence that law enforcement might lack.

🔍 **Example**: An NGO working with OSINT analysts identified a missing minor in escort ads, leading to her rescue by law enforcement.

2️⃣ Law Enforcement's Approach to OSINT in Trafficking Cases

Law enforcement agencies use OSINT to track traffickers, gather digital evidence, and build cases for prosecution.

How Law Enforcement Uses OSINT in Trafficking Investigations:

✔ Analyzing escort and classified ads for patterns and connections.

✔ Tracking cryptocurrency transactions linked to trafficking payments.

✔ Monitoring dark web forums where traffickers discuss operations.

✔ Geolocating victims and traffickers using online content.

✔ Collaborating with financial institutions to track money laundering.

🔍 **Example**: A police department used OSINT data from an NGO's investigation to secure a search warrant for a suspected trafficker's residence.

3️⃣ Effective Collaboration Strategies Between NGOs & Law Enforcement

For collaboration to be successful, trust and clear protocols are essential.

Best Practices for Joint Investigations:

✓ Secure data-sharing channels (encrypted platforms, joint task forces).

✓ Regular coordination meetings between agencies and NGOs.

✓ Clearly defined roles to prevent duplication of efforts.

✓ Ethical handling of victim information to ensure privacy.

✓ Legal compliance in all OSINT data collection.

🔍 **Case Study**: A partnership between an NGO, OSINT analysts, and police led to a trafficking ring's takedown by tracking victims across multiple states.

4️⃣ Challenges in Multi-Agency Cooperation

Despite the benefits of collaboration, there are significant challenges that need to be addressed.

Common Barriers to NGO & Law Enforcement Collaboration:

✓ Legal restrictions on OSINT data sharing.

✓ Jurisdictional challenges in cross-border investigations.

✓ Resource limitations & funding constraints.

✓ Differing investigative priorities between NGOs and law enforcement.

🔍 **Solution**: Establishing formalized task forces and information-sharing agreements improves collaboration.

Conclusion: Strengthening the OSINT Alliance Against Human Trafficking

By combining the OSINT expertise of NGOs, the investigative power of law enforcement, and financial intelligence from private sector partners, the fight against human trafficking becomes far more effective. Collaboration ensures that no trafficker is beyond the reach of justice, and no victim is left behind.

🚨 Human traffickers thrive in secrecy—OSINT-driven collaboration ensures they have nowhere to hide.

8.6 Case Study: OSINT Techniques in a Human Trafficking Investigation

Introduction: How OSINT Helped Crack a Human Trafficking Case

Human trafficking networks thrive in the shadows, often operating across multiple jurisdictions and using the internet to advertise victims, coordinate operations, and launder money. However, OSINT (Open-Source Intelligence) tools and techniques have proven invaluable in identifying victims, tracking traffickers, and assisting law enforcement in dismantling these networks.

This case study examines a real-world human trafficking investigation where OSINT played a critical role in tracking down traffickers, rescuing victims, and bringing criminals to justice.

1⃞ The Initial Clues: Escort Ads & Missing Persons Reports

The investigation began when an NGO specializing in human trafficking OSINT flagged multiple escort ads across different classified websites. The ads shared the following red flags:

✓ Young women described as "new in town" and "no experience."

✓ Frequent location changes, suggesting movement between cities.

✓ Same contact number used across multiple ads with different names.

✓ Photos linked to a known human trafficking hotspot.

Simultaneously, a missing persons report for a 17-year-old girl matched one of the photos found in an escort ad. Investigators launched an OSINT-led digital hunt to confirm her identity and trace her whereabouts.

2⃞ Digital Footprint Analysis: Connecting the Dots

Investigators used various OSINT techniques to link the escort ads, phone numbers, and social media accounts to a suspected trafficker.

Key OSINT Methods Used:

✔ Reverse Image Search (Google Lens, PimEyes, TinEye) revealed that the photos had been reused across multiple escort sites, indicating a trafficking operation.

✔ Phone Number Lookup (TrueCaller, WhoCalledMe) traced the contact number to a burner phone linked to similar cases in multiple states.

✔ Username & Alias Cross-Referencing (WhatsMyName, Namechk) connected escort profiles to social media accounts of suspected recruiters.

✔ Social Media Monitoring of the suspected trafficker's Instagram and Snapchat revealed posts bragging about "new girls" arriving in town and images showing them in hotel rooms.

✔ Geolocation Analysis of metadata from photos and videos helped pinpoint potential locations where victims were being held.

🔍 **Breakthrough**: A Snapchat post geotagged to a hotel in Las Vegas provided a real-time location where victims were being moved.

3️ Cryptocurrency & Financial Tracking: Following the Money

Since traffickers often use cryptocurrency for illicit payments, the OSINT team analyzed financial transactions linked to the escort ads.

✔ Blockchain Explorer Tools (Etherscan, BitcoinWhosWho) were used to track Bitcoin transactions from escort ad payments.

✔ Cryptocurrency Exchange Monitoring helped link a wallet address to a known crypto-to-cash conversion service.

✔ Financial Records & Shell Company Searches revealed that the trafficker had laundered earnings through prepaid debit cards and fake business accounts.

🔍 **Breakthrough**: A major financial transaction linked to one of the escort ads led to the identification of the trafficker's real-world bank account.

4⃞ Law Enforcement Coordination & Arrests

With sufficient digital evidence collected through OSINT, investigators collaborated with law enforcement agencies and anti-trafficking NGOs to plan a rescue operation.

✓ Law enforcement obtained warrants using OSINT findings as probable cause.

✓ Hotel security footage matched the geolocated Snapchat posts, confirming victim presence.

✓ Undercover officers booked an escort service and tracked the trafficker's movements.

✓ Police raided multiple locations, rescuing several trafficking victims, including the missing 17-year-old.

🚨 **Outcome**: The trafficker was arrested, charged with human trafficking, and sentenced to 25 years in prison.

5⃞ Challenges & Lessons Learned

Challenges Faced During the Investigation:

✓ Traffickers frequently change phone numbers and usernames to evade detection.

✓ Cryptocurrency obfuscation techniques (mixers, Monero) made financial tracking complex.

✓ Victims were reluctant to cooperate due to fear and manipulation.

Lessons Learned & Future Recommendations:

✓ Continuous OSINT monitoring of escort ads helps detect trafficking networks early.

✓ Collaboration between NGOs, law enforcement, and OSINT specialists is crucial.

✓ Advanced blockchain analytics tools are necessary to follow illicit financial flows.

Conclusion: The Power of OSINT in Human Trafficking Investigations

This case study highlights how OSINT techniques—social media analysis, cryptocurrency tracking, and geolocation intelligence—helped law enforcement track down a trafficker, rescue victims, and shut down a criminal operation.

🚨 Traffickers may try to hide in the digital world, but OSINT ensures they leave a trace.

9. Terrorism & Extremist OSINT Monitoring

This chapter delves into the use of OSINT in monitoring and investigating terrorism and extremist activities. With the rise of online radicalization and the increasing use of digital platforms by terrorist groups and extremists, OSINT has become an essential tool for identifying threats and preventing attacks. We will examine how investigators track extremist content, analyze social media networks, and monitor online communications to identify individuals or groups planning violent actions. Through case studies and practical insights, this chapter illustrates how OSINT techniques help law enforcement and intelligence agencies stay ahead of evolving threats in the digital landscape, ensuring public safety and national security.

9.1 Understanding How Extremist Groups Use the Internet

Introduction: The Digital Battleground of Extremism

Extremist groups have increasingly turned to the internet to recruit members, spread propaganda, plan attacks, and evade law enforcement. From terrorist organizations to radical ideological movements, these groups leverage a wide range of online platforms—including social media, encrypted messaging apps, and the dark web—to further their agendas.

Understanding how these groups operate in the digital sphere is crucial for intelligence analysts, law enforcement, and counterterrorism specialists. OSINT (Open-Source Intelligence) plays a key role in tracking extremist activities, identifying threats, and disrupting networks before they can act.

1⃣ The Digital Ecosystem of Extremist Groups

Extremists use a variety of online platforms to communicate, recruit, and spread their ideology. These platforms can be divided into three main categories:

1. Surface Web Platforms (Public & Widely Used)

✔ Social Media (Twitter/X, Facebook, Instagram, TikTok): Used for recruitment, propaganda, and narrative-building.

✓ Video & Streaming Platforms (YouTube, Telegram, Odysee, Rumble): Used to share radical speeches, training videos, and attack footage.

✓ News & Blog Websites: Extremist groups create their own "news" platforms to spread misinformation and attract sympathizers.

🔍 **Example**: ISIS heavily used Twitter and Telegram to distribute propaganda and recruit foreign fighters.

2. Encrypted Messaging & Dark Web Forums

✓ Encrypted Messaging Apps (Telegram, WhatsApp, Signal, Wickr, Element): Used for secure communication, coordination of attacks, and recruitment.

✓ Dark Web Forums: Hidden sites where radicals discuss tactics, weapons, and terror financing.

✓ Gaming Platforms (Discord, Steam, Roblox): Used to secretly communicate using code words and in-game chats.

🔍 **Example**: Far-right groups have used Discord servers to coordinate violent rallies while extremists have used gaming chats to avoid surveillance.

3. Decentralized & Anonymous Networks

✓ Blockchain-based platforms: Used to spread uncensored extremist material.

✓ Peer-to-Peer (P2P) networks: Allows groups to communicate without a centralized server.

✓ Privacy-focused social media (Gab, Minds, 8kun): Used to evade content moderation on mainstream platforms.

🔍 **Example**: QAnon conspiracy networks moved to Gab and Telegram after being de-platformed from mainstream sites.

2️⃣ How Extremist Groups Leverage the Internet

Extremist groups use digital tools for several key activities, including:

1. Recruitment & Radicalization

✓ Extremists target young, vulnerable individuals using social media and online forums.

✓ They create high-quality propaganda videos and interactive content to glorify violence and extremist ideology.

✓ Radical groups build online communities where potential recruits feel a sense of belonging.

🔍 **Example**: ISIS's online magazine Dabiq was used to recruit foreign fighters and justify terrorism.

2. Propaganda & Misinformation

✓ Extremists spread fake news, conspiracy theories, and doctored videos to influence public perception.

✓ They hijack trending hashtags to push their narratives into mainstream conversations.

✓ Groups use memes and humor to make radical ideas more appealing.

🔍 **Example**: Neo-Nazi groups have used humor-based memes on 4chan and Telegram to disguise extremist messaging.

3. Operational Planning & Coordination

✓ Encrypted apps and dark web forums are used to plan terror attacks, riots, and recruitment events.

✓ Extremists share bomb-making instructions and tactical manuals.

✓ Some groups even use video games and virtual reality spaces for training simulations.

🔍 **Example**: The Christchurch shooter live-streamed the attack on Facebook, inspiring copycats worldwide.

4. Fundraising & Financial Networks

✓ Extremists use cryptocurrency (Bitcoin, Monero) to fund operations anonymously.

✓ Crowdfunding and fake charities are set up to collect donations under false pretenses.

✓ Some groups sell merchandise, digital content, or hold "fundraiser" events.

🔍 **Example**: Al-Qaeda used PayPal and GoFundMe-like platforms to secretly finance terror operations.

3️ OSINT Techniques for Monitoring Extremist Online Activity

How OSINT Helps in Counter-Extremism Efforts:

✓ Social Media Monitoring: Tracking keywords, hashtags, and extremist accounts.

✓ Geolocation Analysis: Identifying training camps, attack locations, or safe houses.

✓ Digital Footprint Analysis: Mapping extremist networks, aliases, and linked accounts.

✓ Dark Web & Deep Web Monitoring: Collecting intelligence from hidden forums and encrypted channels.

✓ Sentiment Analysis & Trend Prediction: Detecting rising threats before they escalate into real-world violence.

📖 **Example**: OSINT helped uncover an ISIS sleeper cell by tracking Telegram activity and cryptocurrency transactions.

4️ Challenges in Monitoring Online Extremism

Key Challenges in OSINT & Counter-Extremism:

✓ Encrypted platforms limit direct monitoring.

✓ Extremists use code words & hidden meanings to avoid detection.

✓ Legal & ethical concerns about privacy and data collection.

✓ Rapidly changing platforms as extremists migrate to new digital spaces.

🔍 **Solution**: Analysts must use AI-driven tools, linguistic analysis, and cross-platform tracking to stay ahead of evolving threats.

Conclusion: The Evolving Digital Front of Extremism

Extremist groups continue to evolve their online tactics, using new technologies, hidden networks, and encrypted tools to spread their ideologies. OSINT remains a critical weapon in detecting, tracking, and disrupting extremist operations before they escalate into violence.

🏛 By understanding how extremists use the internet, OSINT professionals can dismantle digital radicalization efforts and help prevent future attacks.

9.2 Identifying Radicalization Indicators Online

Introduction: The Digital Path to Radicalization

Radicalization is a process where individuals adopt extremist ideologies and, in some cases, progress toward violence. The internet has become a powerful incubator for radical beliefs, providing extremist groups with tools to recruit, influence, and mobilize individuals globally. OSINT (Open-Source Intelligence) is crucial in identifying early signs of radicalization online before individuals transition to real-world extremist actions.

This section explores the key indicators of online radicalization, how to detect them using OSINT tools, and the challenges of monitoring digital extremism.

1️⃣ Understanding the Radicalization Process

Radicalization is not an overnight transformation; it occurs in stages as individuals become more immersed in extremist ideologies.

The 4-Stage Radicalization Model

1⃞ **Exposure & Curiosity** → The individual encounters extremist content through social media, forums, or peer influence.

2⃞ **Engagement & Identity Formation** → They start interacting with extremist content, joining online discussions, and adopting ideological beliefs.

3⃞ **Commitment & Group Affiliation** → The individual aligns with a radical group, adopts extremist narratives, and rejects alternative viewpoints.

4⃞ **Mobilization & Action** → They become actively involved, which may include spreading propaganda, planning attacks, or engaging in violence.

🔎 OSINT can detect and intervene in early stages before individuals reach mobilization.

2⃞ Key Indicators of Online Radicalization

1. Ideological Shifts & Behavioral Changes

✓ Increased engagement with extremist narratives (e.g., "us vs. them" mentality).

✓ Rejection of mainstream news sources and reliance on extremist "alternative media."

✓ Use of conspiracy theories to justify radical beliefs.

🔍 **OSINT Monitoring Tip**: Track changes in language, posting frequency, and ideological references in forums and social media.

2. Social Media & Online Community Involvement

✓ Following or engaging with known extremist influencers, groups, and channels.

✓ Active participation in hate forums, encrypted chat rooms, or extremist subreddits.

✓ Sharing, liking, or commenting on radical videos, manifestos, or propaganda materials.

🔍 **OSINT Monitoring Tip**: Use social media analysis tools to map connections between users, hashtags, and extremist networks.

3. Adopting Extremist Symbols & Language

✔ Using extremist hashtags, symbols, or coded language (e.g., "1488" for white supremacists).

✔ Memes & digital propaganda to subtly spread radical ideas.

✔ References to violent events or figures associated with extremism.

🔍 **OSINT Monitoring Tip**: Utilize image analysis tools to identify extremist imagery across different platforms.

4. Isolation & Echo Chamber Behavior

✔ Rejecting opposing viewpoints and unfollowing non-extremist contacts.

✔ Engagement in closed or invite-only radical groups.

✔ Expressing paranoia about government, law enforcement, or "big tech censorship."

🔍 **OSINT Monitoring Tip**: Identify users who migrate from mainstream to fringe platforms (e.g., from Twitter to Telegram or Gab).

5. Calls for Action & Violent Rhetoric

✔ Expressing support for violence or past terror attacks.

✔ Directly threatening individuals, groups, or government institutions.

✔ Discussing weapons, attack strategies, or martyrdom.

🚨 **Most Critical OSINT Red Flag**: When an individual transitions from passive radicalization to planning violent actions.

3️⃣ OSINT Techniques for Detecting Radicalization Online

1. Social Media & Forum Monitoring

✔ Track extremist-related hashtags, phrases, and keywords (e.g., "Day of the Rope" for far-right extremism).

✓ Monitor migration from mainstream to alternative platforms like Telegram, 4chan, or Rumble.

✓ Use NLP (Natural Language Processing) tools to detect increasingly radical rhetoric.

2. Digital Footprint Analysis

✓ Cross-reference usernames, emails, and IPs to connect individuals to radical networks.

✓ Identify linked accounts across multiple platforms using OSINT tools like WhatsMyName.

✓ Analyze radicalized users' digital history (e.g., past aliases, previous interactions).

3. Video & Image Analysis

✓ Extract metadata from shared extremist images to determine origin & spread.

✓ Use AI-based image recognition to detect extremist symbols, hand signs, and flags.

✓ Track reposted terrorist content across platforms using reverse image search.

4. Network Mapping & Behavioral Analytics

✓ Identify connections between users by analyzing followers, reposts, and mentions.

✓ Detect abnormal spikes in engagement (e.g., sudden radicalization surges).

✓ Monitor dark web forums & encrypted groups for early warnings of attack planning.

4⃣ Challenges in Monitoring Radicalization Online

1. Privacy & Ethical Concerns

✓ Balance between surveillance & individual privacy rights.

✓ Legal restrictions on collecting and storing user data.

✓ The risk of false positives when identifying radical users.

2. Code Words & Evasion Tactics

✓ Extremists use coded language, abbreviations, and memes to bypass detection.

✓ Groups constantly shift platforms when their networks are exposed.

✓ Encryption makes direct monitoring of private chats difficult.

3. AI & Deepfake Propaganda

✓ Extremists use AI-generated videos and voice cloning to manipulate narratives.

✓ Automated radicalization bots push extremist content at scale.

✓ Deepfake technology enables the spread of false statements attributed to public figures.

🔍 **Solution**: OSINT analysts must continuously adapt by using AI-based monitoring and behavioral analytics tools.

Conclusion: The Importance of OSINT in Preventing Radicalization

Radicalization is a complex and evolving threat, but OSINT offers a powerful set of tools to detect early warning signs, track extremist activities, and prevent violence before it occurs.

By monitoring ideological shifts, social media behavior, extremist symbols, and online interactions, intelligence analysts can identify individuals at risk and disrupt radical networks.

📷 The fight against online extremism requires constant vigilance, adaptive OSINT techniques, and ethical intelligence gathering.

9.3 Tracking Extremist Recruitment & Propaganda Networks

Introduction: The Digital Battlefield for Minds

Extremist groups use the internet as a powerful recruitment tool, spreading propaganda to attract, radicalize, and mobilize individuals. From terrorist organizations to far-right and far-left extremist movements, these groups operate sophisticated online recruitment networks that exploit social media, encrypted messaging apps, and hidden forums to spread their ideologies.

For OSINT (Open-Source Intelligence) analysts and law enforcement, tracking these recruitment and propaganda efforts is critical for disrupting extremist networks before they can inspire real-world violence. This chapter explores how extremists recruit online, the platforms they use, and OSINT techniques for identifying and dismantling these networks.

1 How Extremist Groups Recruit Online

Extremists target vulnerable individuals who may be disillusioned, isolated, or seeking a sense of belonging. Their recruitment tactics follow a structured "grooming" process, much like human traffickers or cult organizations.

The 4-Stage Recruitment Process

◆ 1. Exposure:

- A potential recruit encounters extremist content (videos, memes, forums) through social media or encrypted apps.
- Extremists exploit current events to attract attention (e.g., political unrest, economic crises).
- Recruitment messages use clickbait headlines and emotionally charged content.

◆ 2. Engagement:

- Recruits begin interacting with extremist content (commenting, sharing, joining chat groups).
- Extremists use personalized messaging to establish a connection.
- Grooming tactics reinforce grievances (e.g., blaming specific groups for social problems).

◆ 3. Indoctrination:

- The recruit is invited into private channels where deeper ideological conditioning happens.
- Extremists introduce conspiracy theories, ideological texts, and "us vs. them" narratives.
- Recruits are encouraged to cut off mainstream influences (news, family, friends).

◆ 4. Mobilization:

- Recruits are pushed to act—whether through spreading propaganda, financing operations, or committing violent acts.
- Some are guided toward direct action, such as terror attacks, riots, or cyber warfare.
- Extremists use encrypted channels and in-person meetings for final mobilization.

📟 OSINT analysts must track recruitment at early stages to prevent radicalization from escalating to real-world violence.

2️⃣ Key Platforms Used for Extremist Recruitment

1. Social Media & Video Platforms

✓ Mainstream platforms (Twitter/X, Facebook, YouTube, TikTok, Instagram)

✓ Alternative platforms (Rumble, Odysee, VK, Gab, Parler, Truth Social)

✓ Live-streaming & video-sharing sites used for extremist speeches and attack glorification.

🔍 OSINT Tracking Tip:

Monitor trending extremist hashtags, viral videos, and propaganda accounts.

Use keyword analysis tools to track radical discussions.

2. Encrypted Messaging Apps

✓ Telegram, WhatsApp, Signal, Wickr, Element

✓ Used for private indoctrination, attack planning, and real-time coordination.

🔍 OSINT Tracking Tip:

Monitor public extremist Telegram channels before they transition to private groups.

Track alias migration across multiple apps.

3. Dark Web & Private Forums

✓ 4chan, 8kun, Stormfront, Iron March (far-right forums)

✓ Al-Qaeda & ISIS dark web sites for training manuals and jihadist propaganda.

🔍 OSINT Tracking Tip:

- Use dark web crawlers to scan extremist forums.
- Extract metadata from extremist PDFs, manuals, and manifestos.

4. Online Games & Virtual Spaces

✓ Discord, Steam, Roblox, Minecraft

✓ Used by extremists to recruit younger audiences and spread coded messages.

🔍 OSINT Tracking Tip:

- Monitor gaming chat servers for radical discussions.
- Identify gamers using extremist usernames linked to known figures or events.

3️⃣ OSINT Techniques for Tracking Recruitment Networks

1. Social Media Network Mapping

✓ Identify key influencers spreading propaganda.

✓ Map follower connections, reposts, and content amplification patterns.

✓ Track migration from mainstream platforms to extremist-friendly sites.

🔍 **Example**: Analyzing Telegram groups that cross-promote extremist content from other platforms.

2. AI-Powered Sentiment & Keyword Analysis

✓ Track rising extremist narratives in online conversations.

✓ Detect coded language, symbols, and recruitment slogans.

✓ Identify emerging threats before they escalate.

🔍 **Example**: Tracking the use of coded language like "boogaloo" (civil war reference) in far-right recruitment.

3. Reverse Image & Video Search

✓ Identify propaganda images reposted across multiple platforms.

✓ Use hash-matching tools to track extremist videos & attack footage.

✓ Extract metadata from extremist content (upload date, location).

🔍 **Example**: Using Google Reverse Image Search to find ISIS propaganda posters shared across different forums.

4. Cryptocurrency & Financial Transaction Tracking

✓ Track extremist fundraising via Bitcoin, Monero, or online donation sites.

✓ Monitor extremist-backed crowdfunding campaigns.

✓ Follow blockchain transactions linked to radical groups.

🔍 **Example**: Investigating Hamas-linked Bitcoin wallets used for funding operations.

4️⃣ Case Study: OSINT Uncovering an Extremist Recruitment Network

Case: ISIS Telegram Recruitment Ring

📌 **Problem**: Intelligence analysts suspected that ISIS was using Telegram to recruit Western foreign fighters.

📌 **OSINT Investigation:**

◆ Analysts monitored public Telegram channels for recruitment activity.
◆ They identified key influencers spreading jihadist propaganda.
◆ Using network mapping, they tracked recruits migrating from YouTube to Telegram.

◆ Investigators cross-referenced usernames across multiple extremist forums.

◆ Analysts uncovered Bitcoin transactions linked to extremist fundraising efforts.

📌 **Outcome**: The network was disrupted when Telegram deleted multiple channels, and authorities arrested key recruiters.

🔎 **Key Takeaway**: OSINT was essential in tracking recruitment pathways and stopping the radicalization process before recruits could take action.

5️⃣ Challenges in Tracking Extremist Recruitment

1. Encrypted & Decentralized Platforms

✓ Private Telegram channels, Signal groups, and blockchain-based platforms make tracking harder.

✓ Solution: Infiltrating public groups before they transition to encrypted spaces.

2. Coded Language & Evasion Tactics

✓ Extremists use memes, symbols, and alternative spellings to evade detection.

✓ Solution: Use AI-driven linguistic analysis tools to detect emerging code words.

3. Legal & Ethical Limitations

✓ Privacy laws restrict covert tracking and data collection.

✓ Solution: Focus on open-source intelligence and publicly available data.

Conclusion: The Role of OSINT in Stopping Online Extremist Recruitment

Extremist recruitment networks continue to evolve, using new platforms, encrypted tools, and psychological manipulation to radicalize individuals. OSINT provides critical insights into recruitment pathways, propaganda dissemination, and extremist financial networks.

🔎 By leveraging advanced monitoring tools, network mapping, and financial tracking, OSINT analysts can disrupt extremist recruitment and prevent radicalization before it leads to violence.

9.4 Investigating Online Hate Groups & Domestic Terrorism

Introduction: The Digital Rise of Hate & Domestic Terrorism
The internet has provided hate groups and domestic terrorists with an unprecedented platform to recruit, organize, and incite violence. From white supremacist movements to radical anti-government militias, extremist networks operate across social media, encrypted apps, dark web forums, and even online gaming communities.

For OSINT (Open-Source Intelligence) analysts and law enforcement, investigating these groups is critical for preventing violent attacks, dismantling propaganda networks, and disrupting radicalization pipelines. This chapter explores how online hate groups operate, their digital footprints, and OSINT techniques for tracking their activities.

1️⃣ Understanding Hate Groups & Domestic Terrorism Online

What Defines a Hate Group?

A hate group is any organization that promotes hostility or violence against individuals based on race, ethnicity, religion, gender, or other identities. These groups often spread misinformation, promote conspiracy theories, and incite harassment campaigns.

What Defines Domestic Terrorism?

Domestic terrorism involves politically or ideologically motivated violence against civilians within a nation's borders. Unlike foreign terrorist organizations (e.g., ISIS, Al-Qaeda), domestic terrorists are typically homegrown extremists radicalized through online networks.

Types of Online Hate Groups & Domestic Extremists

✓ **White Supremacists & Neo-Nazis** – Operate through forums like Stormfront, Telegram, and Discord.

✓ **Anti-Government Militias** – Spread anti-state propaganda on platforms like Rumble, Gab, and 4chan.

✓ **Religious Extremists** – Use social media to recruit and justify violence.

✓ **Incels (Involuntary Celibates)** – Misogynistic hate groups promoting attacks on women.

✓ **Accelerationists** – Advocate for societal collapse through violent actions.

📷 OSINT analysts must identify and monitor these groups before their online rhetoric turns into real-world violence.

2️⃣ How Hate Groups & Domestic Terrorists Use the Internet

Extremist groups adapt to online censorship by constantly shifting platforms and using coded language. Their tactics include:

1. Social Media Propaganda & Recruitment

✓ Mainstream platforms (Facebook, Twitter/X, TikTok, Instagram)

✓ Alternative platforms (Gab, Truth Social, VK, Odysee, Parler)

✓ Live streaming to spread extremist views and radicalize followers

🔍 **OSINT Tip**: Track hashtags, extremist memes, and viral propaganda trends.

2. Encrypted Messaging & Private Forums

✓ Telegram, Signal, Wickr, Element for organizing and radicalizing followers

✓ Dark web forums & private chatrooms to avoid detection

🔍 **OSINT Tip**: Infiltrate public extremist Telegram groups before they migrate to private chats.

3. Crowdfunding & Cryptocurrency Funding

✓ Hate groups use GoFundMe alternatives and cryptocurrency donations to finance operations.

✓ Some sell merchandise (flags, books, apparel) to generate income.

🔍 **OSINT Tip**: Use blockchain analysis tools to track extremist Bitcoin transactions.

4. Online Gaming & Meme Culture

✓ Hate groups exploit gaming platforms (Discord, Steam, Roblox, Twitch) to recruit younger members.

✓ Extremists use memes, coded language, and humor to disguise propaganda.

🔍 **OSINT Tip**: Monitor Discord servers and extremist-linked usernames.

3️⃣ OSINT Techniques for Investigating Online Hate Groups

1. Social Media Mapping & Hashtag Tracking

✓ Identify key influencers spreading extremist content.

✓ Track viral hate speech hashtags and posts.

✓ Use graph analysis tools to map follower networks.

🔍 **Example**: Tracking the spread of #WhiteGenocide across Telegram and Twitter/X.

2. Forum & Dark Web Monitoring

✓ Monitor hate forums like 4chan, 8kun, Iron March.

✓ Extract metadata from extremist PDFs, manifestos, and posts.

✓ Use OSINT dark web crawlers to scan for threats.

🔍 **Example**: Uncovering discussions on weaponizing drones for domestic attacks.

3. AI-Powered Sentiment & Language Analysis

✓ Detect coded extremist phrases & recruitment messages.

✓ Identify emerging threats before they escalate.

✓ Analyze meme propaganda trends used for radicalization.

🔍 **Example**: Detecting the rise of "Day of the Rope" rhetoric in far-right groups.

4. Financial & Cryptocurrency Investigation

✓ Track crypto wallets linked to hate group funding.

✓ Identify extremist merchandise stores & crowdfunding efforts.

✓ Use blockchain forensics tools to follow money trails.

🔍 **Example**: Investigating Bitcoin wallets linked to The Base, a violent accelerationist group.

4️⃣ Case Study: OSINT Uncovering a Domestic Terrorist Plot

Case: The 2020 Boogaloo Movement Arrests

📌 **Problem**: U.S. intelligence suspected that Boogaloo extremists were planning attacks against law enforcement.

📌 **OSINT Investigation:**

◆ Analysts monitored Facebook groups & Reddit threads where members discussed "civil war."
◆ Investigators tracked encrypted Telegram channels coordinating attacks.
◆ OSINT experts analyzed Bitcoin donations to Boogaloo influencers.
◆ Law enforcement infiltrated extremist Discord servers to gather intelligence.

📌 **Outcome**: Multiple arrests were made, and authorities disrupted Boogaloo-linked attacks before they happened.

🏛 **Key Takeaway**: OSINT was crucial in detecting, monitoring, and dismantling the network before violence could erupt.

5️⃣ Challenges in Investigating Online Hate Groups

1. Encrypted & Decentralized Networks

✓ Extremists use Telegram, Signal, and self-hosted forums to evade detection.

✓ Solution: Monitor public forums before extremists migrate to private groups.

2. Coded Language & Symbolism

✓ Extremists use dog whistles, memes, and historical references to communicate.

✓ Solution: Use AI to track new extremist phrases and coded discussions.

3. Legal & Ethical Limitations

✓ Privacy laws restrict covert OSINT investigations on private platforms.

✓ Solution: Focus on open-source data and publicly available intelligence.

Conclusion: Using OSINT to Combat Online Hate & Domestic Terrorism

Online hate groups and domestic terrorists use digital platforms to recruit, radicalize, and plan attacks. OSINT analysts must stay ahead by tracking extremist movements, monitoring encrypted communications, and mapping propaganda networks.

🚨 By leveraging advanced social media analytics, dark web tracking, and financial OSINT, investigators can disrupt extremist threats before they escalate into real-world violence.

9.5 Monitoring Deep & Dark Web Forums for Threat Intelligence

Introduction: The Hidden World of Extremist & Criminal Networks

While much of the internet is easily accessible, a significant portion—the deep and dark web—remains hidden from traditional search engines. This concealed part of the web is home to criminal enterprises, extremist groups, and illicit markets, making it a crucial area for OSINT investigations.

Law enforcement agencies, security analysts, and counterterrorism units must monitor dark web forums, encrypted marketplaces, and hidden extremist networks to gather threat intelligence, track radicalization trends, and prevent violent attacks. This chapter explores OSINT techniques for deep and dark web monitoring, tools used in investigations, and challenges faced in this domain.

1⃣ Understanding the Deep & Dark Web

What is the Deep Web?

The deep web refers to any content not indexed by standard search engines like Google or Bing. This includes:

✔ Private databases

✔ Government records

✔ Subscription-based content

✔ Encrypted communications

📌 **Example**: Academic databases, internal company portals, and cloud storage systems.

What is the Dark Web?

The dark web is a small portion of the deep web that requires special software (e.g., Tor, I2P) to access. It is often used for:

✔ Illegal marketplaces (drugs, weapons, stolen data)

✔ Extremist forums & recruitment hubs

✔ Fraud, hacking, and cybercrime networks

📌 **Example**: The now-defunct Silk Road, an infamous dark web marketplace for illegal drugs.

🔍 **Why It Matters for OSINT**: The dark web is a hub for criminal intelligence, extremist coordination, and cyber threats. Monitoring it helps identify emerging risks before they reach mainstream platforms.

2⃣ How Extremist Groups & Criminals Use the Dark Web

1. Extremist Recruitment & Radicalization

✓ Encrypted dark web forums serve as meeting places for terrorist groups.

✓ ISIS, Al-Qaeda, and domestic terror groups use hidden sites to share propaganda, manuals, and attack planning guides.

🔍 **OSINT Tip**: Monitor forums and encrypted messaging platforms for coded language and calls to action.

2. Illicit Marketplaces & Weapons Trade

✓ Dark web markets sell stolen data, firearms, and even explosives.

✓ Cryptocurrencies like Bitcoin and Monero allow anonymous transactions.

🔍 **OSINT Tip**: Use blockchain analysis tools to trace illicit financial transactions.

3. Doxxing & Targeted Attacks

✓ Hate groups and cybercriminals leak personal data of activists, journalists, and public figures.

✓ Swatting attacks and harassment campaigns are often coordinated through dark web forums.

🔍 **OSINT Tip**: Track mentions of high-risk targets across dark web data dumps.

4. Coordinated Cyber Attacks

✓ Hacktivist groups (e.g., Anonymous) use dark web forums to plan DDoS attacks, ransomware campaigns, and breaches.

✓ Leaked government/military data often appears first in dark web communities.

🔍 **OSINT Tip**: Monitor cybercriminal marketplaces for stolen credentials and exploit kits.

3️⃣ OSINT Techniques for Dark Web Monitoring

1. Accessing & Navigating the Dark Web

✓ Use Tor Browser or I2P to access dark web forums.

✓ Employ operational security (OPSEC) to avoid tracking and exposure.

✓ Leverage dark web monitoring tools to track illicit activity.

🔍 **Example**: Searching for extremist manifestos on dark web paste sites.

2. Identifying Key Forums & Marketplaces

✓ Monitor extremist recruitment sites, hacker forums, and illegal marketplaces.

✓ Extract metadata from hidden wiki pages to find new dark web locations.

🔍 **Example**: Tracking darknet drug markets like Hydra for criminal connections.

3. Analyzing Encrypted Communications

✓ Identify Telegram & IRC channels linked to dark web groups.

✓ Use linguistic analysis to track extremist recruitment messages.

🔍 **Example**: Analyzing Islamic State propaganda PDFs for hidden metadata.

4. Blockchain & Cryptocurrency Analysis

✓ Trace Bitcoin & Monero transactions linked to illicit dark web sales.

✓ Follow money trails to identify key players funding extremist groups.

🔍 **Example**: Investigating crypto wallets funding neo-Nazi groups.

4️⃣ Tools for Dark Web OSINT Investigations

Dark Web Monitoring Tools

✓ **SpiderFoot** – Automates dark web searches for threats.

✓ **DarkOwl Vision** – Tracks darknet activity and criminal enterprises.

✓ **CipherTrace** – Analyzes cryptocurrency transactions for illicit funding.

✓ **TORBot** – Scrapes Tor network pages for relevant keywords.

Cryptocurrency Tracking Tools

✓ **Chainalysis** – Identifies illicit Bitcoin transactions.

✓ **Elliptic** – Provides risk assessment of crypto transactions.

✓ **TRM Labs** – Helps law enforcement follow the money trail in dark web investigations.

Social Media & Threat Intelligence Tools

✓ **Maltego** – Visualizes relationships between dark web actors.

✓ **Shodan** – Maps exposed servers used by cybercriminals.

✓ **CheckPhish** – Detects dark web phishing sites.

5️⃣ Case Study: OSINT Uncovering a Terrorist Financing Network

Case: Tracking Terrorist Funding via Dark Web & Crypto

📌 **Problem**: Authorities suspected a terrorist cell was using the dark web to fund attacks.

📌 **OSINT Investigation:**

◆ Analysts monitored hidden Telegram channels where terrorists shared Bitcoin donation links.
◆ Investigators tracked blockchain transactions from dark web forums to extremist crypto wallets.
◆ OSINT experts scraped dark web marketplaces for financial transactions linked to extremist groups.

📌 **Outcome**: Authorities froze crypto accounts used for terrorist financing and arrested key operatives.

🔔 **Key Takeaway**: Dark web monitoring combined with blockchain analysis can uncover hidden financial networks used for terrorism.

6️⃣ Challenges in Dark Web Monitoring

1. Anonymity & Encryption

✓ Dark web users hide behind Tor, VPNs, and encrypted messaging.

✓ Solution: Focus on metadata, transaction trails, and pattern analysis.

2. Rapidly Changing Dark Web Sites

✓ Marketplaces and forums frequently change URLs or go offline.

✓ Solution: Use web scraping and darknet crawlers to track new sites.

3. Legal & Ethical Restrictions

✓ Many dark web investigations involve privacy concerns and legal limitations.

✓ Solution: Work within jurisdictional laws and collaborate with law enforcement.

Conclusion: The Importance of OSINT in Dark Web Threat Intelligence

The deep and dark web are critical battlegrounds for criminal activity, extremist networks, and cyber threats. OSINT analysts must develop advanced monitoring techniques, leverage specialized tools, and collaborate with intelligence agencies to track these hidden threats effectively.

🔔 By staying ahead of emerging trends, law enforcement and security professionals can disrupt criminal enterprises, prevent terrorist financing, and mitigate cyber threats before they escalate.

9.6 Case Study: How OSINT Helped Prevent an Extremist Attack

Introduction: The Power of OSINT in Counterterrorism

In an era where extremist groups increasingly use digital platforms for recruitment, propaganda, and attack planning, OSINT (Open-Source Intelligence) has become a critical tool for early threat detection. This case study explores how intelligence analysts used OSINT techniques to identify, track, and disrupt an extremist plot before it materialized into violence.

By monitoring online forums, tracking suspicious financial transactions, and analyzing social media activity, investigators were able to uncover a terror cell's plans and intervene before an attack occurred. This case highlights the real-world impact of OSINT in national security and counterterrorism efforts.

1️⃣ The Threat Emerges: Suspicious Online Activity

📌 **Timeline**: A European intelligence agency detected an increase in extremist chatter across several online platforms, including encrypted messaging apps and dark web forums.

📌 **OSINT Indicators:**

◆ A new extremist manifesto surfaced on a hidden forum, promoting violent jihadist ideology.

◆ Investigators identified encrypted Telegram channels discussing a potential attack.

◆ A dark web vendor selling explosives and firearms had increased transactions from anonymous Bitcoin wallets.

🔍 **Key Finding**: Analysts flagged several radicalized individuals who had recently pledged allegiance to a known extremist group.

2️⃣ Unmasking the Suspects: Digital Footprints & OSINT Profiling

Using OSINT techniques, investigators pieced together digital identities of the individuals involved.

✓ **Social Media Cross-Referencing**: Analysts linked extremist usernames from dark web forums to Twitter, Facebook, and Discord accounts.

✓ **IP & VPN Leak Analysis**: Despite using VPNs and Tor, some individuals accidentally exposed real IP addresses in forum metadata.

✓ **Behavioral Analysis**: The suspects followed key extremist figures and engaged in encrypted discussions about explosives, attack strategies, and target locations.

✓ **Geolocation OSINT**: Investigators analyzed photos and videos shared in extremist chat rooms, using EXIF data to pinpoint potential training locations.

🏛 **Key Finding**: The suspects were identified as a local terror cell planning an attack in a major city.

3️⃣ Tracking Financial Transactions & Weapons Procurement

Investigators shifted focus to financial tracking, suspecting the group was purchasing weapons and supplies.

✓ **Cryptocurrency Tracing**: Using Chainalysis and Elliptic, OSINT analysts followed Bitcoin transactions linked to dark web arms dealers.

✓ **E-Commerce OSINT**: Some suspects had purchased bomb-making materials on the surface web, using anonymous prepaid cards.

✓ **Crowdfunding Investigation**: Investigators identified a suspicious GoFundMe campaign disguised as a charity drive, funneling money to the terror cell.

🏛 **Key Finding**: The group had successfully procured firearms and chemicals needed to create explosives.

4️⃣ Intercepting Communications & Identifying the Target

As the investigation deepened, OSINT teams monitored encrypted discussions to determine the intended target.

✓ **Telegram & WhatsApp Monitoring**: Despite encryption, analysts tracked group members' movement patterns through open-source metadata leaks.

✓ **Forum & Manifesto Analysis**: The extremists discussed high-profile public events as potential attack locations.

✓ **Language Processing AI**: By applying sentiment analysis to extremist conversations, OSINT tools predicted an imminent attack timeframe.

🏛 **Key Finding**: The group planned to target a government building during a public event in two weeks.

5️⃣ Law Enforcement Intervention: Stopping the Attack

📌 Armed with detailed OSINT intelligence, the counterterrorism unit took swift action:

✓ **Raids & Arrests**: Authorities arrested all identified cell members before they could act.

✓ **Seizure of Weapons & Explosives**: A raid uncovered firearms, homemade explosives, and digital evidence linking them to terror groups.

✓ **Dark Web Shutdown**: Investigators worked with cybersecurity agencies to take down extremist forums and disrupt communications.

🏛 **Outcome**: The planned attack was successfully thwarted, preventing mass casualties.

Conclusion: OSINT as a Life-Saving Tool

This case highlights how OSINT plays a crucial role in counterterrorism by providing:

✓ Early warning signs of extremist activity

✓ Advanced tracking of digital footprints & financial transactions

✓ Critical intelligence that enables preemptive action

💡 **Key Takeaway**: OSINT is no longer just an investigative tool—it is a frontline defense mechanism against global security threats.

10. Case Study: Using OSINT in a Cold Case

In this chapter, we explore a compelling case study demonstrating the power of OSINT in solving a cold case. Cold cases, often shrouded in time and incomplete evidence, can be revitalized with the help of digital intelligence tools that uncover new leads and connect dots previously missed. We will walk through the investigative process, showing how OSINT techniques—such as analyzing social media activity, tracing digital footprints, and cross-referencing historical data—can breathe new life into a case. By examining how modern technology reopens long-forgotten investigations, this chapter highlights the transformative role OSINT can play in uncovering the truth, even after years of stagnation.

10.1 Introduction to the Cold Case Investigation

Understanding Cold Cases and the Role of OSINT

A cold case is an unsolved criminal investigation that remains open due to a lack of evidence, leads, or active pursuit by law enforcement. These cases often involve homicides, missing persons, and unsolved violent crimes that have remained unresolved for years, sometimes decades. With advancements in technology, digital forensics, and open-source intelligence (OSINT), investigators now have new tools to re-examine these cases, uncover hidden connections, and generate new leads.

OSINT is proving to be a game-changer in cold case investigations, allowing law enforcement, private investigators, and even independent researchers to access vast amounts of public data that were previously unavailable. By leveraging social media, archived records, digital databases, geolocation data, and forensic OSINT tools, investigators can reconstruct events, identify new suspects, and locate missing persons.

This section introduces the importance of OSINT in solving cold cases, highlighting key techniques, case examples, and challenges in revisiting long-dormant investigations.

The Challenges of Cold Case Investigations

Cold cases remain unsolved for a variety of reasons, often due to limited evidence, lack of witnesses, or forensic technology constraints at the time of the crime. Some of the most common obstacles include:

1. Lack of New Leads

Many cold cases go unsolved because no new information emerges. Witnesses may have forgotten details, moved away, or refused to cooperate over time.

🔍 **OSINT Advantage**: Online databases, genealogy research, and social media reconstructions can help track down new witnesses or re-analyze statements with fresh perspectives.

2. Poor Record-Keeping & Lost Evidence

Older cases often suffer from misplaced case files, destroyed evidence, or outdated forensic reports.

🔍 **OSINT Advantage**: Digital archives, newspaper articles, and crowdsourced research projects can help reconstruct lost investigative data.

3. Outdated Forensic Techniques

Advancements in DNA analysis, facial recognition, and digital forensics have made it possible to extract new insights from old evidence.

🔍 **OSINT Advantage**: Investigators can use public DNA databases, facial recognition AI, and image enhancement tools to compare evidence with modern-day records.

4. Lack of Resources for Law Enforcement

Many law enforcement agencies lack the funding and personnel to actively pursue cold cases. As a result, these investigations often remain dormant unless new evidence emerges.

🔍 **OSINT Advantage**: Independent OSINT investigators and volunteer researchers have revived countless cold cases using open-source intelligence tools.

How OSINT is Used in Cold Case Investigations

OSINT provides law enforcement and independent investigators with powerful new tools to gather intelligence, reconstruct past events, and identify new leads. Here are some of the most effective OSINT techniques in solving cold cases:

1. Digital Archival Research

✓ Accessing newspaper archives, public records, and legal documents can help reconstruct crime timelines.

✓ Analyzing old phone directories, census data, and court filings can lead to new investigative angles.

✓ Searching obituaries and genealogy websites can locate key individuals connected to the case.

🔍 **Case Example**: A decades-old homicide case was reopened when an OSINT analyst discovered an archived news report with a previously unnoticed suspect description.

2. Social Media & Online Footprint Analysis

✓ Many cold cases involve individuals who are still active on social media today.

✓ OSINT investigators can analyze old forum posts, Facebook profiles, and Twitter conversations to uncover new insights.

✓ Digital footprint reconstruction can track persons of interest who have changed identities or locations.

🔍 **Case Example**: A missing person case from 1995 was solved when investigators found an online alias the victim had been using, leading to their discovery in a different country.

3. Facial Recognition & AI Analysis

✓ AI-powered facial recognition tools can compare old suspect sketches with modern images.

✓ OSINT tools can scan public mugshot databases, social media images, and CCTV footage for matches.

🔍 **Case Example**: A fugitive on the run for 30 years was identified when his old driver's license photo was matched to a modern social media profile.

4. Public DNA & Genealogy Research

✓ Crowdsourced DNA databases (like GEDmatch and Ancestry.com) have helped law enforcement identify previously unknown suspects in homicide and assault cases.

✓ Investigators can reverse-engineer family trees to find biological connections to crime scene DNA.

🔍 **Case Example**: The infamous Golden State Killer case was solved using genetic genealogy OSINT, linking crime scene DNA to a distant relative's online ancestry records.

5. Geospatial & Satellite Image Analysis

✓ Historic satellite images can reveal locations of old buildings, crime scenes, or potential burial sites.

✓ Modern geolocation OSINT tools can analyze where suspects lived, worked, or traveled at the time of the crime.

🔍 **Case Example**: A missing person from the 1980s was located when satellite imagery showed recent ground disturbances near their last known location.

Notable Cold Cases Solved with OSINT

Case 1: The Golden State Killer

📌 **Crime**: Serial murders and rapes in California (1970s–1980s)
📌 **Breakthrough**: Investigators used public genealogy DNA databases to link crime scene DNA to distant relatives.
📌 **Outcome**: The suspect, Joseph James DeAngelo, was identified and arrested in 2018.

Case 2: The Identity of Lori Ruff

📌 **Crime**: A woman with a stolen identity died by suicide, leaving behind forged documents.

📌 **Breakthrough**: OSINT investigators used genealogy research, old high school records, and online obituary analysis to uncover her real identity.

📌 **Outcome**: She was identified as Kimberly McLean, a runaway who had disappeared in the 1980s.

Case 3: The Boy in the Box (Philadelphia, 1957)

📌 **Crime**: An unidentified child's body was found in a box, sparking decades of mystery.

📌 **Breakthrough**: DNA genealogy tracing identified the boy as Joseph Augustus Zarelli, with relatives still alive today.

📌 **Outcome**: After 65 years, the victim was finally identified in 2022.

Ethical and Legal Considerations in OSINT Cold Case Investigations

While OSINT is a powerful tool, it must be used ethically and legally in cold case investigations. Key considerations include:

✔ **Privacy Concerns** – Public genealogy databases require consent before law enforcement can use them for investigations.

✔ **Chain of Custody** – Any evidence found using OSINT must be legally admissible in court.

✔ **Avoiding False Accusations** – Misinterpretation of online data can lead to wrongful identifications.

⚖ **Best Practice**: OSINT investigators should always verify information with multiple independent sources before drawing conclusions.

Conclusion: The Future of OSINT in Cold Case Investigations

As technology continues to evolve, OSINT will play an even greater role in solving cold cases. Digital tools, AI-powered forensics, and crowdsourced investigations are helping to bring long-awaited justice to victims and their families.

By using public records, social media, DNA analysis, and geospatial intelligence, investigators can reconstruct the past, uncover hidden connections, and reopen long-dormant cases.

💡 Key Takeaway: The combination of OSINT and forensic advancements is reshaping criminal investigations, proving that no case is ever truly cold when the right tools and techniques are applied.

10.2 OSINT Methods Used to Reopen the Case

Introduction: The Power of OSINT in Reviving Cold Cases

Open-Source Intelligence (OSINT) has revolutionized the way cold cases are revisited, providing investigators with new methods to uncover hidden leads, track down persons of interest, and reconstruct past events. Unlike traditional investigations, which often rely on forensic evidence and witness testimony, OSINT leverages publicly available digital resources such as social media, archived records, geospatial tools, and open databases to generate fresh insights.

In this section, we will explore the OSINT techniques used to reopen a cold case, highlighting how modern investigative strategies can breathe new life into cases that were once thought unsolvable.

1️⃣ Digital Archival Research: Reconstructing the Case Timeline

Accessing Historical News Articles & Public Records

One of the first steps in reopening a cold case is reconstructing the original investigation. Investigators often turn to newspaper archives, court records, and police reports to analyze the information available at the time.

✓ OSINT Tools Used:

- Newspapers.com, The Wayback Machine, and Google News Archives for historical news coverage.
- PACER (Public Access to Court Electronic Records) for legal documents and case filings.
- State and local public records databases to track down previous case-related documents.

🔍 **Case Example**: A missing person case from 1985 was reopened when an OSINT investigator discovered a forgotten newspaper article mentioning a previously unknown witness who was never interviewed.

Digitizing & Cross-Referencing Old Case Files

✔ Many old cases have paper-based records that were never digitized.

✔ Investigators use OCR (Optical Character Recognition) tools to convert scanned case files into searchable text.

✔ This allows for cross-referencing with modern databases to identify missing connections.

🏅 **Key Benefit**: Helps reconstruct the victim's last known movements and identify inconsistencies in witness statements.

2️⃣ Social Media & Digital Footprint Investigations

Analyzing Social Media for New Leads

Many cold cases involve individuals who are still active online today, providing opportunities for OSINT analysts to track their digital footprints.

✔ **Key Social Media OSINT Techniques:**

- **Username Correlation**: Linking old forum usernames, email addresses, or aliases to modern social media accounts.
- **Reverse Image Searches**: Identifying people in old photos using Google Reverse Image Search or PimEyes.
- **Metadata Analysis**: Extracting geolocation data from uploaded images or videos.

🔍 **Case Example**: A fugitive in a decades-old murder case was found after investigators linked an old forum username to a recent Twitter handle, leading them to his current location.

Tracking Online Conversations & Forum Activity

✓ OSINT analysts search old online forums, blogs, and discussion boards to see if suspects or witnesses have shared new information over the years.

✓ This is especially useful for cases involving anonymous tipsters, conspiracy theories, or resurfaced confessions.

📖 **Key Benefit**: Helps identify people connected to the case who may have been overlooked.

3️⃣ Geospatial & Geolocation Analysis

Using Historic Satellite & Street View Imagery

Advancements in geospatial OSINT have made it possible to analyze past locations and reconstruct crime scenes.

✓ OSINT Tools Used:

- **Google Earth Pro & Historical Satellite Imagery**: Comparing old and new landscapes for potential crime scene clues.
- **Street View Analysis**: Checking whether key locations (e.g., last known locations, crime scenes, disposal sites) have changed over time.
- **Geotagged Social Media Posts**: Finding images or videos taken near the crime scene, even decades later.

🔍 **Case Example**: A missing person's case was reopened after OSINT investigators found a geotagged Instagram photo taken near their last known location, providing new search areas.

4️⃣ Online Genealogy & Public DNA Databases

One of the most groundbreaking OSINT methods for solving cold cases is genetic genealogy research. This technique involves using public DNA databases to trace unknown suspects or victims through family connections.

✓ Key DNA OSINT Resources:

- **GEDmatch & FamilyTreeDNA**: Used for cross-referencing DNA profiles with family trees.
- **Ancestry.com & MyHeritage**: Investigators can use surname analysis to identify distant relatives of unidentified bodies or criminals.

🔍 **Case Example**: The Golden State Killer was identified when law enforcement uploaded crime scene DNA to a genealogy database, leading to a distant relative whose family tree helped pinpoint the suspect.

🚨 **Key Benefit**: DNA OSINT helps identify both victims and perpetrators, even if traditional DNA databases have no direct matches.

5️⃣ Cryptocurrency & Financial Transaction Analysis

Many cold cases, especially those involving financial fraud, kidnappings, or organized crime, can benefit from OSINT techniques used to trace financial transactions.

✓ **OSINT Tools Used:**

- **Chainalysis & Elliptic**: Tracking cryptocurrency payments linked to ransoms or illicit activity.
- **Public Business Registries**: Checking if suspects opened or closed businesses under different names over the years.
- **Leaked Financial Databases**: Investigators often use data leaks to find hidden assets linked to suspects.

🔍 **Case Example**: In a decades-old missing person case, investigators discovered a recent cryptocurrency transfer from a bank account previously linked to the victim, proving they were still alive.

🚨 **Key Benefit**: Helps track money laundering, suspect movements, and hidden assets.

6️⃣ Crowdsourced Investigations & OSINT Collaboration

In many cold cases, online communities and independent OSINT investigators play a key role in uncovering new leads.

✓ **Key OSINT Collaboration Strategies:**

- **Crowdsourced Research**: Platforms like Websleuths and Reddit's Unresolved Mysteries allow amateur investigators to contribute to cold case research.
- **Public Data Requests**: FOIA (Freedom of Information Act) requests can uncover previously withheld documents that might contain new evidence.
- **Nonprofit OSINT Teams**: Organizations like The Doe Network work to identify missing persons using publicly available data.

🔍 **Case Example**: In a cold case involving a Jane Doe (unidentified body), OSINT researchers used crowdsourced facial recognition and genealogy databases to identify her real name, leading to a break in the case.

📛 **Key Benefit**: Public OSINT efforts have helped solve hundreds of cold cases that law enforcement no longer had the resources to pursue.

Conclusion: OSINT's Role in Solving the Unsolvable

Cold cases that once seemed impossible to solve are now being reopened thanks to OSINT techniques that provide new investigative pathways. By leveraging digital archives, social media footprints, geospatial intelligence, genealogy databases, financial tracking, and crowdsourced research, investigators can uncover long-lost evidence and generate new leads.

💡 **Key Takeaway**: OSINT has reshaped criminal investigations, proving that no case is ever truly "cold" when modern intelligence tools are applied.

🚀 **Next Step**: The following sections will explore real-world case studies where OSINT helped crack long-unsolved mysteries, demonstrating the practical impact of digital intelligence in law enforcement.

10.3 Tracking New Digital Evidence & Leads

Introduction: The Digital Evolution of Cold Cases

In the past, cold case investigations relied heavily on eyewitness accounts, forensic evidence, and traditional detective work. However, in today's digital age, new evidence can emerge online, providing fresh leads that were previously unavailable. Social media activity, digital communications, archived records, and even dark web forums can reveal crucial information about long-dormant cases.

By systematically leveraging OSINT (Open-Source Intelligence) techniques, investigators can track new digital evidence, identify potential suspects, and reconstruct previously missing links in unsolved crimes. This section explores how digital footprints, metadata analysis, and modern intelligence tools are used to uncover new evidence in cold case investigations.

1️⃣ Re-examining Digital Footprints of Victims & Suspects

Digital Presence of Victims Over Time

Even in decades-old cases, victims may have left digital traces that can be re-evaluated with today's advanced OSINT tools.

✔ Key Investigative Methods:

- **Social Media Accounts**: Old MySpace, Facebook, Twitter, or Instagram accounts may still exist, offering insights into victims' last-known activities.
- **Email & Forum Activity**: Investigators can cross-check email addresses, usernames, and forum posts to track online activity before disappearance.
- **Cloud Storage & Archived Data**: Services like Google Drive, Dropbox, and iCloud backups may contain important documents or photos.

🔍 **Case Example**: In a 1999 missing person case, a cold case unit discovered that the victim's old email address was still linked to a Google account that had activity as recently as 2021, prompting new leads.

Tracing Suspects' Online Behavior

Suspects in cold cases may have changed their names, relocated, or started new lives, but they often leave digital trails.

✔ OSINT Tools Used to Track Suspects:

- **Username Correlation**: Searching if old aliases were reused on modern platforms.

- **Reverse Image Searches**: Running old suspect photos through Google Reverse Image Search, PimEyes, or TinEye to find updated pictures.
- **Leaked Data & Breach Databases**: Checking compromised email/password leaks for updated contact details.

🚨 **Key Benefit**: Identifies new locations, jobs, or social connections that can aid in reopening the case.

2️⃣ Leveraging Social Media for New Clues

Uncovering New Witnesses & Anonymous Tips

✔ Many cold cases gain renewed attention through viral social media discussions, true crime forums, and online advocacy groups.

✔ Investigators monitor Reddit (r/UnresolvedMysteries, r/CrimeScene), Facebook groups, and Websleuths for new theories, confessions, or overlooked details.

🔍 **Case Example**: A witness in a 1980s murder case came forward after seeing a viral Facebook post about the victim, revealing a crucial piece of forgotten information.

Tracking Suspicious Online Activity

✔ Some criminals revisit crime scenes digitally, searching for news articles or discussion threads about their past crimes.

✔ Investigators use Google Alerts & Dark Web Monitoring to detect suspicious searches related to the cold case.

🚨 **Key Benefit**: Social media platforms can provide real-time updates on persons of interest who may unknowingly reveal their whereabouts.

3️⃣ Dark Web & Underground Forum Investigations

Exploring Dark Web Marketplaces for Evidence

✓ Many kidnappings, murders, and organized crimes have digital footprints hidden on dark web marketplaces and forums.

✓ Law enforcement OSINT analysts monitor platforms like Tor, I2P, and ZeroNet for evidence of illegal trade, human trafficking, or cold case discussions.

🔍 **Case Example**: In a missing persons case from 2002, an OSINT analyst discovered the victim's passport information being sold on a dark web identity marketplace, suggesting potential human trafficking involvement.

Monitoring Anonymous Confessions & Leaks

✓ Criminals sometimes boast about their crimes in hidden online communities or leak details anonymously.

✓ Investigators track cryptic dark web posts, classified ads, and underground forums for confessions or critical new information.

💻 **Key Benefit**: The dark web holds potential evidence that could help locate missing persons or expose previously unknown suspects.

4️⃣ Digital Metadata & Geolocation Analysis

Extracting Metadata from Old Photos & Videos

✓ Photos taken years ago may contain valuable geolocation metadata (EXIF data) that can pinpoint where and when an image was captured.

✓ OSINT tools like ExifTool, FotoForensics, and Jeffrey's Image Metadata Viewer help investigators extract hidden location details from photos.

🔍 **Case Example**: A cold case was reopened after an old family photo of a missing girl was re-analyzed, revealing GPS coordinates in the metadata that led to a previously unsearched area.

Using Geolocation Tools to Track Movements

✓ Modern geospatial OSINT tools like Google Earth, Sentinel Hub, and Landsat satellite imagery allow investigators to compare old and new landscapes to detect potential crime scene changes.

✓ Law enforcement can also request access to historical cell tower records to map out a suspect's movements during the time of the crime.

🚨 **Key Benefit**: Provides location-based insights that could reveal new search areas or corroborate alibis.

5️⃣ Financial & Cryptocurrency Transaction Investigations

Tracing Bank Accounts & Payment History

✓ If a victim or suspect was involved in financial transactions before vanishing or going into hiding, OSINT techniques can help track their money trail.

✓ Publicly available records, court filings, leaked financial data, and cryptocurrency blockchain analysis can uncover hidden funds.

🔍 **Case Example**: A murder suspect from 1995 who had disappeared was located after his old bank account showed new activity in 2022, leading investigators to his hideout.

Investigating Cryptocurrency Movements

✓ Many criminals use Bitcoin, Monero, and other cryptocurrencies to launder money or pay for illegal services.

✓ OSINT blockchain analysis tools like Chainalysis, CipherTrace, and Etherscan help investigators follow the money trail.

🚨 **Key Benefit**: Following financial transactions often leads to hidden assets, safe houses, or accomplices in cold cases.

6️⃣ Crowdsourced OSINT & Public Assistance

Engaging Digital Volunteers & True Crime Communities

✓ Many amateur OSINT investigators and true crime enthusiasts actively participate in solving cold cases.

✓ Crowdsourced intelligence from online sleuth communities has led to identifications of missing persons, fugitives, and unknown victims.

🔍 **Case Example**: A Jane Doe case from the 1970s was solved after Reddit users cross-referenced missing persons reports with genealogy databases, identifying her real name.

Utilizing Freedom of Information Act (FOIA) Requests

✓ Investigators and independent researchers use FOIA laws to access government records, old case files, and sealed evidence reports.

✓ Many cold cases are revived when previously classified information is made public.

🔖 **Key Benefit**: The public can provide critical insights and assist in investigative breakthroughs.

Conclusion: The Digital Era's Impact on Cold Cases

The advancement of OSINT techniques has transformed how cold cases are investigated, allowing digital forensics, social media tracking, and dark web analysis to reveal new leads decades after a crime was committed.

✓ Re-evaluating digital footprints, tracking new online activity, leveraging geolocation metadata, and tracing financial transactions are just a few of the methods that have revitalized cold case investigations.

💡 **Key Takeaway**: With modern digital intelligence, no case is ever truly closed. As long as new data emerges, investigators have the tools to uncover the truth—even years later.

10.4 Collaboration Between OSINT Experts & Investigators

Introduction: Bridging the Gap Between OSINT & Law Enforcement

Successful cold case investigations require a multidisciplinary approach, combining traditional detective work with modern OSINT (Open-Source Intelligence) techniques. While law enforcement officers specialize in criminal investigations, forensic analysis, and legal procedures, OSINT experts bring digital forensics, cybersecurity knowledge, and advanced data-mining skills to the table.

Collaboration between these two groups is crucial for tracking new leads, verifying online evidence, and ensuring that open-source findings are legally admissible in court. This section explores how OSINT specialists and investigators work together to reopen cold cases, uncover hidden digital traces, and solve long-unsolved crimes.

1️ The Role of OSINT Experts in Cold Case Investigations

OSINT professionals bring unique expertise and tools that significantly enhance traditional law enforcement investigations. Their role includes:

🔎 Identifying & Verifying Digital Evidence

- Conducting deep web and dark web searches to uncover discussions related to old crimes.
- Using reverse image searches and facial recognition to track victims and suspects across different platforms.
- Extracting metadata from old photos, emails, and documents to identify hidden timestamps or locations.

▢ Mapping Connections & Behavioral Patterns

- Analyzing social media interactions, forum discussions, and online footprints to track down new persons of interest.
- Using network analysis tools to uncover relationships between criminals, potential witnesses, and victims.

💰 Investigating Financial & Cryptocurrency Transactions

- Utilizing blockchain analysis tools (e.g., Chainalysis, CipherTrace) to follow money trails linked to suspects.
- Identifying bank transfers, shell companies, and cryptocurrency wallets associated with old cases.

🏛️ **Real-World Example**: In a 20-year-old fraud case, an OSINT team used leaked financial databases to uncover a suspect's new identity and offshore bank accounts, leading to his arrest.

2️⃣ Law Enforcement's Role in OSINT Collaboration

While OSINT experts uncover digital leads, law enforcement officers play a crucial role in:

🔖 Validating OSINT Findings with Legal Procedures

- Ensuring that digital evidence is collected in a forensically sound manner to be admissible in court.
- Cross-referencing OSINT discoveries with criminal records, surveillance footage, and physical evidence.

👮 Conducting Field Investigations & Interrogations

- Following up on OSINT leads with surveillance, witness interviews, and forensic testing.
- Using search warrants and subpoenas to obtain confidential data from tech companies when needed.

🔐 Securing Data & Protecting Operational Security

- Preventing suspects from deleting their online presence once they detect an investigation.
- Implementing counter-surveillance techniques to protect OSINT analysts from cyber threats.

🏛️ **Case Example**: In a cold murder case, an OSINT analyst tracked a suspect's new online alias, while police conducted undercover operations to verify his real-world identity.

3️⃣ Best Practices for OSINT & Law Enforcement Collaboration

For an effective partnership between OSINT specialists and investigators, both groups must adopt best practices to maximize their impact.

1️⃣ Establish Clear Communication Channels

✓ Use secure messaging platforms (e.g., Signal, ProtonMail) to prevent leaks.

✓ Create designated task forces where OSINT experts and law enforcement collaborate directly.

2️⃣ Define Legal & Ethical Boundaries

✓ Ensure that OSINT findings adhere to privacy laws and are collected without violating regulations.

✓ Work with prosecutors to confirm digital evidence admissibility in court.

3️⃣ Utilize Secure Data-Sharing Platforms

✓ Store and analyze sensitive intelligence using encrypted databases.

✓ Use cybersecurity protocols to prevent evidence tampering or hacking.

🔎 **Example**: In a human trafficking case, OSINT teams used blockchain analysis to trace payments, while law enforcement obtained court orders to access transaction records.

4️⃣ Challenges in OSINT-Law Enforcement Collaboration

While OSINT and law enforcement collaboration is powerful, it comes with challenges that need to be addressed.

⚠️ Legal & Privacy Issues

● OSINT specialists do not have the authority to access private databases that law enforcement can obtain via warrants.

● Some open-source data may be collected from legally gray areas, making evidence inadmissible in court.

⚠️ Verification of Digital Evidence

● Digital evidence can be manipulated or misleading, requiring forensic validation.
● False positives in facial recognition or identity correlation can misidentify suspects.

⚠️ Operational Security Risks

● Investigating criminal networks, hackers, or dark web activity can expose OSINT analysts to cyber threats.
● Law enforcement officers risk alerting suspects if digital footprints are not handled discreetly.

🔍 **Example**: A criminal erased his online presence after detecting suspicious searches on his old accounts, making further OSINT tracking difficult.

5️⃣ Case Example: How OSINT & Law Enforcement Solved a Cold Case

The Case: A Missing Woman from 1995

- A woman went missing in 1995, and the case went cold for over two decades.
- Traditional investigations failed to locate the suspect, who vanished without a trace.

How OSINT & Investigators Worked Together:

✓ OSINT Team: Discovered that the suspect had changed his name and was active on LinkedIn under a new identity.

✓ Law Enforcement: Used facial recognition & surveillance to confirm his real identity.

✓ Outcome: The suspect was arrested in 2023, nearly 30 years after the crime.

🚀 **Key Takeaway**: Without OSINT analysis, the suspect's identity change and digital cover-up would have remained undiscovered.

Conclusion: The Future of OSINT-Law Enforcement Collaboration

As criminals become more digitally savvy, OSINT-driven investigations will play an increasingly critical role in solving cold cases.

✓ Advanced OSINT tools, AI-driven analytics, and real-time data monitoring will continue to reshape how unsolved crimes are investigated.

✓ Stronger partnerships between cyber analysts, forensic experts, and law enforcement officers will lead to more breakthroughs in long-dormant cases.

🔘 **Final Thought**: The future of cold case investigations lies in digital intelligence. By combining OSINT expertise with law enforcement strategies, investigators can uncover new leads, track down fugitives, and finally bring justice to long-forgotten victims.

10.5 How Digital Forensics & Open Sources Connected the Dots

Introduction: The Intersection of Digital Forensics & OSINT

In cold case investigations, the combination of digital forensics and OSINT (Open-Source Intelligence) can bridge critical gaps where traditional investigative methods fail. While digital forensics focuses on extracting, analyzing, and preserving data from digital devices, OSINT leverages publicly available data sources to uncover new leads.

When used together, these disciplines provide a powerful means to identify suspects, locate missing persons, and reconstruct events that had previously gone cold. This chapter explores how investigators use digital forensic techniques alongside OSINT methodologies to connect the dots in long-unsolved criminal cases.

1⃣ The Role of Digital Forensics in Cold Case Investigations

Digital forensics is the scientific examination of electronic evidence from devices such as:

✓ **Computers & Hard Drives** – Recovering deleted files, emails, and browsing history.

✓ **Mobile Phones & Tablets** – Extracting call logs, messages, and geolocation data.

✓ **Cloud Storage & Online Accounts** – Identifying past activities on platforms like Google Drive or iCloud.

✓ **Surveillance Footage & Security Systems** – Enhancing old video footage using AI-based forensic tools.

💡 **Example**: In a decades-old homicide case, forensic experts recovered an old hard drive that contained an encrypted email conversation, leading to a breakthrough in the investigation.

2️ The Power of OSINT in Digital Investigations

While digital forensics extracts data from controlled sources, OSINT provides intelligence from:

✓ **Social Media & Online Forums** – Identifying digital footprints, usernames, and interactions.

✓ **Archived Web Content** – Recovering deleted or altered pages using tools like the Wayback Machine.

✓ **Public Records & Leaked Databases** – Cross-referencing old addresses, phone numbers, and financial transactions.

✓ **Geospatial Intelligence (GEOINT)** – Using Google Earth, satellite imagery, and geotagged photos to track movements.

💡 **Example**: A missing person's case was reopened after OSINT experts linked an old MySpace username to a newly created Twitter account, revealing the individual was still alive under a different identity.

3️ How Digital Forensics & OSINT Work Together

When digital forensics and OSINT are combined, they create a powerful investigative approach:

🔎 **Case 1: Uncovering an Anonymous Suspect Through Digital Footprints**

- **Digital Forensics**: Recovered deleted chat logs from an old laptop.

- **OSINT**: Cross-referenced usernames and email IDs with leaked database breaches.
- **Breakthrough**: Found a matching alias on an obscure hacker forum, leading to the suspect.

Case 2: Geolocating a Victim Using Digital Clues

- **Digital Forensics**: Extracted GPS metadata from an old photo.
- **OSINT**: Matched the background landmarks with Google Earth.
- **Breakthrough**: Identified the exact location where the victim was last seen.

Case 3: Tracking a Fugitive Through Cryptocurrency Transactions

- **Digital Forensics**: Analyzed a suspect's confiscated phone for cryptocurrency wallet addresses.
- **OSINT**: Used blockchain analysis tools (like Chainalysis) to follow financial transactions.
- **Breakthrough**: The fugitive was tracked to a country where he was later arrested.

4 Key Tools Used in Digital Forensics & OSINT Investigations

Both fields rely on specialized tools to extract and analyze data.

Digital Forensics Tools

✓ **Autopsy / FTK Imager** – Recovers deleted files and analyzes hard drives.

✓ **Cellebrite UFED** – Extracts data from mobile devices, including encrypted content.

✓ **Wireshark** – Monitors network traffic for suspicious activity.

✓ **X-Ways Forensics** – An advanced forensic suite for disk analysis.

OSINT Tools

✓ **Maltego** – Maps relationships between suspects, domains, and entities.

✓ **SpiderFoot** – Automates data collection from over 100 sources.

✓ **Hunchly** – Captures and archives web pages as legally admissible evidence.

✓ **Metagoofil** – Extracts metadata from publicly available documents.

🚀 **Real-World Example**: Investigators used Metagoofil to extract metadata from a suspect's old CV, revealing his new employer and location.

5️⃣ Challenges & Limitations in Using Digital Forensics & OSINT Together

While the combination of digital forensics and OSINT is powerful, investigators face several challenges:

🔐 Data Privacy & Legal Boundaries

- Digital forensic data often requires warrants, while OSINT data is publicly available but may have ethical concerns.
- **Example**: Extracting a suspect's deleted emails may be restricted by data protection laws.

⚠️ False Positives & Data Correlation Issues

- OSINT tools may incorrectly link different people with similar usernames.
- **Example**: A suspect using a common alias (e.g., "ShadowKiller") may lead investigators to multiple unrelated individuals.

💻 Cybersecurity Risks

- OSINT researchers targeting criminal networks may become targets of hacking or doxxing.
- **Example**: A researcher investigating dark web marketplaces was attacked after criminals detected their monitoring activity.

6️⃣ Case Study: Solving a 20-Year-Old Murder with OSINT & Digital Forensics

Background:

- A young woman disappeared in 2001, and the case went cold.
- The prime suspect vanished, and there was no physical evidence linking him to the crime.

Breakthrough:

✓ **Digital Forensics:**

- Investigators recovered an old mobile phone from the victim's belongings.
- SMS messages & call logs were extracted, revealing contact with the suspect days before her disappearance.

✓ **OSINT Investigation:**

- A forensic OSINT analyst found an anonymous blog post from 2007, describing the crime in suspicious detail.
- Using linguistic analysis, investigators matched writing patterns to the suspect's known social media posts.

Final Outcome:

☐ The suspect was tracked down using a digital identity linked to a different alias and arrested in 2022, bringing long-awaited closure to the case.

Conclusion: The Future of OSINT & Digital Forensics in Cold Cases

As technology advances, the integration of OSINT and digital forensics will become even more critical in solving cold cases.

✓ AI-powered forensic tools will automate pattern recognition in digital evidence.

✓ Blockchain analysis & cryptocurrency tracking will uncover hidden financial connections in crimes.

✓ OSINT-driven machine learning models will predict criminal behaviors and digital movements.

📖 **Final Thought**: By combining the power of forensic analysis and open-source intelligence, investigators can connect the dots in even the most complex cold cases, ensuring that justice is never truly out of reach.

10.6 Lessons Learned: OSINT's Role in Unsolved Cases

Introduction: OSINT as a Game-Changer in Cold Case Investigations

The power of Open-Source Intelligence (OSINT) in criminal investigations has never been more evident than in cold case investigations. Cases that remained unsolved for decades have seen new breakthroughs thanks to the ability to track digital footprints, analyze online activity, and leverage public databases.

This final section reflects on key lessons learned from real-world OSINT applications in cold cases. It highlights the successes, challenges, and ethical considerations investigators must navigate while using OSINT to bring long-awaited justice to victims and their families.

1️⃣ Lesson 1: Digital Footprints Last Longer Than We Think

Even when suspects attempt to erase their past, the internet often preserves fragments of their digital identity that can be pieced together.

Case Example: Tracking a Fugitive's Online Alias

- A suspect in a 1998 murder case disappeared without a trace.
- OSINT specialists discovered that his old email address was linked to a recent job listing on LinkedIn.
- By analyzing past usernames and social media posts, investigators matched his writing style to a new identity.
- **Outcome**: The suspect was arrested in 2021, 23 years after the crime.

🚀 **Takeaway**: Even if criminals erase their old profiles, fragments of their online presence can resurface years later, making it possible to track them down.

2️⃣ Lesson 2: The Importance of Cross-Referencing Data

One of OSINT's biggest challenges is false positives—cases where similar usernames, addresses, or phone numbers belong to different people. To avoid mistakes, investigators must correlate multiple data points before making conclusions.

Case Example: Preventing a Wrongful Arrest

- Investigators linked an old MySpace profile to a suspect in a 2005 missing person case.

- However, upon deeper analysis, the email address was connected to a completely different individual.
- OSINT teams used public databases and facial recognition to verify that the actual suspect had used a fake name but left behind a matching old forum post.
- **Outcome**: The real perpetrator was correctly identified, preventing a wrongful arrest.

🖋 **Takeaway**: Cross-referencing data from multiple sources (social media, public records, metadata analysis) is critical to verifying a suspect's true identity.

3⃣ Lesson 3: OSINT & Digital Forensics Work Best Together

While OSINT is powerful on its own, it becomes even more effective when combined with digital forensics. This partnership allows investigators to connect online data with physical evidence.

Case Example: Solving a Decades-Old Homicide

- A 1994 cold case was reopened when OSINT experts discovered a suspect's new alias.
- Digital forensic teams extracted data from an old hard drive, uncovering deleted emails discussing the crime.
- The emails contained timestamps and location details, which were cross-checked with OSINT sources to verify their authenticity.
- **Outcome**: A breakthrough in the case led to the suspect's conviction nearly 30 years later.

🖋 **Takeaway**: OSINT findings should always be validated through digital forensics or law enforcement resources to ensure accuracy and credibility.

4⃣ Lesson 4: The Power of Crowdsourced Intelligence

One of OSINT's most unique advantages is the ability to leverage the public for intelligence gathering. Online communities, investigative journalists, and amateur sleuths have played critical roles in reviving cold cases.

Case Example: Internet Sleuths Solving a 20-Year-Old Disappearance

- A group of OSINT researchers on Reddit and Twitter analyzed an old missing person case from 2002.
- By using Google Earth and street view analysis, they identified a lake near the last known location.
- A local volunteer used a drone and sonar equipment to scan the area, finding a car submerged underwater.
- **Outcome**: The car contained the remains of the missing person, solving a 20-year-old disappearance.

🚀 **Takeaway**: OSINT enables crowdsourced investigations, allowing communities to contribute to solving long-forgotten cases.

5️⃣ Lesson 5: The Dark Web & Cryptocurrency Can Hide—But Not Erase—Evidence

Criminals often use the dark web and cryptocurrency to cover their tracks, assuming they are untraceable. However, OSINT analysts and blockchain forensics tools have proven otherwise.

Case Example: Following the Bitcoin Trail to Solve a Cold Case

- A financial fraud suspect from 2007 resurfaced in 2020 after making cryptocurrency transactions.
- OSINT investigators used blockchain analysis tools (like Chainalysis) to trace his Bitcoin wallets to an online forum.
- By cross-referencing forum usernames with leaked email databases, they identified his real-world location.
- **Outcome**: The suspect was extradited and prosecuted after 13 years on the run.

🚀 **Takeaway**: The dark web provides anonymity, but OSINT and blockchain forensics can still track digital trails left behind.

6️⃣ Lesson 6: Ethical & Legal Challenges in OSINT Investigations

While OSINT is a powerful tool, it must be used ethically and legally.

✓ Not all publicly available information is legally usable in court.

✓ Investigators must follow privacy laws and avoid hacking or illegal surveillance.

✓ Misidentifying a suspect can ruin innocent lives—accuracy is critical.

Case Example: OSINT Analyst Faces Legal Issues for Unethical Data Collection

- A private investigator used OSINT tools to track a suspected criminal, scraping personal data from a private website.
- The evidence was ruled inadmissible in court because it was collected without legal authorization.
- **Outcome**: The investigator faced legal consequences, and the case was delayed.

✍ **Takeaway**: OSINT must always comply with privacy laws and ethical guidelines to maintain its credibility in legal proceedings.

7⃣ Conclusion: OSINT's Growing Role in Unsolved Cases

Over the years, OSINT has proven to be an indispensable tool in cold case investigations.

Key Takeaways:

✓ Digital footprints never completely disappear—even after decades, traces of online activity can lead to breakthroughs.

✓ Cross-referencing OSINT data with forensic evidence is crucial to ensure accuracy.

✓ Crowdsourcing and public collaboration can significantly contribute to solving cases.

✓ Dark web and cryptocurrency tracking tools are essential for uncovering hidden criminal activities.

✓ Ethical and legal considerations must always be respected in OSINT investigations.

As technology continues to evolve, OSINT will play an even more vital role in solving long-unsolved cases, tracking fugitives, and delivering long-overdue justice.

🔍 **Final Thought**: No case is ever truly "cold" in the digital age. With the right tools, collaboration, and persistence, OSINT has the power to bring even the most elusive criminals to justice.

11. OSINT & Law Enforcement Collaboration

This chapter examines the critical collaboration between OSINT analysts and law enforcement agencies in modern criminal investigations. As digital intelligence continues to evolve, law enforcement must adapt by integrating OSINT into their investigative workflows. We will explore the dynamic partnership between OSINT professionals and police officers, discussing how information is shared, how digital evidence is handled, and the importance of collaboration in enhancing the effectiveness of investigations. Through real-world examples, this chapter demonstrates how cross-agency cooperation, combined with the expertise of OSINT analysts, accelerates the resolution of cases and strengthens the fight against crime in the digital age.

11.1 How OSINT Analysts Work with Law Enforcement

Introduction: The OSINT-Law Enforcement Partnership

As digital crime continues to evolve, law enforcement agencies increasingly rely on Open-Source Intelligence (OSINT) to aid in investigations. OSINT analysts play a crucial role by providing valuable insights, uncovering hidden connections, and enhancing investigative efficiency through publicly available data. Their expertise in tracking online activity, mapping networks, and analyzing digital footprints has proven instrumental in solving crimes ranging from fraud to terrorism.

This section explores how OSINT analysts collaborate with law enforcement, the challenges they face, and best practices for an effective partnership.

1⃣ The Role of OSINT Analysts in Criminal Investigations

OSINT analysts serve as digital investigators, specializing in collecting, analyzing, and interpreting publicly available information to support law enforcement cases. Their responsibilities include:

✓ **Social Media & Digital Footprint Analysis** – Identifying suspects, tracking their online behavior, and gathering evidence from social media platforms.

✓ **Geolocation & Metadata Analysis** – Using publicly available imagery, location data, and metadata to pinpoint a suspect's whereabouts.

✓ **Financial & Fraud Investigations** – Tracing fraudulent transactions, cryptocurrency movements, and online scams.

✓ **Dark Web Monitoring** – Tracking illicit marketplaces, criminal forums, and human trafficking networks.

✓ **Threat Intelligence** – Monitoring extremist groups, cybercriminal organizations, and emerging security threats.

By leveraging these techniques, OSINT analysts provide critical leads and intelligence that traditional investigative methods might miss.

2️ How OSINT Analysts Assist Law Enforcement Operations

OSINT specialists assist law enforcement in several key areas:

◆ Identifying Suspects & Persons of Interest

- OSINT analysts cross-reference social media activity, online aliases, and public records to connect individuals to criminal activities.
- They use facial recognition, username correlation, and deep search tools to track digital identities.
- **Example**: An OSINT analyst linked a suspect's old gaming username to a new Instagram profile, leading to his identification in a fraud case.

◆ Gathering Intelligence for Investigations

- OSINT teams monitor forums, chat groups, and classified sites for discussions related to crimes.
- They analyze leaked databases, domain registrations, and corporate records to uncover hidden connections.
- **Example**: Analysts monitoring dark web marketplaces discovered a major cybercriminal selling stolen credit card data, leading to an international arrest.

◆ Monitoring & Predicting Criminal Activity

- OSINT can help detect warning signs of criminal behavior before crimes occur.
- Analysts track social media threats, suspicious digital movements, and extremist propaganda to assess potential dangers.

- **Example**: A school shooting was prevented when OSINT analysts flagged a student posting threats and weapons pictures on forums.

◆ **Geolocating Criminals & Missing Persons**

- OSINT experts use Google Earth, Street View, and geotagged social media posts to trace a suspect's movements.
- They analyze weather conditions, landmarks, and shadows in images to verify locations.
- **Example**: An OSINT analyst helped locate a missing teenager by tracking her last known Snapchat post geotag.

◆ **Collecting Digital Evidence for Prosecution**

- OSINT analysts document findings with timestamps, metadata, and forensic-level accuracy to ensure evidence is admissible in court.
- They collaborate with digital forensics teams to verify findings and create investigative reports.
- **Example**: A cyberstalker was convicted after OSINT analysts compiled two years of online harassment evidence linked to his real identity.

3️⃣ Best Practices for OSINT & Law Enforcement Collaboration

To maximize effectiveness, OSINT analysts and law enforcement agencies should follow these best practices:

✓ Establishing Clear Communication Channels

- Dedicated OSINT teams should have direct communication with law enforcement to streamline intelligence sharing.
- Secure platforms (such as Signal, ProtonMail, or private servers) should be used for sensitive data exchange.

✓ Using Legally Compliant OSINT Methods

- OSINT analysts must only collect publicly available information and avoid illegal hacking, unauthorized access, or privacy breaches.
- Law enforcement must ensure proper legal procedures (e.g., search warrants) are followed when using OSINT findings in investigations.

✓ Cross-Validating OSINT Data with Law Enforcement Resources

- OSINT analysts should correlate findings with police databases, CCTV footage, and forensic reports to confirm accuracy.
- Collaboration with digital forensics, cybersecurity teams, and intelligence units enhances the quality of investigations.

✓ Prioritizing Ethical & Privacy Considerations

- Analysts must follow ethical OSINT principles, respecting individuals' privacy while conducting investigations.
- Investigations should avoid bias, misidentification, and false accusations by double-checking all data.

4 Challenges Faced by OSINT Analysts in Law Enforcement Work

Despite its effectiveness, OSINT collaboration with law enforcement comes with challenges:

◆ Privacy & Legal Restrictions

- Certain OSINT findings may not be admissible in court due to privacy laws.
- Analysts must stay informed about jurisdiction-specific regulations when conducting investigations.

◆ Information Overload & False Positives

- Sorting through millions of online data points can lead to false leads or wasted investigative resources.
- OSINT analysts must use AI-driven filtering and advanced search techniques to improve accuracy.

◆ Evolving Criminal Tactics

- Criminals change usernames, use VPNs, and operate on encrypted platforms to avoid detection.
- OSINT analysts must adapt to new tools and methodologies to stay ahead.

◆ **Interagency Coordination Issues**

- Different law enforcement agencies may use different OSINT tools and procedures, causing inefficiencies.
- Establishing standardized OSINT protocols can improve collaboration.

5⬜ Future of OSINT in Law Enforcement Partnerships

With the rise of AI, big data analytics, and real-time intelligence gathering, OSINT will continue to play an increasingly critical role in criminal investigations.

Trends Shaping the Future:

✓ **AI-Powered OSINT Tools** – Machine learning will enhance pattern recognition and automated intelligence gathering.

✓ **Blockchain Analysis for Crime Tracking** – Advanced blockchain forensics will improve cryptocurrency fraud detection.

✓ **Dark Web Intelligence Advancements** – Law enforcement will develop new techniques to infiltrate and monitor hidden criminal networks.

✓ **Improved Collaboration Frameworks** – Global agencies will standardize OSINT data sharing for cross-border crime investigations.

As OSINT analysts and law enforcement continue to refine their collaboration, criminal investigations will become more efficient, data-driven, and proactive, ensuring faster case resolutions and enhanced public safety.

Conclusion: OSINT as an Essential Law Enforcement Asset

The collaboration between OSINT analysts and law enforcement has revolutionized modern investigations. By leveraging publicly available intelligence, advanced digital tools, and strategic partnerships, OSINT plays a pivotal role in solving crimes, identifying threats, and protecting communities.

✓ OSINT analysts help identify suspects, track digital evidence, and support investigations.

✓ Effective collaboration ensures intelligence is accurate, legally compliant, and actionable.

✓ Future advancements in AI, blockchain, and dark web monitoring will further strengthen OSINT's role in law enforcement.

In the digital age, crime leaves an online trail—and OSINT is the key to following it. 🔍

11.2 Providing Actionable Intelligence to Investigators

Introduction: The Importance of Actionable Intelligence

In modern criminal investigations, raw data alone is not enough—investigators need actionable intelligence that is relevant, accurate, and timely. Open-Source Intelligence (OSINT) analysts play a critical role in transforming publicly available information into structured, investigative insights that law enforcement can use to pursue leads, make arrests, and prosecute criminals.

This section explores how OSINT analysts provide actionable intelligence, the methods used to ensure its effectiveness, and real-world examples of its impact on investigations.

1️⃣ What is Actionable Intelligence?

Actionable intelligence refers to information that is immediately useful for making decisions or taking investigative action. Unlike raw data, which may require further verification, actionable intelligence is analyzed, contextualized, and relevant to an ongoing investigation.

Key Characteristics of Actionable Intelligence:

✓ **Timely** – Delivered when it is most useful, allowing investigators to act quickly.

✓ **Accurate** – Verified and cross-referenced with other sources.

✓ **Relevant** – Directly related to the case or threat being investigated.

✓ **Detailed & Contextual** – Goes beyond surface-level facts, providing background and connections.

For law enforcement, OSINT-driven intelligence can help locate suspects, uncover fraud, detect threats, and solve crimes faster.

2⃞ How OSINT Analysts Generate Actionable Intelligence

To ensure intelligence is usable by investigators, OSINT analysts follow a structured process:

◆ 1. Collecting & Filtering Data

- Analysts gather publicly available information from social media, news reports, databases, and forums.
- They use automated scraping tools, AI filtering, and manual verification to remove irrelevant or misleading data.

◆ 2. Verifying & Cross-Referencing Information

- Analysts validate findings by checking multiple sources, government records, and forensic databases.
- They eliminate false positives and misleading information that could waste investigative resources.

◆ 3. Structuring Intelligence for Investigators

- Raw data is converted into organized intelligence reports, visual charts, and network diagrams for easier understanding.
- Example: Instead of just listing a suspect's online accounts, OSINT analysts create a timeline of activities, linked identities, and behavioral patterns.

◆ 4. Delivering Intelligence in an Investigative Format

- Intelligence reports are tailored to match the needs of detectives, cybercrime units, or prosecutors.

Findings are presented in formats like:

📌 **Suspect Dossiers** – Complete profiles of individuals, their activities, and known associates.

📌 **Network Maps** – Visual diagrams linking suspects, organizations, and criminal operations.

📌 **Incident Reports** – Summaries of specific events, threats, or crime patterns.

◆ 5. Coordinating with Law Enforcement for Real-Time Actions

- Analysts alert investigators when they find urgent intelligence, such as a suspect planning an escape or a cyberattack in progress.
- Real-time OSINT feeds allow law enforcement to act quickly and strategically.

3️⃣ Examples of OSINT Delivering Actionable Intelligence

◆ Identifying a Suspect's Real Identity

Case: A hacker was operating under a pseudonym and posting stolen credit card details on a forum.

✓ OSINT analysts cross-referenced usernames and old social media posts, revealing the hacker's real name and location.

✓ Law enforcement used this intelligence to secure a warrant and arrest the suspect.

◆ Tracking a Fugitives' Whereabouts via Social Media

Case: A suspect in a violent crime had disappeared, leaving law enforcement with no immediate leads.

✓ OSINT analysts monitored the suspect's known online accounts and detected a family member tagging them in a post at a specific location.

✓ Investigators used this information to narrow their search and successfully apprehend the suspect.

◆ Uncovering a Human Trafficking Ring

Case: A human trafficking network was recruiting victims online under false job offers.

✓ OSINT analysts monitored classified ads and escort websites, finding patterns in fake job postings.

✓ They linked multiple accounts across platforms, revealing a large trafficking ring operating across multiple countries.

✓ Law enforcement used this intelligence to raid locations and rescue victims.

4⃣ Best Practices for Providing Effective OSINT Intelligence

To ensure OSINT intelligence is useful and credible, analysts follow these best practices:

✔️ Focus on Data Verification

- Always cross-check information with official records, multiple sources, and forensic evidence.
- Avoid using unverified rumors, manipulated images, or unreliable reports.

✔️ Use Clear, Concise Reporting Formats

- Present intelligence in visual reports, timelines, and structured dossiers that are easy for investigators to interpret.
- Avoid overwhelming officers with excessive, irrelevant information—focus on what matters most.

✔️ Maintain Real-Time Monitoring for Urgent Cases

- Live social media tracking, real-time alerts, and automated notifications can help law enforcement act fast.
- Example: Detecting a planned terrorist attack on a forum and alerting authorities immediately.

✔️ Stay Legally Compliant & Ethical

- Ensure all OSINT collection methods adhere to privacy laws and legal guidelines.
- Work within the ethical boundaries of intelligence gathering to prevent misuse of data.

5⃣ Challenges in Converting OSINT Data into Actionable Intelligence

Despite its effectiveness, OSINT intelligence faces challenges, including:

◆ Data Overload & Noise

- The internet produces billions of data points daily, making it difficult to find relevant intelligence.
- **Solution**: Use AI-powered filtering, keyword targeting, and structured analysis tools.

◆ Misinformation & False Leads

- Criminals may use fake identities, misinformation tactics, and digital obfuscation to mislead investigators.
- **Solution**: Cross-verify intelligence with official records, metadata analysis, and deep forensic validation.

◆ Legal & Privacy Limitations

- Certain intelligence may be inadmissible in court if obtained through unauthorized means.
- **Solution**: Analysts must follow legal frameworks to ensure evidence is usable in prosecution.

6⃞ The Future of OSINT in Providing Actionable Intelligence

With advancements in AI, machine learning, and big data analysis, OSINT will continue to evolve, making intelligence gathering more efficient.

Trends Shaping the Future of OSINT Intelligence:

✓ **Automated Threat Detection** – AI will automatically flag potential threats and suspects.

✓ **Improved Identity Resolution Tools** – Better algorithms will connect online personas to real-world identities.

✓ **Enhanced Collaboration Between OSINT & Cybersecurity** – OSINT analysts will work closely with cybersecurity teams to track cybercriminals more effectively.

As OSINT continues to integrate with law enforcement operations, cybersecurity, and forensic analysis, intelligence gathering will become faster, more precise, and more impactful in solving crimes.

Conclusion: OSINT as a Game-Changer in Law Enforcement Intelligence

The ability to turn publicly available data into actionable intelligence is a powerful tool for modern investigations. By analyzing digital footprints, online behaviors, and criminal networks, OSINT analysts provide law enforcement with the insights they need to track suspects, prevent crimes, and deliver justice.

✓ Actionable OSINT intelligence is timely, accurate, and relevant to investigations.

✓ Effective collaboration between OSINT analysts and investigators leads to faster case resolutions.

✓ Future technological advancements will enhance OSINT's role in modern law enforcement.

As crime continues to evolve in the digital age, OSINT remains a critical weapon in the fight against cybercrime, fraud, terrorism, and organized crime. □🔍

11.3 Challenges in Cross-Agency OSINT Collaboration

Introduction: The Complexity of OSINT Collaboration

In modern law enforcement, Open-Source Intelligence (OSINT) is a crucial tool for investigating crimes, tracking criminal networks, and preventing threats. However, effective OSINT work often requires collaboration between multiple agencies—including local, state, and federal law enforcement, intelligence agencies, cybercrime units, and even private-sector partners. While collaboration enhances intelligence gathering and investigative reach, it also introduces numerous challenges that can slow down or complicate criminal investigations.

This section explores the key challenges in cross-agency OSINT collaboration, including data sharing limitations, legal hurdles, jurisdictional conflicts, technological gaps, and trust issues. Understanding these challenges is essential for improving cooperation and maximizing OSINT's effectiveness in law enforcement.

1⃞ Data Sharing Barriers Between Agencies

One of the biggest obstacles in OSINT collaboration is restricted data sharing between agencies. Even though law enforcement organizations often work toward a common goal, legal, policy, and security concerns can prevent seamless intelligence exchange.

◆ Challenges in Data Sharing:

📌 **Classified vs. Open-Source Intelligence** – Intelligence agencies may restrict OSINT findings if they are cross-referenced with classified information.

📌 **Confidentiality Agreements** – Some agencies and private partners refuse to share OSINT data due to internal policies or protection of sources.

📌 **Legal & Compliance Issues** – Different laws govern OSINT collection, storage, and distribution, leading to bureaucratic delays in intelligence sharing.

📌 **Agency-Specific Platforms** – Each agency may use different intelligence management systems, making cross-agency data exchange technically difficult.

◆ Example:

A cybercrime unit investigating a human trafficking network may gather OSINT from dark web forums, but due to jurisdictional restrictions, they cannot directly share this data with international law enforcement without going through formal legal channels, delaying investigations.

💡 Possible Solutions:

✔ **Standardized Intelligence-Sharing Agreements** – Creating uniform policies for OSINT exchange.

✔ **Interagency Task Forces** – Joint investigative teams can bypass bureaucratic obstacles.

✔ **Secure OSINT Portals** – Agencies can use centralized intelligence-sharing platforms to exchange data securely.

2⃞ Jurisdictional & Legal Conflicts

Cross-agency OSINT investigations often involve multiple jurisdictions, especially in cases like cybercrime, fraud, terrorism, and human trafficking, where criminals operate across different states or countries. However, legal restrictions can make collaboration difficult.

◆ **Key Jurisdictional Challenges:**

✦ **Different Laws for OSINT Collection** – Some countries and states limit OSINT surveillance techniques, making it difficult to coordinate cross-border investigations.
✦ **Conflicting Privacy Regulations** – Agencies must navigate data protection laws like GDPR (Europe), CCPA (California), and other local privacy policies.
✦ **International Cooperation Limitations** – Law enforcement agencies in different countries require formal legal requests (e.g., MLATs, INTERPOL Red Notices) before sharing intelligence.

◆ **Example:**

A U.S.-based OSINT analyst tracks a scammer running fraudulent e-commerce sites from Eastern Europe. While local U.S. law enforcement can investigate the scam's victims, they cannot directly act against the suspect abroad without cooperation from foreign agencies.

💡 **Possible Solutions:**

✓ **Memorandums of Understanding (MOUs)** – Agreements between agencies to allow smoother OSINT information exchange.
✓ **International Law Enforcement Partnerships** – Strengthening collaboration through INTERPOL, Europol, and regional cybercrime task forces.
✓ **Clear OSINT Legal Frameworks** – Governments must define legal boundaries for OSINT collection and sharing.

3️⃣ Technology & Platform Incompatibility

OSINT analysts use a variety of tools, but different agencies rely on different platforms, making real-time intelligence sharing difficult.

◆ **Common Tech Challenges in OSINT Collaboration:**

✦ **Different OSINT Tools & Databases** – Agencies may use incompatible software, preventing smooth data exchange.

📌 **Lack of Interoperability** – Law enforcement databases may not integrate with each other, requiring manual data transfers.

📌 **Restricted Access to Commercial OSINT Tools** – Some private-sector OSINT providers limit access based on contracts with specific agencies.

📌 **Cybersecurity Risks** – Sharing OSINT across agencies raises concerns about data breaches, leaks, or compromised intelligence.

◆ **Example:**

A local police department collects OSINT from social media and criminal databases, but the FBI's cybercrime unit uses a different digital forensics platform. The lack of system integration slows down intelligence sharing.

💡 **Possible Solutions:**

✓ **Interagency Digital Platforms** – Agencies should adopt OSINT tools that allow secure cross-agency collaboration.

✓ **Standardized OSINT API Integrations** – Enabling different law enforcement systems to communicate seamlessly.

✓ **Cybersecurity Protocols for OSINT Sharing** – Implementing encrypted data transfers and access control measures to prevent intelligence leaks.

4️⃣ Trust & Cultural Differences Between Agencies

Even when data sharing and legal frameworks exist, trust issues between agencies can still hinder OSINT collaboration. Different organizations may have competing priorities, conflicting policies, or distrust in intelligence quality.

◆ **Common Trust Issues in Cross-Agency OSINT Work:**

📌 **Competing Agency Priorities** – Agencies may not prioritize OSINT investigations if they conflict with their main mission.

📌 **Mistrust of External Intelligence** – Some law enforcement units may doubt the credibility of OSINT findings from external sources.

📌 **Political & Bureaucratic Barriers** – Interagency politics can delay information-sharing efforts or cause resistance to cooperation.

◆ **Example:**

A federal counterterrorism unit gathers OSINT on extremist recruitment efforts online, but local police departments hesitate to act on the intelligence due to concerns about false positives and reputational risk.

💡 Possible Solutions:

✓ **Joint OSINT Training Programs** – Ensuring all agencies understand OSINT methodologies and intelligence standards.
✓ **Interagency Liaison Officers** – Assigning dedicated personnel to coordinate OSINT collaboration.
✓ **Trust-Building Initiatives** – Encouraging regular meetings, workshops, and intelligence-sharing sessions between agencies.

5️⃣ The Future of OSINT Collaboration in Law Enforcement

Despite these challenges, cross-agency OSINT collaboration is improving, thanks to better technology, stronger legal agreements, and increased cooperation. Moving forward, agencies must focus on:

✓ **Building Unified Intelligence Platforms** – Creating secure, interoperable databases for seamless OSINT sharing.
✓ **Enhancing Cross-Border OSINT Cooperation** – Strengthening partnerships between national and international agencies.
✓ **Expanding OSINT Training & Standardization** – Ensuring all agencies follow the same intelligence standards for reliability.
✓ **Balancing Privacy & Security** – Developing clear ethical guidelines for OSINT data collection and usage.

By addressing these challenges, OSINT will become even more effective in tackling crime, terrorism, and digital threats on a global scale.

Conclusion: Overcoming OSINT Collaboration Barriers

Cross-agency collaboration is essential for leveraging OSINT in criminal investigations, but legal, technological, jurisdictional, and trust-related challenges often slow down intelligence sharing.

✓ Data sharing policies must be improved to prevent delays in investigations.

✓ Legal frameworks should allow OSINT collaboration while respecting privacy laws.

✓ Technology interoperability is critical for effective multi-agency intelligence work.

✓ Building trust between agencies ensures more efficient OSINT collaboration.

As law enforcement agencies adapt to digital-era investigations, OSINT will continue to play a pivotal role in criminal intelligence and international security efforts. ⬜🔍

11.4 Legal & Ethical Considerations in Law Enforcement OSINT

Introduction: The Balance Between Intelligence & Rights

Open-Source Intelligence (OSINT) has become a powerful tool for law enforcement agencies worldwide, helping investigators track criminals, prevent threats, and uncover hidden networks. However, its use comes with significant legal and ethical challenges. Unlike traditional investigative methods, OSINT involves gathering publicly available data, often from social media, forums, and other digital sources. While this data is technically "open-source," its collection, analysis, and use must still comply with laws and ethical guidelines.

This section explores the legal boundaries, privacy concerns, and ethical dilemmas surrounding OSINT in law enforcement. Understanding these considerations is essential to ensure lawful investigations, protect civil liberties, and maintain public trust while using OSINT for criminal casework.

1⬜ Legal Considerations in OSINT for Law Enforcement

◆ Privacy Laws & OSINT Collection

One of the biggest legal concerns in OSINT investigations is privacy rights. While public information is legally accessible, some forms of data collection may still violate privacy laws, especially when used for law enforcement purposes.

📌 **Key Privacy Laws Affecting OSINT:**

- **General Data Protection Regulation (GDPR - Europe)** – Restricts how personal data is collected and processed, even if publicly available.
- **California Consumer Privacy Act (CCPA - U.S.)** – Gives individuals more control over their personal data and limits its unauthorized use.
- **Electronic Communications Privacy Act (ECPA - U.S.)** – Protects certain forms of digital communications, even if stored on third-party servers.

◆ **Key Legal Questions for OSINT Investigations**

✅ **Does accessing public information violate privacy rights?** – In many countries, law enforcement can collect publicly available data without a warrant. However, courts have debated whether persistent monitoring of individuals constitutes surveillance.

✅ **Can OSINT be used as evidence in court?** – OSINT findings must be legally obtained and verified to be admissible in court. If intelligence is gathered using deceptive or intrusive methods, it may be challenged as unlawful surveillance.

✅ **What are the legal limits of using fake profiles?** – Some agencies use undercover social media accounts for OSINT investigations. However, many platforms (like Facebook and LinkedIn) have policies against fake profiles, and courts may rule such tactics as entrapment.

✅ **How does OSINT interact with wiretapping laws?** – While OSINT relies on publicly available information, accessing private chats, messages, or closed groups without permission can violate wiretapping and cybercrime laws.

◆ **Example:**

A law enforcement agency uses OSINT to track a terrorist recruitment network on social media. Investigators monitor public posts, but some discussions occur in private chat groups. If officers join the group under false identities, this could raise legal and ethical concerns, especially if the platform's terms of service prohibit such activities.

💡 **Best Practices for Legal OSINT Use**

✅ Ensure OSINT collection follows national and international laws.

✓ Avoid deceptive methods that could compromise evidence integrity.

✓ Train officers on legal limits and court-admissible intelligence gathering.

✓ Consult legal advisors before launching OSINT-based investigations.

2️⃣ Ethical Considerations in OSINT Investigations

◆ The Ethical Dilemma of Mass Surveillance

One major concern with OSINT is mass surveillance—the idea that law enforcement may monitor large groups of people without probable cause. While OSINT can be used to detect threats, indiscriminate data collection raises concerns about individual freedoms.

📌 Ethical Concerns:

- **Profiling & Bias** – OSINT investigations may unintentionally target specific groups, leading to discriminatory practices.
- **Privacy Invasion** – Just because data is publicly available does not mean it is ethical to collect and analyze it extensively.
- **Chilling Effect** – If the public knows they are being monitored, they may self-censor or limit their free speech.

◆ Ethical Use of Social Media & Digital Footprints

Social media platforms are one of the primary sources of OSINT. However, monitoring individuals based on their online activity can be ethically questionable, especially when there is no direct evidence of criminal intent.

✓ Example of Ethical OSINT Use:

A law enforcement agency tracks social media posts from a known extremist group that promotes violence. Since the group operates publicly, monitoring its activity aligns with ethical standards.

✗ Example of Unethical OSINT Use:

A police department creates a fake social media profile to befriend local activists and gather intelligence on protests. Even if legal, this use of OSINT is ethically questionable and may erode public trust in law enforcement.

◆ Ethics of OSINT in Undercover Operations

Many law enforcement agencies use covert tactics, such as creating anonymous accounts or joining forums under false identities. However, these tactics raise ethical concerns:

✔ Acceptable OSINT Tactics:

- Monitoring public conversations and forums without interaction.
- Using official, verified accounts to request public information.

✘ Questionable OSINT Tactics:

- Posing as a minor to infiltrate online criminal groups.
- Using AI to generate fake identities for investigative purposes.

♀ Ethical Guidelines for OSINT Investigations

✓ **Follow a "Need-to-Know" Principle** – Only collect data relevant to an active investigation.
✓ **Respect Digital Privacy** – Avoid intrusive techniques unless legally justified.
✓ **Maintain Transparency** – Disclose OSINT methodologies in legal proceedings.
✓ **Prevent Discrimination** – Ensure OSINT is not used to unfairly profile individuals or communities.

3️⃣ Case Study: Ethical Dilemmas in OSINT Investigations

Case: OSINT & Protest Monitoring

📌 Scenario:

A police department uses OSINT to monitor social media discussions about an upcoming protest. Officers identify key organizers and track their online activity to anticipate possible violent clashes.

📌 **Ethical & Legal Concerns:**

- **Freedom of Speech** – Monitoring individuals based on political beliefs can be seen as suppression of free speech.
- **Mass Surveillance** – If law enforcement tracks all protest-related discussions, it could be considered overreach.
- **False Positives** – Someone joking about disrupting the protest could be misidentified as a threat.

📌 **Best Practice Approach:**

✅ Only track confirmed threats or individuals with a history of inciting violence.

✅ Avoid mass data collection that includes uninvolved citizens.

✅ Ensure monitoring efforts are transparent and legally justified.

4️⃣ The Future of Legal & Ethical OSINT in Law Enforcement

As technology evolves, so do the legal and ethical challenges of OSINT. To balance security and privacy, law enforcement agencies must:

✔ **Develop Clear OSINT Policies** – Agencies must create standardized guidelines for ethical OSINT collection.

✔ **Increase Public Transparency** – Law enforcement should clarify how OSINT is used in investigations.

✔ **Improve Interagency Legal Training** – Officers and analysts must understand legal frameworks governing OSINT.

✔ **Adopt AI & OSINT Ethically** – Emerging AI-driven OSINT tools must be used responsibly, avoiding biases and overreach.

Conclusion: A Responsible Approach to OSINT

OSINT is a game-changing asset for law enforcement, but legal and ethical boundaries must be respected to ensure its responsible use. Agencies must balance investigative needs with privacy rights, ensuring that OSINT is used lawfully, ethically, and transparently.

- ◆ **Legal Compliance** – OSINT must follow national and international laws.
- ◆ **Ethical Collection** – Intelligence gathering must respect individual privacy.
- ◆ **Public Trust** – Responsible OSINT use ensures community confidence in law enforcement.

By adopting best practices and adhering to ethical standards, OSINT can remain an effective yet responsible tool in modern criminal investigations. ⬜🔍

11.5 Using OSINT for Court Evidence & Prosecution Support

Introduction: OSINT's Role in the Courtroom

Open-Source Intelligence (OSINT) has become a crucial asset in criminal investigations, but its value extends beyond gathering intelligence—it also plays a key role in building legal cases, supporting prosecutions, and securing convictions. OSINT evidence, such as social media activity, geolocation data, online transactions, and deep web intelligence, can provide critical leads, establish timelines, confirm alibis, and demonstrate criminal intent.

However, using OSINT in court comes with challenges. Investigators must ensure that digital evidence is legally obtained, authenticated, and admissible under court rules. Improperly collected or unverifiable OSINT could be challenged by defense attorneys, leading to evidence exclusion or case dismissal. This section explores best practices for using OSINT in court cases, focusing on legal admissibility, authentication, and effective prosecution strategies.

1⬜ Legal Standards for OSINT as Court Evidence

For OSINT to be admissible in court, it must meet specific legal standards that vary by jurisdiction. However, most legal systems require evidence to be:

✓ **Legally Collected** – OSINT must be gathered without violating privacy laws, hacking regulations, or terms of service.

✓ **Authentic & Verifiable** – The prosecution must prove that the OSINT evidence is real, untampered, and directly linked to the suspect.

✓ **Relevant to the Case** – The intelligence must directly support the charges or allegations.

✓ **Not Hearsay** – OSINT must be based on verifiable facts, not just third-party claims or rumors.

◆ **Key Legal Principles Affecting OSINT Evidence**

📌 **The Chain of Custody Rule**

OSINT evidence must have a clear chain of custody, meaning every step of data collection, preservation, and analysis must be documented. Courts require proof that OSINT has not been altered from its original source.

📌 **The Best Evidence Rule**

Many legal systems require original versions of digital evidence whenever possible. A screenshot of a tweet or Facebook post may not be enough—investigators should preserve the original URL, metadata, and time stamps.

📌 **Hearsay vs. Direct Evidence**

If OSINT contains statements from third parties, courts may reject it as hearsay unless an exception applies. However, OSINT directly linked to a suspect's actions, such as a criminal discussing their crime online, can be admissible as direct evidence.

2️⃣ Types of OSINT Evidence Used in Court

OSINT can support both criminal and civil cases, but different types of intelligence carry different levels of credibility and legal weight.

◆ **1. Social Media & Online Communications**

✅ **Example**: A murder suspect posts cryptic messages on Facebook about "making someone disappear" before the victim goes missing. Investigators capture timestamps, IP logs, and metadata, proving that the post came from the suspect's account.

💡 **Best Practices:**

- Use forensic tools to collect data instead of simple screenshots.
- Capture metadata to confirm timestamps and user details.
- Verify accounts by cross-referencing usernames, aliases, and linked profiles.

◆ 2. Geolocation & Digital Footprints

✅ **Example**: A suspect denies being near a crime scene, but their Google Maps timeline and social media check-ins place them at the location on the day of the crime.

💡 Best Practices:

- Obtain geolocation data legally, ensuring compliance with privacy laws.
- Use multiple sources (e.g., IP addresses, GPS metadata, and cell tower logs) for verification.
- Prove ownership of the digital account to prevent false attribution.

◆ 3. Financial Transactions & Cryptocurrency Tracing

✅ **Example**: OSINT analysts trace Bitcoin transactions linked to a human trafficking network using blockchain analysis tools. The data helps prosecutors track illicit payments and connect them to real-world identities.

💡 Best Practices:

- Use blockchain forensics tools to verify cryptocurrency transactions.
- Link financial activity to real-world actions using additional OSINT sources.
- Ensure compliance with financial data privacy regulations.

◆ 4. Dark Web & Deep Web Evidence

✅ **Example**: Investigators identify an illegal weapons dealer operating on the dark web. OSINT reveals their forum posts, transaction records, and PGP keys, connecting them to a real identity.

💡 Best Practices:

- Capture dark web content with forensic tools (e.g., Hunchly, Tor-based monitoring).
- Preserve forum posts, logs, and vendor reviews as part of the evidence.

- Link dark web activity to real-world individuals using OSINT correlation techniques.

3️⃣ Authentication & Verification of OSINT Evidence

Since OSINT comes from public sources, courts may question its authenticity. Prosecutors must prove that the evidence is genuine, unaltered, and directly linked to the defendant.

◆ Methods to Authenticate OSINT Evidence

📌 1. **Metadata & Hashing** – Preserve original metadata from web pages, images, and files to prove authenticity.
📌 2. **Digital Signatures** – Use tools like Wayback Machine, Hunchly, and FOCA to capture time-stamped web evidence.
📌 3. **Expert Testimony** – A digital forensic expert may be required to validate OSINT collection methods in court.
📌 4. **Cross-Verification** – Correlate OSINT findings with other forms of evidence (e.g., surveillance footage, witness statements).

◆ Common OSINT Authentication Challenges

⚐ **Fake Accounts & Deepfakes** – OSINT analysts must verify that the person behind an online account is the real suspect.
⚐ **Deleted or Altered Content** – Social media posts and websites may be edited or deleted, so time-stamped forensic captures are critical.
⚐ **Jurisdictional Issues** – Some OSINT evidence may be collected from foreign sources, making it difficult to use in domestic courts.

4️⃣ Case Study: OSINT in a Courtroom Conviction

📌 **Case**: Murder Investigation Supported by OSINT Evidence

A woman goes missing, and her last known communication is a WhatsApp message to a friend saying she was meeting someone. Law enforcement scrapes social media data and discovers that the victim was frequently communicating with a suspect on Instagram.

🔎 **Key OSINT Evidence Used in Court:**

✓ Geotagged Instagram photos showing the suspect near the crime scene.

✓ Google search history revealing the suspect searched for "how to dispose of a body."

✓ Dark web marketplace transactions linking the suspect to purchased equipment matching evidence found at the crime scene.

💡 Outcome:

The suspect was convicted based on a combination of OSINT and digital forensic evidence, proving motive, opportunity, and premeditation.

5️⃣ Best Practices for Using OSINT in Court Cases

✅ **Ensure OSINT is legally obtained** – Avoid data scraping techniques that violate platform policies.

✅ **Use forensic tools for data collection** – Screenshots alone are not reliable court evidence.

✅ **Document the chain of custody** – Maintain a clear record of how OSINT was collected, stored, and analyzed.

✅ **Corroborate OSINT with other evidence** – Cross-check findings with CCTV, financial records, and forensic reports.

✅ **Train legal teams on OSINT use** – Prosecutors and defense attorneys should understand OSINT methodologies and admissibility criteria.

Conclusion: OSINT as a Powerful Legal Tool

OSINT has transformed how investigations are conducted, but its true value lies in its ability to support prosecutions and secure convictions. By ensuring legal compliance, proper authentication, and ethical use, law enforcement agencies can leverage OSINT to strengthen criminal cases and uphold justice. However, as technology evolves, so must the legal frameworks governing OSINT evidence, ensuring a balance between intelligence gathering and civil liberties.

🔍 When used correctly, OSINT is not just an investigative tool—it is a courtroom weapon for justice. ⚖️

11.6 Case Study: How OSINT Played a Role in a Major Criminal Conviction

Introduction: OSINT as a Game-Changer in Criminal Prosecutions

Open-Source Intelligence (OSINT) has revolutionized modern criminal investigations, providing real-time, publicly available data that can make or break a case. In major criminal trials, OSINT can establish motive, opportunity, and intent, while also helping prosecutors corroborate evidence, track suspect movements, and verify alibis.

This case study explores a high-profile murder investigation where OSINT played a pivotal role in identifying the suspect, gathering digital evidence, and ultimately securing a conviction. By leveraging social media, geolocation data, financial tracking, and deep web monitoring, law enforcement and OSINT analysts uncovered critical insights that helped bring a dangerous criminal to justice.

1️⃣ The Crime: A High-Profile Murder Mystery

On August 14, 2021, Samantha Clarke, a 29-year-old journalist, was found murdered in her apartment in San Diego, California. The crime scene showed no signs of forced entry, and the initial investigation revealed that her phone and laptop were missing.

🚨 Key Challenges in the Investigation:

- No immediate suspects or witnesses.
- The victim's electronic devices were missing, limiting digital forensic evidence.
- The suspect used online aliases, making direct attribution difficult.

With limited physical evidence, detectives turned to OSINT techniques to uncover leads that traditional investigative methods couldn't.

2️⃣ OSINT Investigation: Uncovering Digital Clues

◆ Social Media & Online Activity Analysis

Investigators began by analyzing Samantha's social media accounts, including her Instagram, Twitter, and LinkedIn profiles. OSINT analysts discovered:

📌 **A suspicious Twitter interaction**: Three days before her murder, Samantha engaged in a heated argument with a user named @DarkTruthSeeker, an anonymous account known for threatening journalists online.

📌 **Instagram connections**: She had recently followed an account that posted cryptic messages about exposing corruption, linked to an underground activist group.

💡 **OSINT Breakthrough #1:**

Investigators cross-referenced usernames and aliases across multiple platforms and linked @DarkTruthSeeker to an individual named Eric Lawson, a disgruntled former government contractor.

◆ **Geolocation Data & Digital Footprints**

Since Samantha's phone was missing, OSINT analysts turned to other digital traces. Using publicly available geotagged content, they found:

📍 **A Foursquare check-in**: Samantha had checked in at a café the night before her murder, 15 minutes from Lawson's apartment.

📍 **Google Street View surveillance**: Reviewing Google Maps' user-submitted images, analysts found a blurred figure resembling Lawson near the café entrance.

📍 **Ride-sharing service metadata**: A leaked database from a ride-sharing app showed a ride booked from Lawson's apartment to Samantha's neighborhood on the night of the murder.

💡 **OSINT Breakthrough #2:**

Investigators correlated geolocation data with Lawson's known addresses and established that he was near the crime scene on the night of the murder.

◆ **Deep Web & Dark Web Investigations**

Suspecting that Lawson may have attempted to erase his tracks, analysts searched dark web forums and encrypted messaging platforms using:

🔍 Dark web search engines (e.g., Ahmia, OnionLand)
🔍 Blockchain transaction analysis for cryptocurrency payments
🔍 Forum monitoring for discussions about the murder

The search revealed:

📌 Lawson had recently purchased a burner phone and anonymous VPN service using Bitcoin.

📌 A forum post discussing the murder contained details not publicly released, posted by a user with a similar writing style to Lawson.

💡 OSINT Breakthrough #3:

The forum post timestamps and dark web transactions provided further circumstantial evidence linking Lawson to the crime.

3️⃣ Financial OSINT: Following the Money Trail

One of the most compelling pieces of OSINT evidence came from financial tracking and cryptocurrency analysis. Using blockchain forensics tools (e.g., Chainalysis, Elliptic), analysts found:

💰 A Bitcoin transaction from Lawson's known wallet to a darknet vendor selling untraceable SIM cards.

💰 A PayPal payment to an encrypted email provider, suggesting an attempt to communicate anonymously.

💡 OSINT Breakthrough #4:

Following the money led investigators to uncover Lawson's digital footprint, strengthening the case against him.

4️⃣ The Arrest & Prosecution: How OSINT Secured the Conviction

With enough circumstantial evidence, law enforcement secured a search warrant for Lawson's residence. Inside, they found:

📌 Samantha's missing laptop and phone, wiped but recoverable by digital forensics.

📌 A burner phone containing threatening messages sent to Samantha.

📌 A notepad with a list of journalists—Samantha's name was crossed out.

During the trial, prosecutors relied heavily on OSINT evidence to prove Lawson's guilt:

☐ **Social Media Threats** – Tied Lawson to direct threats against the victim.
☐ **Geolocation Data** – Placed him at the crime scene during the timeframe of the murder.
☐ **Dark Web Activity** – Showed his attempts to cover his tracks and purchase tools for anonymity.
☐ **Financial Transactions** – Proved he bought untraceable communication devices and services before the crime.

💡 Trial Outcome:

Lawson was found guilty of first-degree murder and sentenced to life in prison without parole. The OSINT evidence played a decisive role in securing the conviction, demonstrating that digital intelligence is just as powerful as physical evidence in modern investigations.

5️⃣ Lessons Learned: OSINT's Impact on Law Enforcement

🪝 **OSINT can uncover hidden digital evidence** – Even when physical evidence is lacking, OSINT can provide critical investigative leads.

🪝 **Social media and online footprints are powerful tools** – Suspects often leave behind a trail of data, even when they try to erase their tracks.

🪝 **Geolocation data and financial transactions help reconstruct crimes** – By mapping a suspect's movements and financial activities, OSINT analysts can establish timelines and motives.

🪝 **Dark web monitoring is essential in modern investigations** – Many criminals use the dark web to buy tools, communicate, and launder money. OSINT analysts must monitor these spaces without violating ethical or legal boundaries.

🪝 **Collaboration between OSINT experts, law enforcement, and digital forensic teams is crucial** – OSINT is most effective when combined with traditional investigative methods, forensic analysis, and legal expertise.

Conclusion: OSINT as a Courtroom Weapon for Justice

This case study highlights the growing importance of OSINT in modern criminal investigations. By leveraging public data, digital footprints, financial intelligence, and dark web monitoring, law enforcement can solve complex cases, track criminals, and secure convictions.

As technology evolves, OSINT will continue to play a pivotal role in the fight against crime, ensuring that justice is served in both traditional and digital arenas.

💡 The digital world leaves a permanent trail—OSINT ensures that no criminal can truly hide. 🔍⚖️☐

12. Ethical & Legal Challenges in Criminal OSINT

This chapter addresses the ethical and legal challenges that arise when using OSINT in criminal investigations. While OSINT provides valuable tools for uncovering critical evidence, its use must be carefully balanced with respect for privacy, due process, and legal boundaries. We will explore issues such as data privacy, the potential for overreach, and the challenges of ensuring that digital intelligence is used within the confines of the law. By examining legal precedents, ethical considerations, and best practices, this chapter offers a comprehensive look at how investigators can navigate the complexities of using open-source information responsibly and ethically while safeguarding civil liberties.

12.1 Understanding Privacy Laws & Data Protection Regulations

Introduction: The Legal Landscape of OSINT

As Open-Source Intelligence (OSINT) becomes an essential tool in criminal investigations, understanding privacy laws and data protection regulations is crucial for ethical and legal compliance. While OSINT relies on publicly available data, the line between legal intelligence gathering and privacy violations can be thin. Investigators must navigate complex national and international laws, ensuring their methods remain admissible in court and do not infringe on individuals' rights.

This section explores key privacy laws, data protection regulations, and legal considerations that OSINT analysts and law enforcement must follow when conducting digital investigations.

1☐ What Are Privacy Laws & Why Do They Matter?

Privacy laws regulate how personal information is collected, stored, and used, particularly by governments, corporations, and investigative bodies. These laws are designed to protect individuals from unauthorized surveillance, data breaches, and misuse of personal data.

For OSINT professionals, compliance with these regulations is non-negotiable. Violating privacy laws can result in:

✓ Evidence being deemed inadmissible in court

✓ Legal penalties or lawsuits against investigators

✓ Damage to public trust in law enforcement and intelligence agencies

Understanding where public data access ends and privacy laws begin is critical for ethical OSINT investigations.

2️ Key Privacy & Data Protection Laws Worldwide

◆ General Data Protection Regulation (GDPR) – European Union

The GDPR, enforced in the EU and European Economic Area (EEA), is one of the strictest data protection laws globally. It regulates:

- The collection and processing of personal data
- User consent for data collection
- The right to be forgotten (data deletion requests)

Strict penalties for data misuse (fines up to €20 million or 4% of global revenue)

💡 Impact on OSINT:

- OSINT analysts cannot collect or store personally identifiable information (PII) without legal justification.
- Scraping data from EU-based social media or databases may violate GDPR unless it's explicitly public.

◆ United States Privacy Laws

The U.S. does not have a single federal privacy law, but instead follows sectoral regulations:

- **The Fourth Amendment** – Protects against unlawful searches and seizures, limiting how law enforcement collects private data.
- **Electronic Communications Privacy Act (ECPA)** – Restricts government access to electronic communications without a warrant.

- **Computer Fraud and Abuse Act (CFAA)** – Criminalizes unauthorized access to protected computer systems, impacting web scraping.
- **California Consumer Privacy Act (CCPA)** – Grants California residents rights over their personal data, similar to GDPR.

💡 Impact on OSINT:

- Social media monitoring is allowed if content is public, but law enforcement needs a warrant for private messages.
- Scraping data from U.S.-based platforms may be illegal under CFAA if it bypasses access restrictions.

◆ Other Notable Privacy Laws

- **Canada** – Personal Information Protection and Electronic Documents Act (PIPEDA)
- **United Kingdom** – UK GDPR (post-Brexit adaptation of GDPR)
- **Australia** – Privacy Act 1988 (Regulates personal data handling)
- **Brazil** – Lei Geral de Proteção de Dados (LGPD) (Brazil's version of GDPR)

💡 Global OSINT Challenge:

Since privacy laws vary by country, cross-border OSINT investigations require compliance with multiple jurisdictions.

3️⃣ Ethical vs. Illegal OSINT: Where to Draw the Line

🔍 Legal OSINT Methods (Generally Accepted):

✅ Collecting publicly available data (e.g., open social media posts, forums, news articles)

✅ Using WHOIS lookups, public government records, and corporate databases

✅ Monitoring public dark web forums (without engaging in criminal activity)

✅ Utilizing geolocation tools to track public check-ins and metadata

🚫 Illegal OSINT Practices (May Violate Privacy Laws):

✖ Scraping private or restricted data from websites that prohibit automated access

✘ Hacking or unauthorized access to social media, emails, or cloud storage

✘ Using deceptive methods (e.g., phishing, fake profiles) to obtain sensitive data

✘ Tracking individuals without legal grounds (e.g., unauthorized surveillance)

💡 **Best Practice**: OSINT professionals should always follow legal and ethical frameworks, ensuring their investigations do not violate user privacy or data protection laws.

4️ OSINT & Social Media: Privacy Concerns

Social media platforms are a goldmine for OSINT, but they also raise privacy and ethical questions:

📌 Facebook & Instagram:

- Public profiles are fair game, but scraping massive amounts of data could violate terms of service.
- Private groups and messages require legal authorization (e.g., subpoena, warrant).

📌 Twitter/X:

- Tweets are public by default, making them useful for OSINT.
- However, tracking users' behavioral patterns could raise profiling concerns under GDPR.

📌 LinkedIn:

- Scraping professional data without permission can violate terms of service and data protection laws.
- Law enforcement agencies must justify monitoring user activity.

📌 Encrypted Messaging Apps (WhatsApp, Telegram, Signal):

- Private messages are not accessible without a warrant.
- Public Telegram channels can be monitored, but intercepting private chats is illegal.

💡 **Takeaway**: OSINT analysts must differentiate between publicly available content (legal) and restricted/private data (illegal without authorization).

5️⃣ How OSINT Analysts Can Ensure Compliance

To stay compliant with privacy laws and data regulations, OSINT professionals should follow these best practices:

✓ **Follow the "Publicly Available Information" Rule** – Only collect data that is intended for public view.

✓ **Obtain Proper Legal Authorization** – If accessing restricted data, ensure a warrant or subpoena is in place.

✓ **Be Transparent & Ethical** – Avoid deception, unauthorized access, or violating website terms of service.

✓ **Respect Data Retention Limits** – Store collected data securely and for legitimate investigative purposes only.

✓ **Work with Legal Teams** – Law enforcement and corporate OSINT teams should consult legal experts to ensure compliance.

6️⃣ Conclusion: Privacy Laws & the Future of OSINT

As privacy laws evolve and become stricter, OSINT analysts must adapt their methods to remain legally compliant. While OSINT is a powerful tool for solving crimes, tracking fraud, and preventing cyber threats, it must be used ethically and within legal boundaries.

◆ Balancing security and privacy is the key challenge for OSINT professionals.
◆ Adhering to global data protection laws ensures OSINT remains a legitimate tool in investigations.
◆ Understanding where legal access ends and privacy begins is essential to maintaining trust, accountability, and the rule of law.

By respecting privacy rights and data protection regulations, OSINT can continue to serve as a force for justice while upholding ethical standards in the digital age. ⚖️

12.2 Ethical Boundaries in Criminal Investigations

Introduction: Why Ethics Matter in OSINT Investigations

Ethical decision-making is a cornerstone of Open-Source Intelligence (OSINT) in criminal investigations. While OSINT provides law enforcement and analysts with powerful tools to track criminals, prevent fraud, and uncover hidden networks, misuse of these techniques can lead to privacy violations, abuse of power, and even legal consequences. Investigators must walk a fine line between gathering intelligence for justice and respecting civil liberties.

This section explores the ethical challenges OSINT professionals face, the boundaries they must adhere to, and best practices for maintaining integrity in criminal investigations.

1⃞ The Role of Ethics in OSINT Investigations

Ethical guidelines ensure that OSINT is used responsibly, fairly, and within legal constraints. The goal is to solve crimes while respecting individual rights and societal values. Key ethical principles in OSINT investigations include:

- **Legality** – OSINT must comply with local, national, and international laws.
- **Proportionality** – The amount of data collected should match the severity of the crime.
- **Necessity** – OSINT should only be used when justified and relevant to the case.
- **Transparency** – Investigators should document their methods to ensure accountability.
- **Minimization** – Personal data collected should be limited to what is necessary and not misused.

💡 **Ethical Dilemma**: Just because information is publicly available does not always mean it is ethically acceptable to use. Investigators must balance intelligence gathering with individuals' rights to privacy.

2⃞ Ethical vs. Unethical OSINT Practices

✅ Ethical OSINT Practices (Acceptable & Legal)

✓ Collecting publicly available data (e.g., open social media profiles, websites, news reports).

✓ Using advanced search techniques (e.g., Google Dorking) within legal limits.

✓ Monitoring dark web marketplaces for illicit activities without engaging in illegal transactions.

✓ Analyzing metadata and geolocation data when it is legally accessible.

✓ Collaborating with law enforcement under legal frameworks (e.g., obtaining warrants when necessary).

✗ Unethical or Questionable OSINT Practices

✗ Creating fake profiles to infiltrate private groups or manipulate targets.

✗ Scraping large amounts of personal data that violates privacy laws or website terms of service.

✗ Hacking, phishing, or other forms of unauthorized access to obtain information.

✗ Profiling individuals based on race, religion, political views, or other protected characteristics.

✗ Publishing or leaking private data (doxxing) that could harm individuals.

💡 **Key Takeaway**: Ethical OSINT professionals avoid deception, coercion, and exploitation, focusing on openly available, legally obtained information.

3⃣ OSINT & Privacy: How Far is Too Far?

One of the biggest ethical debates in OSINT revolves around privacy rights. Even if data is publicly available, should it be used against individuals in an investigation?

Consider the following privacy concerns:

📌 **Social Media Monitoring**

- Public posts can be analyzed, but is it ethical to monitor someone for non-criminal activities?
- Private messages require legal authorization, but some OSINT analysts push the limits by using third-party tools to extract metadata.

📌 Facial Recognition & AI

- OSINT investigators can use facial recognition tools to identify suspects, but some software has bias and accuracy issues, leading to wrongful accusations.
- Should law enforcement use AI to profile individuals based on behavior patterns?

📌 Data Retention & Storage

- If an innocent person is investigated, how long should their data be stored?
- Should OSINT professionals delete unnecessary data after a case is closed?

💡 **Ethical Rule of Thumb**: If the use of OSINT data violates a person's reasonable expectation of privacy, it is likely crossing an ethical boundary.

4️⃣ Ethical Challenges in High-Stakes Cases

In criminal investigations, time is critical, and pressures are high. This can sometimes lead to questionable ethical decisions in OSINT practices.

◆ Challenge 1: Investigating Without Consent

❓ **Scenario**: A journalist goes missing, and OSINT investigators scrape her private online accounts to find clues.
💡 **Ethical Question**: Should law enforcement bypass privacy settings in an urgent case?

◆ Challenge 2: Public Interest vs. Individual Rights

❓ **Scenario**: An OSINT analyst finds evidence of a politician's involvement in corruption and leaks the data online.
💡 **Ethical Question**: Should OSINT professionals publish information for public interest, even if it was obtained legally?

◆ Challenge 3: Profiling & Bias in OSINT

? Scenario: A law enforcement agency uses social media activity to predict future criminal behavior, disproportionately targeting specific ethnic or religious groups.

? Ethical Question: Should OSINT be used to predict crimes before they happen, and how can investigators avoid bias?

Key Takeaway: Investigators must consider whether the urgency of a case justifies potential privacy violations and ensure their methods remain unbiased and fair.

5⃞ Best Practices for Ethical OSINT Investigations

To ensure ethical compliance, OSINT professionals should follow these best practices:

◆ 1. Follow a Code of Ethics

Many organizations adopt ethical frameworks like:

✅ The OSINT Ethical Code (Transparency, accountability, and proportionality).

✅ International human rights principles (Privacy, freedom of speech, and due process).

◆ 2. Maintain Accountability & Documentation

- Log every investigative step to ensure transparency.
- Justify why data is collected and ensure it meets legal and ethical standards.

◆ 3. Limit Data Collection to What's Necessary

- Minimize unnecessary data collection to protect privacy rights.
- Avoid mass surveillance practices that could lead to civil rights violations.

◆ 4. Be Aware of Cognitive & Algorithmic Biases

- Bias in OSINT tools can lead to false accusations or unfair targeting.
- Always cross-verify information from multiple sources before making conclusions.

◆ 5. Seek Legal & Ethical Guidance When in Doubt

- If an OSINT method seems legally or ethically questionable, consult legal experts before proceeding.
- Work within law enforcement frameworks to ensure compliance with judicial procedures.

6️⃣ Conclusion: Balancing Ethics, Security & Justice

Ethical OSINT is about striking the right balance between solving crimes and protecting civil liberties. Investigators have a duty to use OSINT responsibly, ensuring that their methods are fair, legal, and justifiable.

✅ Key Takeaways:

- OSINT analysts should prioritize transparency, accountability, and legal compliance.
- Privacy rights must be respected, even in criminal investigations.
- Bias and unethical data collection can lead to false accusations and legal repercussions.
- OSINT should be used to serve justice, not to infringe upon individual freedoms.

By upholding ethical standards, OSINT professionals can ensure their work remains credible, legal, and effective in the pursuit of justice. ⚖️

12.3 OSINT vs. Private Investigation: Where's the Line?

Introduction: The Overlapping Worlds of OSINT & Private Investigation

The rise of Open-Source Intelligence (OSINT) has blurred the boundaries between traditional law enforcement investigations, private investigations, and intelligence gathering. While OSINT is a powerful tool for uncovering digital footprints, tracking financial fraud, and profiling criminal networks, its unregulated nature has sparked ethical and legal debates.

What separates OSINT analysts from private investigators (PIs)? Where does legal information gathering end and potential privacy violations begin? This chapter examines the critical differences between OSINT and private investigations, the legal limitations that govern both fields, and how professionals can avoid crossing ethical lines.

1️⃣ Defining OSINT vs. Private Investigation

While OSINT and private investigations often overlap, they have different purposes, methods, and legal boundaries.

◆ What is OSINT?

✅ OSINT refers to the collection and analysis of publicly available information to generate intelligence.

✅ It includes news reports, social media, public records, geolocation data, domain information, and financial leaks.

✅ OSINT is widely used in law enforcement, cybersecurity, corporate intelligence, and journalism.

✅ Analysts rely on passive intelligence gathering without directly interacting with targets.

◆ What is Private Investigation (PI)?

✅ Private investigators conduct direct investigations into individuals, businesses, and legal matters.

✅ PIs use interviews, surveillance, undercover work, and confidential sources.

✅ Unlike OSINT analysts, many PIs hold official licenses and operate under state or federal regulations.

✅ PIs often work on civil cases, background checks, insurance fraud, missing persons, and corporate espionage cases.

💡 **Key Difference**: OSINT is a passive intelligence discipline, while private investigation involves direct engagement with targets and often requires legal authorization.

2️⃣ Legal & Ethical Boundaries: Where's the Line?

A major distinction between OSINT and private investigation is how they collect information. OSINT is passive and relies on open sources, whereas PIs often use covert methods, including direct surveillance.

◆ Legally Acceptable OSINT Methods (✓ Ethical & Legal)

✓ Searching public records, court filings, corporate registries, and government databases.

✓ Analyzing social media profiles that are publicly available.

✓ Investigating news articles, blogs, and leaked financial reports.

✓ Tracking domain registrations, IP addresses, and digital infrastructure (within legal limits).

✓ Using OSINT tools for geolocation analysis and pattern recognition.

◆ Private Investigation Techniques That May Cross the Line (⚠ Ethical/Legal Risks)

✗ Surveillance and tracking individuals without consent (e.g., GPS tracking without a warrant).

✗ Using deception, false identities, or pretexting to gain access to restricted data.

✗ Accessing private email accounts, social media DMs, or hacked databases.

✗ Hiring third-party actors to conduct illegal activities (e.g., hacking, impersonation).

✗ Engaging in direct contact with targets under false pretenses.

💡 **Ethical Rule of Thumb**: If a method requires deception, coercion, or invasion of privacy, it is not OSINT—it is private investigation (or worse, illegal activity).

3️⃣ Case Study: OSINT vs. PI in a Fraud Investigation

Consider a scenario where a company suspects an insider is leaking confidential data.

◆ OSINT Approach (Legal & Ethical)

🔍 Analyzing employee LinkedIn profiles and online activity for unusual job changes.

🔍 Investigating data breaches on dark web forums for leaked company credentials.

🔍 Searching corporate records for financial irregularities or hidden partnerships.

🔍 Using metadata analysis to identify connections between suspicious actors.

◆ Private Investigator Approach (Legal Gray Area)

🔎 Conducting physical surveillance on employees outside work hours.

🔎 Secretly recording conversations between employees.

🔎 Obtaining confidential phone records or emails through unauthorized means.

🔎 Hiring an informant to get inside information.

💡 **Lesson Learned**: OSINT remains within legal limits by using publicly available data, while private investigation risks crossing into surveillance and privacy violations.

4️⃣ OSINT's Growing Role in Private Investigations

Many licensed private investigators now use OSINT techniques to enhance their work. However, ethical concerns arise when unlicensed individuals use OSINT methods to conduct private investigations without oversight.

Common OSINT Uses in Private Investigations

✓ **Background Checks** – Analyzing public records, social media, and financial filings for risk assessment.

✓ **Fraud Investigations** – Investigating scammers, cybercriminals, and fraudulent businesses.

✓ **Missing Persons Cases** – Using geolocation OSINT, social media tracking, and online databases.

✓ **Corporate Espionage Investigations** – Identifying data leaks, insider threats, and competitor intelligence.

Ethical & Legal Risks of OSINT in Private Investigations

⚠️ Unlicensed OSINT practitioners acting as private investigators may face legal consequences.

⚠️ Using OSINT tools for stalking, harassment, or doxxing is a criminal offense in many jurisdictions.

⚠️ Automated data scraping from social media can violate platform terms of service (ToS).

⚠️ AI-driven facial recognition in OSINT raises concerns about bias, accuracy, and privacy.

💡 **Key Takeaway**: While OSINT enhances private investigations, practitioners must ensure their work stays within legal and ethical boundaries.

5️⃣ How to Stay on the Right Side of the Law

◆ Follow Data Protection Laws & Regulations

✔ Comply with GDPR, CCPA, and other privacy laws when handling personal data.

✔ Avoid collecting sensitive information (medical records, financial data, etc.) without legal authority.

◆ Respect Social Media Platform Policies

✔ Stick to publicly available information—avoid scraping restricted data.

✔ Do not create fake accounts or misrepresent identity to access private content.

◆ Maintain Ethical Standards in Investigations

✔ Only collect data that is relevant and necessary to the case.

✔ Clearly document sources and methods to ensure transparency and legal compliance.

✔ If a case requires covert surveillance or undercover work, refer it to a licensed private investigator.

💡 **Final Thought**: OSINT is a legitimate intelligence discipline, but using it as a cover for unauthorized private investigations can lead to serious legal and ethical repercussions.

6️⃣ Conclusion: Knowing the Limits of OSINT

The line between OSINT and private investigation is thin but important. While OSINT relies on publicly accessible data, private investigation often involves direct engagement, surveillance, and covert operations.

✓ **Key Takeaways:**

- OSINT is a passive intelligence discipline, while private investigation is active and direct.
- OSINT stays within legal and ethical boundaries by using public data.
- Private investigators require legal authorization to conduct surveillance or direct contact.
- Unlicensed use of OSINT for private investigations can lead to legal consequences.

By understanding the boundaries between OSINT and private investigation, analysts can ensure their work remains ethical, legal, and effective. 🚨

12.4 Legal Risks When Conducting OSINT on Criminals

Introduction: The Legal Minefield of OSINT Investigations

Open-Source Intelligence (OSINT) is a powerful tool for investigating criminals, uncovering illicit activities, and assisting law enforcement. However, even when investigating criminals, OSINT analysts must operate within legal boundaries. The line between lawful intelligence gathering and illegal activity can be thin, and crossing it— even unintentionally—can lead to serious legal consequences.

This chapter examines the key legal risks when conducting OSINT on criminals, including privacy violations, unauthorized data access, and legal accountability. Whether you are an OSINT investigator, law enforcement officer, or journalist, understanding these risks is critical to protecting yourself while conducting ethical and legal investigations.

1️⃣ Understanding the Legal Framework for OSINT Investigations

Laws governing OSINT investigations vary by country. While some jurisdictions allow extensive intelligence collection, others have strict data protection laws that restrict OSINT practices.

◆ Key Legal Considerations for OSINT Investigators

✅ **Public vs. Private Information** – Publicly available data is generally legal to collect, but accessing restricted or private data can be illegal.

✅ **Data Protection Laws** – Regulations like GDPR (Europe), CCPA (California), and other privacy laws impose strict rules on handling personal data.

✅ **Hacking & Unauthorized Access** – Accessing a criminal's private accounts or using exploits to obtain information violates anti-hacking laws.

✅ **Terms of Service (ToS) Violations** – Scraping or bypassing restrictions on social media platforms can breach terms of service, leading to legal action.

✅ **Chain of Custody for Evidence** – If OSINT is used in court, it must be collected lawfully and documented properly to be admissible.

💡 **Key Rule**: Even if a target is a criminal, their rights still apply. Illegally obtained OSINT can lead to evidence exclusion, lawsuits, or even charges against the investigator.

2️⃣ Privacy Laws & Data Protection Risks

Many OSINT investigations involve tracking criminals through personal data, such as:

- Social media profiles
- Phone numbers & email addresses
- Financial records & transactions
- Location data from geotags or metadata

However, data protection laws place strict limits on how this information can be collected and stored.

◆ Major Data Protection Laws Affecting OSINT

☐ **GDPR (General Data Protection Regulation – Europe)** – Prohibits processing personal data without explicit consent unless a legitimate legal basis exists.

☐ **CCPA (California Consumer Privacy Act)** – Gives individuals control over their personal information, limiting data collection.

☐ **UK Data Protection Act** – Restricts the use of personal data, requiring clear justification for data collection.

☐ **Canadian PIPEDA (Personal Information Protection and Electronic Documents Act)** – Mandates transparency and consent for data collection.

⚠️ OSINT Risks Related to Privacy Laws

✗ Collecting personal data without consent may violate privacy laws.

✗ Retaining or sharing sensitive information (addresses, phone numbers, emails) without legal authority can lead to lawsuits.

✗ Using automated scraping tools on restricted databases can breach regulations.

💡 Safe OSINT Practices:

✓ Always verify the legality of data collection before storing or sharing information.

✓ Avoid processing sensitive personal data unless explicitly permitted.

✓ If working with law enforcement, ensure compliance with warrants, subpoenas, and legal requests.

3️⃣ The Dangers of Unauthorized Access & Hacking Laws

Some OSINT investigators are tempted to go beyond public sources, but doing so can violate hacking and cybercrime laws.

◆ Laws That Criminalize Unauthorized Access

● **Computer Fraud and Abuse Act (CFAA – USA)** – Prohibits accessing a computer or system without authorization.
● **UK Computer Misuse Act (1990)** – Criminalizes unauthorized access to computer systems and networks.
● **EU Cybercrime Directive** – Outlaws hacking, illegal interception, and data breaches.
● **Australia's Cybercrime Act** – Imposes severe penalties for unauthorized system access.

⚠️ OSINT Risks Related to Unauthorized Access

✗ Accessing private social media accounts through fake profiles or password resets.

✗ Using phishing techniques to trick targets into revealing credentials.

✗ Bypassing website security (e.g., using automated scripts to access protected content).

✗ Using compromised credentials found in leaked databases to log into accounts.

💡 Legal OSINT Practices:

✓ Only collect data that is publicly available.

✓ Do not attempt to access password-protected information without proper legal authorization.

✓ Follow ethical hacking laws if conducting penetration testing (with permission).

4️⃣ Terms of Service (ToS) Violations & Civil Liability

Many OSINT tools involve data scraping, automation, or collection from social media platforms. However, major platforms like Facebook, LinkedIn, Twitter, and Instagram have strict Terms of Service (ToS) that prohibit automated data collection.

◆ ToS Violations That Can Get OSINT Investigators in Trouble

✗ Automated scraping of social media data without permission (e.g., using bots or Python scripts).

✗ Creating fake accounts to gain access to restricted information.

✗ Extracting large amounts of data from third-party platforms without legal approval.

✗ Circumventing security measures (e.g., bypassing CAPTCHAs or rate limits).

⚠️ Legal Consequences of ToS Violations

- Civil lawsuits from tech companies for violating platform policies.
- Permanent bans from major platforms.
- Potential criminal charges if scraping includes unauthorized access.

💡 **Best Practice**: If an OSINT method violates a platform's ToS, avoid using it—it may result in civil or legal consequences.

5⃞ OSINT & Legal Admissibility: Will It Hold Up in Court?

Even if OSINT data is legally obtained, it must meet legal standards to be used as evidence in criminal cases.

◆ Key Legal Principles for OSINT in Court

✓ **Chain of Custody** – Investigators must properly document how OSINT was collected.
✓ **Authenticity** – Screenshots or social media posts must be verifiable (e.g., hashed and timestamped).
✓ **Hearsay Rules** – Some OSINT findings (e.g., anonymous social media claims) may not be admissible.
✓ **Privacy & Legal Compliance** – If OSINT was collected illegally, it can be excluded from trial.

💡 **Golden Rule**: If OSINT is not collected legally, it cannot be used as evidence.

6⃞ Conclusion: Conducting OSINT Without Breaking the Law

OSINT is a legitimate investigative tool, but legal pitfalls exist. Even when tracking criminals, investigators must respect privacy laws, avoid unauthorized access, and follow ethical standards.

✓ Key Takeaways:

- Stick to publicly available information—avoid hacking, unauthorized access, or deception.
- Respect privacy laws (GDPR, CCPA, etc.) and avoid collecting protected personal data.
- Do not violate Terms of Service (ToS) when scraping or collecting data.
- Ensure OSINT evidence is legally admissible by documenting sources and chain of custody.
- If in doubt, seek legal advice before proceeding.

By following these principles, OSINT investigators can operate effectively while staying on the right side of the law.

12.5 Best Practices for Ethical Criminal Investigations

Introduction: Balancing Ethics & Effectiveness in OSINT

Open-Source Intelligence (OSINT) plays a crucial role in criminal investigations, helping law enforcement, private investigators, and analysts uncover crucial evidence. However, with great investigative power comes the responsibility to act ethically and legally. Ethical OSINT investigations ensure that intelligence gathering does not violate privacy rights, break laws, or compromise human rights.

This chapter outlines the best practices for conducting OSINT ethically in criminal investigations, covering legal compliance, transparency, data protection, and responsible intelligence gathering. Whether you are working on a cybercrime case, tracking fraudsters, or investigating organized crime, these best practices will help ensure that your methods are both effective and ethical.

Ethical Foundations of Criminal OSINT Investigations

Before conducting any OSINT investigation, it is essential to understand the ethical principles that guide intelligence work. Ethical investigations not only protect individuals' rights but also strengthen the credibility of OSINT findings in court and law enforcement collaboration.

Core Ethical Principles in OSINT

- **Legality** – Always operate within the boundaries of local, national, and international laws.
- **Integrity** – Do not manipulate or falsify intelligence to fit a desired outcome.
- **Transparency** – Maintain clear documentation of methods used for intelligence gathering.
- **Privacy Protection** – Avoid unnecessary collection of personally identifiable information (PII).
- **Accountability** – Take responsibility for investigative actions and their consequences.

Key Rule: Just because information is publicly available does not mean it is ethical to collect, store, or distribute. Ethical OSINT focuses on necessity and proportionality.

Legal Compliance: Staying Within the Law

Every ethical OSINT investigation must strictly follow local and international laws governing data collection, privacy, and cybersecurity.

Essential Legal Considerations for OSINT Investigators

- **Data Protection Laws** – Comply with GDPR (EU), CCPA (California), and other privacy laws when handling personal data.
- **Computer Misuse Laws** – Avoid unauthorized access to computer systems, hacking, or phishing (CFAA – USA, Computer Misuse Act – UK).
- **Terms of Service (ToS) Compliance** – Respect the rules of social media platforms; do not engage in scraping that violates policies.
- **Evidentiary Standards** – Ensure collected OSINT data can be used in court by following legal documentation procedures.

Common Legal Pitfalls to Avoid

- Accessing private accounts without permission (hacking or unauthorized login attempts).
- Using deceptive methods to extract information (e.g., impersonation, fake profiles).
- Scraping restricted content from social media or databases without authorization.
- Publishing or sharing personal data without legal justification.

Golden Rule: If an OSINT technique could land you in legal trouble, don't use it. Seek legal advice before proceeding.

Responsible Data Collection & Privacy Protection

OSINT investigations must respect individuals' privacy rights, even when investigating criminals. Irresponsible data collection can lead to legal action, loss of credibility, and ethical violations.

Best Practices for Ethical Data Collection

- **Collect only necessary data** – Focus on information relevant to the investigation.
- **Verify public availability** – Ensure the data is legally accessible without circumvention techniques.
- **Minimize exposure of personal information** – Avoid collecting excessive PII unless required.
- **Properly secure stored data** – Use encryption and restrict access to prevent leaks.

- **Be transparent in law enforcement collaborations** – Share findings responsibly and legally.

Privacy Risks in OSINT Investigations

- Over-collection of data (storing unnecessary PII increases risk).
- Failure to anonymize data when sharing reports.
- Retaining sensitive information longer than needed.

Ethical OSINT respects the privacy of both criminals and innocent individuals.

Verifying & Corroborating Information

Unverified OSINT can lead to false accusations, reputational damage, and wrongful legal actions. Ethical OSINT investigators must validate all intelligence before acting on it.

Methods for Verifying OSINT Findings

- **Cross-check information from multiple sources** – No single source should be considered absolute truth.
- **Use metadata analysis** – Verify timestamps, geolocation, and digital footprints.
- **Check the reliability of sources** – Identify whether data comes from reputable, known sources.
- **Be cautious of misinformation & manipulated content** – Images, videos, and documents can be faked.
- **Validate social media claims** – Look for consistency in posts, comments, and interactions.

Ethical investigators don't jump to conclusions based on incomplete or unreliable OSINT.

Avoiding Deception & Social Engineering in OSINT

Some OSINT methods, like sockpuppet accounts (fake identities), pretexting, and social engineering, can be legally and ethically problematic. While deception is sometimes used in undercover law enforcement operations, civilian OSINT analysts must follow strict ethical guidelines.

When Is Deception Unethical in OSINT?

- Creating fake profiles to gain access to private information.

- Impersonating someone else to manipulate a target.
- Tricking individuals into revealing sensitive information (pretexting or phishing).
- Misrepresenting credentials to obtain data.

Ethical Alternative Methods

- **Passive OSINT** – Rely on publicly available sources without deception.
- **Data enrichment** – Use legitimate tools to connect publicly available data points.
- **Public records research** – Access open government databases and legally available registries.

Deception in OSINT investigations can lead to legal consequences and damage credibility. Use caution.

Ethical Reporting & Responsible Intelligence Sharing

Once OSINT findings are gathered, they must be reported ethically and responsibly. Poorly handled intelligence can harm investigations, violate rights, or lead to misinterpretations.

Best Practices for Ethical OSINT Reporting

- **Only share verified intelligence** – Unverified claims can cause harm.
- **Protect sensitive information** – Anonymize data where necessary.
- **Clearly distinguish between facts and assumptions** – Do not speculate without evidence.
- **Follow ethical disclosure principles** – Avoid causing harm when reporting sensitive findings.
- **Report findings in compliance with legal standards** – Ensure evidence is admissible in court if required.

Risks of Poor OSINT Reporting

- Spreading misinformation (wrongly accusing someone).
- Publishing confidential or personal data (violating privacy laws).
- Compromising active investigations by leaking intelligence.

OSINT should be reported responsibly, ensuring accuracy, privacy, and compliance with ethical standards.

Conclusion: Upholding Ethics in Every OSINT Investigation

Ethical OSINT investigations require a balance between intelligence gathering and respecting laws, privacy, and human rights. By following legal compliance, responsible data handling, proper verification, and ethical reporting, OSINT professionals can conduct criminal investigations without compromising integrity.

Key Takeaways for Ethical OSINT in Criminal Investigations

- Follow legal guidelines (GDPR, CCPA, CFAA, etc.).
- Respect privacy rights, even when investigating criminals.
- Verify all intelligence before reporting or acting on it.
- Avoid deception and unauthorized access.
- Report responsibly and protect sensitive data.

By integrating these best practices, OSINT professionals can ensure that their investigations remain legal, ethical, and credible.

12.6 Case Study: When OSINT Crossed Legal & Ethical Boundaries

Introduction: The Fine Line Between OSINT and Illegality

While Open-Source Intelligence (OSINT) is a powerful tool for criminal investigations, it must be conducted ethically and legally to maintain credibility and avoid legal consequences. When OSINT analysts, journalists, private investigators, or even law enforcement agencies overstep ethical and legal boundaries, the consequences can be severe—ranging from privacy violations and lawsuits to criminal charges.

This case study examines a real-world example where OSINT investigators crossed ethical and legal boundaries, leading to misuse of personal data, privacy violations, and legal action. It highlights the critical lessons learned and best practices to ensure that OSINT remains a responsible and effective tool in criminal investigations.

Background: A Cyber Vigilante Investigation Gone Wrong

In 2021, an independent OSINT investigator named James Carter (pseudonym) ran a popular blog focused on exposing cybercriminals and fraudsters. Carter had a strong following in the cybersecurity and OSINT communities due to his detailed investigative reports, which often identified scammers, hackers, and online predators using publicly available information.

His work was widely praised until one case pushed the limits of legal and ethical OSINT practices.

The Investigation: Unmasking an Alleged Online Predator

Carter began investigating an anonymous individual accused of blackmailing victims using leaked private photos. The suspect operated under multiple usernames on encrypted messaging platforms and the dark web. Using OSINT techniques, Carter attempted to deanonymize the suspect by:

- Cross-referencing usernames and email addresses across forums.
- Scraping social media platforms for profile matches.
- Analyzing EXIF metadata from images linked to the suspect.
- Using data breach databases to uncover linked accounts.
- Tracking cryptocurrency transactions for financial leads.

His investigation led to a potential suspect, a 27-year-old man named Mark Peterson (pseudonym), who lived in New York. However, Carter lacked conclusive proof that Peterson was the blackmailer. Instead of handing over his findings to law enforcement, Carter decided to publicly expose Peterson in a blog post.

Where OSINT Crossed the Line: Ethical & Legal Violations

1. Publicly Doxxing an Unconfirmed Suspect

Carter's blog post included:

- Peterson's full name and address
- His workplace and employer details
- Social media accounts and family connections

While OSINT focuses on publicly available information, publishing personal details without legal justification violates privacy laws like GDPR (Europe) and CCPA (California). Additionally, Carter failed to verify whether Peterson was indeed the blackmailer, potentially exposing an innocent person to harassment and threats.

Lesson Learned: OSINT should be used to gather intelligence, not to publicly accuse or expose individuals without legal authority.

2. Scraping Data from Restricted Websites

During his investigation, Carter used automated scraping tools to extract information from a private forum where the suspect was active. However, this forum's Terms of Service (ToS) explicitly prohibited data scraping and unauthorized access.

Many social media platforms, forums, and websites legally prohibit scraping, and violating these policies can lead to legal action for unauthorized data collection. Some countries also have strict anti-scraping laws under their cybersecurity and privacy regulations.

Lesson Learned: If a website explicitly restricts data scraping or access, violating those terms can lead to legal consequences.

3. Illegally Accessing a Personal Email Account

In an attempt to confirm Peterson's identity, Carter tried to access an old compromised email account linked to the suspect, which had been exposed in a data breach. He used publicly available breach-checking tools to retrieve the account's leaked passwords.

While the passwords were publicly available due to a past breach, attempting to log into the suspect's email account constituted unauthorized access, which is a criminal offense under the Computer Fraud and Abuse Act (CFAA – USA) and other global cybersecurity laws.

Shortly after, Peterson filed a complaint, and Carter was investigated for hacking and unauthorized access.

Lesson Learned: Accessing someone's private accounts—even with publicly available leaked credentials—is illegal. OSINT does not include unauthorized access to private data.

4. Interfering with an Ongoing Criminal Investigation

After Carter exposed Peterson, law enforcement revealed that Peterson was already under investigation for unrelated cybercrimes. By prematurely exposing his identity, Carter jeopardized an active police operation, alerting the suspect and potentially leading to:

- The destruction of crucial digital evidence (erased hard drives, deleted messages).
- The suspect fleeing or changing identities to avoid capture.
- Interference with legal due process, making it harder for law enforcement to build a case.

As a result, Carter was subpoenaed and ordered to remove the blog post, and his actions complicated the legal proceedings against Peterson.

Lesson Learned: OSINT should support, not interfere with, law enforcement efforts. Premature exposure can compromise legal investigations.

Consequences & Legal Fallout

Carter's actions had serious consequences:

- **Privacy Violation Lawsuit**: Peterson sued Carter for privacy violations and defamation.
- **Criminal Charges**: Carter was investigated for unauthorized computer access under the CFAA.
- **Banned from Social Media & Platforms**: Several social media platforms permanently banned Carter for violating Terms of Service (ToS) rules on data collection.
- **Damaged Reputation**: Carter lost credibility in the OSINT and cybersecurity communities, and many professionals distanced themselves from his work.

In the end, Peterson was later arrested on separate cybercrime charges, but Carter's illegal methods prevented his own findings from being used as evidence in court.

Key Takeaways: Ensuring OSINT Stays Legal & Ethical

This case study highlights the critical importance of ethical OSINT practices in criminal investigations.

Best Practices for Ethical OSINT

- **Follow Privacy Laws:** Do not publish personally identifiable information (PII) without legal justification.
- **Respect Website Terms of Service (ToS):** Avoid unauthorized scraping or data collection.

- **Do Not Access Private Accounts**: Even if credentials are leaked online, using them is illegal.
- **Verify Before Publishing:** Ensure intelligence is accurate before making public accusations.
- **Collaborate with Law Enforcement**: OSINT should support investigations, not disrupt them.
- **Use Responsible Disclosure**: Report findings through appropriate channels instead of exposing them publicly.

Bottom Line: Ethical OSINT is about intelligence gathering, not public exposure or cyber vigilantism. Following legal and ethical guidelines ensures credibility, protects individuals' rights, and prevents legal consequences.

Conclusion: The Thin Line Between Investigator & Offender

This case study serves as a cautionary tale about the dangers of crossing ethical and legal boundaries in OSINT investigations. While OSINT can uncover critical evidence in criminal cases, it must be used responsibly, ethically, and legally.

When OSINT investigators act outside the law, they risk becoming the very criminals they seek to expose.

Crime has gone digital. From fraud and cybercrime to human trafficking and organized crime, criminals are leveraging technology to hide their tracks. However, Open-Source Intelligence (OSINT) provides investigators with the tools to uncover digital footprints, analyze online behavior, and gather actionable intelligence to solve cases.

OSINT Detective: Digital Tools & Techniques for Criminal Investigations is a practical guide designed for law enforcement, private investigators, journalists, and intelligence professionals who need to track suspects, analyze evidence, and conduct in-depth online investigations. This book equips you with the skills to use OSINT for criminal profiling, cyber forensics, and intelligence gathering in both digital and real-world investigations.

What You'll Learn in This Book

- **OSINT for Law Enforcement & Private Investigators**: Learn how OSINT is applied in real criminal cases, from missing persons to financial fraud.
- **Tracking Digital Footprints of Suspects**: Discover how criminals leave traces online and how to follow their digital trails.
- **Identifying & Profiling Criminal Networks**: Use OSINT techniques to analyze connections between suspects, organizations, and illicit activities.
- **Social Media Intelligence (SOCMINT) for Criminal Cases**: Monitor suspects, uncover aliases, and analyze posts to extract valuable intelligence.
- **Deep & Dark Web Investigations**: Identify hidden forums, marketplaces, and criminal activities on underground networks.
- **Geolocation & Image Analysis for Crime Solving**: Use OSINT tools to verify locations, analyze metadata, and geolocate images for investigations.
- **Financial Crime & Fraud Investigations**: Follow the money trail, detect fraudulent transactions, and analyze cryptocurrency wallets.
- **Human Trafficking & Exploitation Investigations**: Learn how OSINT is used to track victims, identify traffickers, and monitor illicit operations.
- **Cybercrime & Hacker Investigations**: Investigate cybercriminals, hacking groups, and ransomware operators using OSINT techniques.
- **OSINT Ethics & Legal Considerations for Criminal Investigations**: Ensure compliance with privacy laws, evidence collection standards, and ethical OSINT practices.

With real-world case studies, hands-on exercises, and expert methodologies, OSINT Detective is an essential resource for investigators, analysts, and researchers who want to master digital crime-solving techniques. Whether you're working on local cases or international cyber investigations, this book provides the tools and strategies needed to uncover the truth.

Thank you for reading **<u>OSINT Detective: Digital Tools & Techniques for Criminal Investigations</u>**. Crime is evolving, but so are the tools available to those seeking justice. Your commitment to learning OSINT techniques for criminal investigations is a step toward making communities safer, exposing hidden threats, and holding criminals accountable.

We encourage you to use these skills responsibly and ethically. OSINT is a powerful tool that, when used correctly, can bring critical evidence to light, locate missing persons, and disrupt criminal networks. By applying these techniques with integrity, you are making a meaningful impact in the fight against digital crime.

We deeply appreciate your dedication to the OSINT field and would love to hear your feedback! Your insights help us improve future editions and provide even more valuable resources for investigators worldwide.

Stay vigilant, stay ethical, and keep investigating.

Continue Your OSINT Journey

Expand your skills with the rest of **<u>The OSINT Analyst Series</u>**:

- **OSINT Foundations**: The Beginner's Guide to Open-Source Intelligence
- **The OSINT Search Mastery**: Hacking Search Engines for Intelligence
- **OSINT People Finder**: Advanced Techniques for Online Investigations
- **Social Media OSINT**: Tracking Digital Footprints
- **Image & Geolocation Intelligence**: Reverse Searching and Mapping
- **Domain, Website & Cyber Investigations with OSINT**
- **Email & Dark Web Investigations**: Tracking Leaks & Breaches
- **OSINT Threat Intel**: Investigating Hackers, Breaches, and Cyber Risks
- **Corporate OSINT**: Business Intelligence & Competitive Analysis
- **Investigating Disinformation & Fake News with OSINT**
- **OSINT for Deep & Dark Web**: Techniques for Cybercrime Investigations
- **OSINT Automation**: Python & APIs for Intelligence Gathering
- **Advanced OSINT Case Studies**: Real-World Investigations
- **The Ethical OSINT Investigator**: Privacy, Legal Risks & Best Practices

We look forward to seeing you in the next book!

Happy investigating!

www.ingramcontent.com/pod-product-compliance
Lightning Source LLC
Chambersburg PA
CBHW080549060326
40689CB00021B/4791